THE JAPANESE BUSINESS LEADERS

THE
JAPANESE BUSINESS
LEADERS

HIROSHI MANNARI

FACULTY OF SOCIOLOGY,
KWANSEI GAKUIN UNIVERSITY

UNIVERSITY OF TOKYO PRESS

Kwansei Gakuin University Research Series, vol. 33

©UNIVERSITY OF TOKYO PRESS, 1974
UTP 3036-57061-5149
ISBN 0-86008-122-2
Library of Congress Catalogue Card Number: 74-84827
Printed in Japan

CONTENTS

TABLES

Part I

Part II

APPENDIX I

APPENDIX II

APPENDIX III

APPENDIX IV

FOREWORD

Gradually we are acquiring in useful and compatible form the basic data necessary for the effective and cross-national study of major segments of recent and contemporary national societies. Professor Mannari's monograph represents a notable contribution to this literature. It is outstanding in several respects.

First, it adds a non-Western dimension to a corpus of scholarship that has been largely Western in reference. The Japanese case is of extraordinary interest in this respect. Japan represents the only truly non-Western society that has achieved the most advanced stages of economic and political modernization. Beyond this, the processes of social, economic, and political change are in the Japanese case documented with a degree of thoroughness and accuracy matched in few other societies. The result is a laboratory for the testing and elaboration of theories of development and convergence that offers unique advantages. Professor Mannari's data and findings should be of great interest and importance to scholars working in these fileds.

Second, the study has appropriate historical depth and perspective. So often studies of this sort suffer from the lack or shallowness of these qualities. The Mannari work is spacious in this respect. The basic data stem from the 1880s and culminate with 1960, a perspective of eighty years. This is both unusual and admirable.

Finally, Professor Mannari is interested in the comparative and cross-national significance of the Japanese experience and, when possible, provides comparable information about the American and British experiences.

The result is a book that provides a great deal of new information of durable value on the social characteristics, career profiles, and mobility of Japanese business leaders over practically the entire course of the most critical stages of the society's modernization. It should be of lasting value to all social scientists with professional interests in this area.

Robert E. Ward, Director
Center for Research in International Studies
Stanford University

ACKNOWLEDGMENTS

This monograph is based on a research project entitled Japan's Leaders: Men and Careers in a Changing Society, started at Kwansei Gakuin University, Nishinomiya City, Japan, during 1960. The research, which included a questionnaire survey of Japanese business leaders, was made possible by the generous interest and assistance of many people. I am indebted first to the Secretariat of the Japan Federation of Employers' Association and specifically to Mr. Hayakawa Masaru, who wrote a letter of introduction to the businessmen who were polled. I must express my gratitude to the many Japanese businessmen who by answering our questionnaire made the study possible.

I wish to thank Dr. Hori Tsuneo, former president of Kwansei Gakuin University, and Professor Kurauchi Kazuta, former president of the Japan Sociological Society, for their advice and recommendations in formulating the research project.

For assistance in designing the study, I must express my appreciation to Dr. James C. Abegglen of Boston Consulting Group, Inc., who aided in planning this project and provided valuable advice regarding the research. The questionnaires used were distributed jointly with him. Dr. Abegglen and I jointly presented an earlier version of chapter 7, Trends of Mobility into Japan's Elite Groups, at the Conference on State and Economic Enterprises in Modern Japan, in Estes Park, Colorado, in June 1963, under the title, Japanese Business Leaders, 1880–1960.

We also conducted a follow-up questionnaire research in 1970 and presented an earlier version of appendix I, Japanese Business Leaders in 1970, at the 1971 Asian Regional Conference on Industrial Relations in Tokyo, Japan, in March 1971 under the title, Japanese Business Leaders in 1960 and 1970.

Professor Ryōke Minoru of Kwansei Gakuin University provided valuable advice on the feudal social status system, and Professor Misumi Jūji of Kyushu University gave important aid in analyzing data on education. Socio-economic historians helped to identify business, political, and intellectual leaders of 1880 and 1920. In this respect I wish to thank Dr. Horie Yasuzō, professor emeritus of Kyoto University, and Professors Sadahira Motoshirō and Yunoki Manabu of Kwansei Gakuin University. For aid in gathering biographical data for the historical study, I wish to thank the librarians of Kwansei Gakuin University, Kyoto University, Kobe University, and the Department of Research of the Mainichi Shimbun, Tokyo.

Some preliminary drafts of the manuscript were read by Professors Charles A. Myers, Everett E. Hagen, Solomon B. Levine, and R. P. Dore, who made many helpful comments. Professor Edward Norbeck of Rice University gave invaluable editorial assistance as well as help with conceptual refinement.

Financial support for the project was contributed by the Asia Foundation, Tokyo Office; the Ford Foundation; The Inter-University Study of Labor Problems in Economic Development; and Kwansei Gakuin University for the publication. I am grateful for their understanding aid.

Special acknowledgment is due two organizations. First, I am indebted to the members of the faculty of the Faculty of Sociology at Kwansei Gakuin University for their continued support of the project and for making possible my leave of absence in 1962–63 for full-time research at the Massachusetts Institute of Technology. Second, I am grateful to Dean Howard W. Johnson of the School of Industrial Management at MIT for accepting me as a visiting scholar there.

Finally, it should be noted that this monograph is part of the Political Modernization of Japan Project of the Center for Japanese Studies at the University of Michigan. The project has been supported by the Carnegie Corporation of New York. The author would like to express his gratitude for this support and also his appreciation to Dr. Robert M. Spaulding, Jr., of the center's staff for his very competent editorial work.

Hiroshi Mannari
Kwansei Gakuin University

INTRODUCTION

The economic growth of a nation is for the most part determined by the quality of leadership groups who direct the march to industrialization.[1] The rapid development of Japanese business and industry emphasizes the importance of detailed knowledge of business and industrial leadership. As large corporations in various industries develop, business leaders not only command the organizations they preside over but also exert an important influence over Japanese society. Furthermore, Japanese business leaders have gained great power and prestige among political and intellectual leaders.

Our concern is to learn who these business leaders are: to learn about their family background, their education, and their career patterns. Who these leaders are, what training they get, and how they circulate are among the most significant facts in understanding the nature of the current Japanese business and industrial world.

This is a study of the recruitment of Japanese business leaders in terms of social stratification and mobility. Classical theories of social stratification[2] emphasize inequalities of wealth, privilege, and power, and the persistence of a rigid system of social classes in which the upper classes remain upper, the lower classes, lower, and the two rarely meet. In every traditional society succession to privileged status through family connections has been common.

---

[1]Kerr, Clark, Dunlop, John T., Harbison, Frederick, and Myers, Charles, *Industrialism and Industrial Man* (Cambridge, Massachusetts: Harvard University Press, 1960), pp. 1–13.

[2]Marx, Karl, "A Note on Class," in *Class, Status, and Power*, 2nd ed., edited by Reinhard Bendix and Seymour Martin Lipset (New York: The Free Press, 1966), pp. 5–6; and Veblen, Thorstein, *The Theory of the Leisure Class* (New York: The Viking Press, 1931).

Modern theories of social stratification,[3] however, emphasize social mobility as a basic characteristic of industrial societies. New talents are necessary in a changing society. With advancement of industrialization, traditional ruling classes find it impossible to adapt to changed conditions and difficult to secure new positions for their own members. Sons of middle and lower classes are more ready to acquire new knowledge and skills required in a dynamic and innovating society.

The emergence of Japan's modern business elite from the prior social class structure can be analyzed in the light of these concepts. This study of social processes in recruiting Japanese business leaders in large corporations, is designed to show whether hereditary and aristocratic principles operate to keep families at the top or whether competitive forces emphasizing individual achievement determine who will be a leader.

Among the principal factors in recruiting business leaders, we must first identify their social origins or family occupational status. The extent to which present-day Japanese business leaders rose above the social class into which they were born (as determined by the occupation of their fathers) in achieving their present positions is the index of occupational or social mobility. Patterns of social mobility of Japanese business leaders are evaluated in terms of the extent to which positions of executive leadership are limited to a single class or open to several classes. It is assumed that recruitment of business leaders from all occupational groups is evidence of more effective use of human resources at all levels of society and thus a more egalitarian and stable society. Limiting positions of leadership to a certain class or family tends to create dissatisfaction and conflict in other classes.

A second factor associated with recruitment of business leaders is education. Higher education has become increasingly important for business leaders in every industrialized country. However, edu-

---

[3]Lipset, Seymour Martin and Bendix, Reinhard, *Social Mobility in Industrial Society* (Berkeley and Los Angeles: University of California Press, 1959), pp. 57–64; and Lenski, Gerhard E., *Power and Privilege* (New York: McGraw-Hill, 1966), pp. 389–433; Smelser, Neil J. and Lipset, Seymour Martin, "Social Structure, Mobility and Development," edited by Neil J. Smelser and Seymour Martin Lipset, *Social Structure and Mobility in Economic Development* (Chicago: Aldine Publishing Company, 1966) pp. 1–50.

cational institutions and the industrial community have different relationships in different countries. Thus data on the educational level of Japanese business leaders and the content of university training reveal a special pattern of cooperation between industry and universities in Japan. While it is true that university or college education provides a chance to achieve business leadership, it is common everywhere that the higher the social class, the better the education of its sons. Analysis of data on formal education and social class backgrounds explains to what extent achievement of leadership positions is related to the influence of family status or to individual merit.

Thirdly, we must deal with the career patterns of business leaders. After a century of industrialization in Japan, a management revolution is almost inevitable, in which bureaucratic or professional managers assume the responsibility for directing enterprises. Furthermore, the Japanese social system, which tends to stress education, strong commitment to an organization, seniority, and appointment (rather than election), encourages the development of a bureaucracy. Analysis of the ways in which Japanese business leaders achieve the top management positions through a bureaucratic career reveals not only the special patterns of recruitment but also the qualities of their business experiences.

This is an empirical research report on the social composition and formation of Japanese business and other elite groups in the modern era. It consists of two parts: first, a study of the occupational mobility of men who were Japanese business leaders in 1960; and second, a historical study of the movement of Japan's business, political and intellectual elites at three points in time: 1880s, 1920, and 1960. An appendix provides a more recent profile of Japanese business leaders. The trends in recruitment of Japanese business leaders from 1960 to 1970 are revealed.

PART I. JAPAN'S BUSINESS LEADERS IN 1960

Those who were business leaders in 1960 may be variously defined. In this study, the terms "business leaders" and "business elite" refer to persons who hold top positions in business organiza-

tions, whose positions are acknowledged to be powerful and prestigious, and who are in publicly recognized positions of leadership.
Without reference to individual fame, reputation, or other indications, the men holding top executive positions in the largest firms
in Japanese business and industry in 1960 are the subjects.

These positions and firms were operationally defined in the following ways. The top executive positions include only the chairman of the board of directors, the president, the vice-president,
and the two most highly placed or senior managing directors
(semmu torishimariyaku and *jōmu torishimariyaku)* of the firms. The
largest firms were identified in terms of amount of capitalization,
the most common measure of size, and a measure that is usually
consistent with such other measures as total assets, number of
employees, or gross sales. Firms whose capitalization exceeded 1
billion yen (approximately $2,780,000) in 1960, numbered about
four hundred, of which 60 percent were in manufacturing and the
rest in service industries.

Executives in the defined positions in the largest firms totalled
1,525. A questionnaire about family occupational background, education, and career was sent to each of them. Replies were received
from 985, who have been considered the top management group in
Japanese business. These executives are not numerous, but all are
in a position to make important decisions in their corporate enterprises. Furthermore, executives in the largest firms are more powerful than those of smaller firms, which are mostly dependent on
larger firms.

Some methodological characteristics of this study should be
mentioned. First, detailed data on the family occupational background, education, and careers of the present Japanese business
leaders were collected by questionnaire. A very high percentage of
returns was achieved, and the accuracy of the data was tested in
various ways. Second, national changes in occupational structure
and level of education were intensively gathered. A comparison of
the elite data with national demographic data helps to tell us what
trends, if any, exist in the recruitment of business leaders, and
should aid in providing answers to various questions concerning
the characteristics and background of leaders. Third, the research
results have been compared with research findings on business

leaders in the United States and the United Kingdom. These comparisons help to evaluate the qualities of Japanese business leaders and the effectiveness of social institutions in recruiting leaders of the nation.

PART II. JAPAN'S ELITE GROUPS, 1880–1960

Part II compares Japan's business elite at three points in time, 1880s, 1920 and 1960, and also compares the business elite with the political and intellectual elites of these years.

The primary purpose of this study is to add a historical dimension to part I. A meaningful study of leadership groups in Japan cannot omit close attention to the historical process: the rapid development of Japanese society from a stable and largely unchanging social order to a modern industrial social order.

There is a curious lack of empirical knowledge of the real historical situation in Japan with regard to recruitment of leadership groups. The question of who the men were who led Japan from a feudal, agrarian society to a modern industrial society remains open. A leading role in the process has been attributed by various scholars to the well-to-do peasantry, to the dispossessed samurai, to the Tokugawa merchants, and finally, to the same men who led the earlier social order. Only a few attempts have been made at systematic study from empirical evidence.

There are two research problems in this part of the study. First, to what extent is present-day leadership continuous or discontinuous with earlier Japanese leadership in terms of social status background and professional training? Second, were there similarities or differences in social composition among Japanese business, political, and intellectual elite groups as modernizing forces?

In this historical study, the business elite in each period includes two hundred men who were chief executives (and excludes the lower executive positions that were included in part I). The political elite in each period includes one hundred senior positions in cabinet, Diet, party hierarchies, the civil service, and labor unions. Similarly, the intellectual elite in each period includes one hundred professional leaders in religion, law, and medicine; scholars and professors; journalists and writers; and artists. Thus, the research design assures an accurate comparison of the three leadership groups at three periods. (A detailed description of the sample is included in appendix III.)

Similar studies on changes in elite formation over the past century have been done already for the United States and the United Kingdom. Again, we have employed comparable methods of research to add the important dimension of historical comparison of the three countries.

THE JAPANESE BUSINESS LEADERS

PART I

OCCUPATIONAL MOBILITY OF THE BUSINESS LEADERS OF 1960

Chapter 1

OCCUPATIONAL CHANGES IN JAPAN 1883–1960

An examination of the family occupational backgrounds and mobility of present-day Japanese business leaders properly begins with an analysis of changes in the occupational structure of the total population. This will permit comparison of data on business leaders with data on the total population during the period in which the leaders grew to maturity.

As a society moves toward industrialization, the rural-agrarian population becomes more and more urban-industrial. Modern Japan has seen a radical shift in labor force from primary into secondary and tertiary industry. How did these changes come about? What were the general trends in movement of labor from one industry to others in recent generations?

An industrial society requires a division of labor different from that of a preindustrial society, and with the new division of labor a different hierarchy of prestige appears. These changes in prestige are often described in terms of one's occupation; that is, one's occupational position in an industrial society fairly well defines one's social status as well as one's economic reward. Industrialization implies a great increase in the number of office workers, skilled workmen, highly trained technicians, and professional men, and the creation of many additional forms of specialized labor. Important positions of leadership are relatively few and carry high prestige. The distribution of occupations over a given period provides an objective measure of how extensively a society has developed managerial and professional talents. How did this process of occupational change proceed in Japan?

National Changes in Industrial Labor Force

After an extensive study of census reports from a number of countries, Colin Clark concluded that a basic concomitant of economic progress is movement of working population from agriculture to manufacturing, and from manufacturing to commerce and services.[1] W.W. Rostow expresses this more specifically: "Before take-off, perhaps 75% of the working force is in agriculture, living on a low, if not merely survival, real wage; by the end of take-off, the figure may drop to 40%, and by maturity, it has in many cases fallen to 20%."[2] We may now ask to what extent the population of Japan has changed along these lines in the course of industrialization.

Statistics for the year 1880, near the beginning of Japan's industrialization, show 82 percent of the working population in primary industry (table 1). No other nation that has achieved industrialization began with such a high proportion of agriculturists.[3] This circumstance implies extreme poverty and primitive economic organization. By 1900, however, Japan's agricultural population had fallen to 70 percent, and thereafter the decline was rapid: to 55 percent in 1920, 44 percent in 1940, and 32 percent in 1960.

Between 1880 and 1960, the total work force increased from 19.5 million to 43.7 million. The population engaged in agriculture rose from 16.1 million in 1880 to 17.3 million in 1900, then decreased to 16.5 million in 1910, and 14.7 million in 1920. It has since remained fairly stable at about 14.3 million. The number of farm households remained nearly constant (about 5.5 million) from 1873 to 1960.[4] However, the proportion of the population in agriculture declined sharply from 1880 to 1960 (82 percent to 32 percent). The fact that the total farm population and number of farm households remained essentially unchanged indicates that

---

[1]Clark, Colin, *The Conditions of Economic Progress*, 2nd ed. (London: Macmillan, 1951), p. 395.

[2]Rostow, W.W., *The Stages of Economic Growth: A Non-Communist Manifesto* (New York: Cambridge University Press, 1960), p. 71.

[3]Clark, p. 425

[4]Namiki, Masayoshi, "The Farm Population in the National Economy Before and After World War II," *Economic Development and Cultural Change* (Chicago: University of Chicago), IX: 1, Part II (Oct. 1960), p. 30.

the mainstream of rural out-migration was made up of surplus labor. In accordance with the Japanese pattern of inheritance, migrants from rural villages to cities are nearly always children other than the eldest son. It has been rare for whole families to move to the city.[5]

Population growth was seen chiefly in secondary and tertiary

Table 1. Distribution of Japanese Labor Force by Type of Industry, 1880–1960 (Percent)

Type of Industry	1880	1900	1920	1940	1960
Agriculture, forestry and fishing	82.3	70.0	55.1	44.3	32.4
Mining	.1	.6	1.6	1.8	1.6
Construction and manufacturing	6.5	13.2	20.0	25.0	28.0
Commerce and finance	5.9	8.8	12.0	15.0	17.9
Transportation and communication	.6	1.6	3.9	4.2	5.1
Public administration, professional, and other	4.6	5.8	7.4	9.7	15.0
Total percent	100.0	100.0	100.0	100.0	100.0
Total population (in thousands)	19,542	24,768	26,624	32,478	43,690

Sources: The 1880–1940 data are from Yamada Yūzō, *Nihon Kokumin Shotoku Suikei Shiryō* (Descriptive Statistical Data on National Income in Japan) revised ed., (Tokyo: Tōyō Keizai Shimpō Sha, 1957) pp. 152–53. The 1960 data are from Bureau of Statistics, Office of the Prime Minister, *Japan Statistical Yearbook 1961* (Tokyo: Japan Statistical Association, 1962), p. 56.

Note: In the second edition of *The Conditions of Economic Progress* (p. 425), Colin Clark estimated that agriculture, forestry, and fishing in 1872 accounted for 85 percent of the total employed population. He revised this proportion to 76 percent in his third edition (1957, p. 516), by excluding women in agriculture. Kazushi Ohkawa and Henry Rosovsky state that "the percentage of labor force engaged in agriculture was 76 percent in 1878–82." (Ohkawa and Rosovsky, "The Role of Agriculture in Modern Japanese Economic Development," *Economic Development and Cultural Change*, (Chicago: University of Chicago), IX: 1, Part II (Oct. 1960), p. 63.

[5]Namiki, p. 29.

industries. In 1880 only 1.3 million people, or 6.6 percent of all employed persons, were in manufacturing, construction, and mining. The number and proportion rapidly increased to 13.7 million or 29.6 percent of the total work force in 1960. Commerce and finance had 1.2 million or 5.9 percent of the work force in 1880. The proportion thereafter increased almost exactly 3 percent every twenty years. A substantial increase in the number employed in public administration, professional and other services is notable in recent years.

In general, the statements by Clark and Rostow agree with the evidence that economic progress in Japan, as elsewhere, induced a rapid shift of labor from primary industries into services as well as into manufacturing. Some additional comments need to be made, however, with respect to the movement of labor in Japan. Regarding structural changes in the work force, subsidiary employment of members of farm households must be taken into account. From the early period to 1940, about one third of the farm households had subsidiary occupations.[6] For millions of peasant families, supplementary nonagricultural pursuits were the chief source of cash income. These included seasonal work in fisheries, sericulture, mat-making, charcoal-making, and construction. It has been reported that tenant farmers engaged in part-time work more often than did landowning farmers.[7] Still other millions combined handicraft industries with commerce, transportation or other services, one or another being given as the chief occupation.[8]

Another characteristic of the Japanese transition to an industrial society is the high proportion of commercial employment. The surplus agricultural population was largely absorbed by commerce. As Colin Clark has said, commerce carried out by working proprietors and their families has been unusually common in Japan.[9]

---

[6]For the periods before 1900 see Hirano, Yoshitarō, *Nihon Shihon-shugi Shakai no Kikō* (The Mechanism of Japanese Capitalism), 6th ed. (Tokyo: Iwanami Shoten, 1940), p. 83; for later periods see *Meiji Taishō Kokusei Sōran* (General Statistics for the Meiji and Taishō Periods) (Tokyo: Tōyō Keizai Shimpō Sha, 1927), p. 507, and *Japan Statistical Yearbook 1961*, p. 71.

[7]Hirano, pp. 81–84, states that 36 percent of all landowning farmers in 1886 and 34 percent in 1891 were engaged in part-time subsidiary work, as compared with 37 percent and 41 percent of all tenant farmers.

[8]Lockwood, William W., *The Economic Development of Japan, Growth and Structural Change, 1868–1938* (Princeton: Princeton University Press, 1964), p. 464.

[9]Clark, p. 436.

Reviewing changes in the labor force during the early years of Japan's industrialization, William W. Lockwood comments:

Japan remained throughout the Meiji Era (1868–1912) a predominantly agricultural country. Farming continued to provide the largest share of the national income, and to afford the principal livelihood for over half of the country's population. Only slowly did it yield to the advance of the newer industries and service trades, where the more dynamic growth was taking place. More rapid transfer to non-agricultural pursuits was held in check by the swelling population, which brought intense competition in the industrial labor market and dammed up the existing farm population on the land.[10]

By about 1900 the population employed in agriculture had not only decreased proportionately but had also decreased slightly in absolute numbers. The surplus population continued to move into industry and commerce, greatly increasing the work force in these sectors of employment. The role of surplus rural population as a source of supply for the urban and industrial labor force continues today to be no less important than during the earlier stages of industrialization. Sons and daughters of farm families continue to enter industrial employment. Agricultural employment represented 38 percent of the total labor force in 1955; by 1960 the proportion had decreased to 32 percent. If women in agriculture (7.4 million women as compared with 6.9 million men) are excluded, the percentage of men engaged in agriculture, fishing, and forestry in 1960 was less than one-fifth (19 percent) of the working population.[11]

This brief examination of changes in the labor force makes it clear that Japan has made a very rapid transition from agriculture to industry, and the movement of the labor force may be regarded as a measure of Japan's industrialization. Industrialization inevitably results in social rearrangements of various kinds, and we now turn to an examination of changes in social structure as related to changes in occupation.

---

[10]Lockwood, p. 462.

[11]Bureau of Statistics, Office of the Prime Minister, *Japan Statistical Yearbook, 1961* (Tokyo: Japan Statistical Association, 1962), p. 56. This annual publication will be cited hereafter as *JSY*.

National Changes in Occupational Structure

In order to understand occupational mobility among the Japanese business leaders of 1960 and to help determine whether or to what extent their positions of leadership were ascribed or achieved, it is necessary to examine the occupational mobility of the Japanese nation as a whole during the life spans of the business leaders.

A concomitant of economic growth is an increase in positions of authority and high prestige, which in turn implies social mobility. Nelson N. Foote and Paul K. Hatt have pointed out that ". . . many studies of social mobility arrive at their conclusions simply by comparing the occupations of sons with the occupations of their fathers without subtracting the influence of the flow of labor into the more advanced occupation."[12] In order to study the occupational mobility of business leaders in Japan, where industrialization took place within the past two or three generations, general economic growth as measured by occupational changes in the nation as a whole must be given special attention to ascertain whether or to what degree business leaders have risen occupationally above the national level. The occupational structure of Japan in 1883, 1920, and 1960 offers a basis for comparing the occupations of grandfathers and fathers of the 1960 business leaders, as well as conveying some information about modern and premodern social structure. The intervals chosen here are approximately forty years; 1883 was selected as the starting point because it is the earliest year for which the desired information is available.

Table 2 shows the national occupational structure as it appears in the census figures for the years we have selected. It should be noted that, owing to changes in census policies, occupational classifications used for the three periods are not identical. The statistics for 1883 lack detail, but they are useful as a basis for inferring the general trend of occupational stratification of the time.

In 1883 about three-fourths of the gainfully employed population were farmers, and the country lacked the high degree of labor specialization characteristic of industrialized societies. Laborers in

---

[12]Foote, Nelson N. and Hatt, Paul K., "Social Mobility and Economic Advancement," *American Economic Review*, Vol. 43 (May 1953), p. 370.

Table 2. Occupational Structure: 1883, 1920 and 1960

	Thousands of Workers			Percent of Workers		
	1883	1920	1960	1883	1920	1960
Government officials	5	34	94	.02	.12	.21
Officials and managers, Private business	n.a.	n.a.	922	n.a.	n.a.	2.11
Professions	201	499	2,137	.93	1.85	4.89
Professors and teachers	97	226	787	.45	.84	1.81
Medical workers	37	108	556	.17	.40	1.27
Priests	67	69	111	.31	.26	.25
Writers and artists		58	75		.21	.17
Lawyers	n.a.	5	22	n.a.	.02	.05
Other professions		33	586		.12	1.34
White collar workers	n.a.	1,299	7,883	n.a.	4.81	18.04
Clerical, public service	181	278	1,610	.83	1.03	3.69
Clerical, private business	n.a.	752	3,434	n.a.	2.78	7.86
Salesworkers	n.a.	269	2,839	n.a.	1.00	6.49
Business owners or managers	1,538	3,260	4,038	7.09	12.08	9.24
Mining, construction, manufacturing	24	1,307	1,843	.11	4.84	4.21
Retailers and wholesalers	1,134	1,217	1,774	5.23	4.51	4.06
Other services	380	736	421	1.75	2.73	.97
Laborers	n.a.	6,863	14,352	n.a.	25.42	32.85
Mining, construction, manufacturing	680	4,102	11,010	3.14	15.18	25.20
Transportation, other services	46	2,761	3,342	.21	10.23	7.65
Farmers	16,882	14,671	14,253	77.84	54.35	32.63
Landlords, owner-operators and tenants	5,861	5,361	5,223	27.02	19.86	11.96
Family members and laborers	11,021	9,310	9,030	50.82	34.49	20.67
Other occupations	2,031[a] 125[b]	360[c]	11[d]	9.36 .58	1.37	.03
Total	21,689	26,995	43,690	100.00	100.00	100.00

a. Miscellaneous job holders
b. Occupation unidentifiable
c. Unearned income only
d. Occupation unclassifiable

Sources and Notes for 1883: The figures for 1883 are primarily from Hirano, Yoshitarō, *Nihon Shihonshugi Shakai no Kikō* (The Mechanism of Japanese Capitalism), 6th ed.

(Tokyo: Iwanami Shoten, 1949), p. 83, based on the census of January, 1883 by the Nōshōmusho (Ministry of Agriculture and Commerce). The census report is included in *Meiji-Zenki Zaisei Shiryō Shūsei* (Materials on Financial and Economic History in the Early Meiji Period) (Tokyo: Kaizōsha, 1931), XVIII: pp. 37–38.

In addition to the above data, which are classified mainly by industry, supplementary statistics on various occupational groups were drawn from *JSY*, 1885. "Government officials" and "clerical" include military as well as civilian personnel. The former include 4,944 men of *chokunin* or *sōnin* rank (military commissioned officers and civilian officials of comparable rank) and 521 civilian district headmen (*kuchō* and *gunchō*). "Clerical" includes 85,373 men of *hannin* or lower rank (military noncommissioned officers and other enlisted men; national government civilian officials and employees of comparable rank) and 96,535 clerks employed by local governments (*kochō, shoki,* and *jimu*). (*Ibid.*, pp. 872, 874, 892.)

Business owners or managers include 2,033 factory owners and 21,824 manufacturers of *sake* and *shōyu* (*ibid.*, pp. 175–83); 1,134,191 households in retail and wholesale, and 379,937 households in service industries (*ibid.*, pp. 233–36). Statistics on the manufacturing industry include 680,224 employees, classified as laborers in the present table. Also classified as laborers are 148,744 servants in private houses and 31,258 soldiers that appear in Hirano's table. No information is available on other categories of laborers or unskilled workmen.

The figures for farmers include people engaged in fishing. The figures for landlords, owner-operators and tenants and number of households in farming and fishing are for 1886, when statistics of this kind were first recorded (*JSY*, 1888, p. 175 and 183). "Other occupations," which embraces 2,031,280 people, is in Japanese *zatsugyō* ("miscellaneous" or, more accurately, "odd jobs"). It is thought that people so classified were principally workmen in various petty handicrafts and peddlers. According to the sources used, the total working population in 1883 was 21,689,000, of which 125,000 were in unidentified occupations.

Sources and Notes for 1920:   The figures are based on the first detailed census of occupations in 1920 (Bureau of Statistics, Imperial Cabinet, *Shokugyō: Kokusei Chōsa Hōkoku*, Vol. II (Occupations: 1920 National Census Report, 1929), and on *JSY*, 1924 and 1929).

A large number of the railroads and all mail, telegraph, and telephone services were owned by the government at this time but were classified under business (transportation and communication) in the 1920 census. (Additional details are shown in the statistics on employed males in 1920. Of the adults in 1920, 382,897 are classified as lacking occupations (*mushokugyō*) and these are not included in the table.

Sources and Notes for 1960:   The principal source is the 1960 census report, as summarized in *JSY*, 1961, p. 57. This does not give the number of priests and lawyers; these were taken from other sources recorded in the same yearbook, pp. 448 and 482.

mining, construction, manufacturing, and service industries accounted for only 3.3 percent of the total. White collar workers in private business were not yet differentiated from servants in merchant families. It is safe to conclude that very little of the labor force was employed in the budding industries of the time. Retail and wholesale activities were carried out by traditional merchants. The number of government officials, military officers, teachers, and clerks in public service stands out prominently against the number of people engaged in traditional businesses and in industry. Outstanding characteristics of employment of the period were that the family formed a work unit and that there were few jobs in industry or allied business concerns except governmental agencies.

Between 1883 and 1920 the total employed population increased 24 percent, or about 5 million. Occupational specialization became more complex. There were significant increases in industrial employment and in the number of professional men, white collar workers, and laborers. Certain occupational groups more than doubled during the period: government officials, professors and teachers, medical workers, white collar workers in clerical and sales positions, business owners or managers, and laborers in manufacturing. Occupational groups that did not expand were retailers and wholesalers. Farmers decreased to 5 percent of the total but still provided a large reservoir of surplus labor for industrial employment in the decades that followed.

The industrial labor force of skilled, semiskilled, and unskilled workers had increased substantially by 1920, and continued to increase in both absolute and relative numbers in later decades. Workers in manufacturing increased more than those in service industries. Officials in public service and professions comprised 1.9 percent and white collar workers, 4.8 percent of the total. Between 1883 and 1920, there were large increases in the number of business owners and managers, particularly in mining, construction, and manufacturing. The number of retail and wholesale workers did not increase in proportion to the general increase in population.

In comparison with the occupational distribution in other countries, the proportion of small business owners in Japan was high throughout the forty-year period of this study and was unusually high in 1920. The proportions are 7 percent in 1883, 13 percent in 1920 (in contrast with 5 percent in the United States), and 9 percent in 1960.[13] One-third (33.6 percent) of the total employed population was classified as *gyōshu* (employer or manager). There are no statistics to indicate whether they were self-employed workers or entrepreneurs engaging a number of employees. We may note, however, that the number of clerks (3.2 percent) and of

[13]Warner, W. Lloyd and Abegglen, James C., *Occupational Mobility in American Business and Industry* (Minneapolis: University of Minnesota Press, 1955), p. 40.

laborers including family workers (63.2 percent) indicates only a one-to-two ratio of employers to employees in 1920.[14]

The exceedingly high proportion of self-employed workers, not only in agriculture but also in manufacturing and trading, is also characteristic of Japanese society. One reason for this is that many farmers and farm households have side occupations, especially in petty handicrafts. It is also noteworthy that among persons engaged in retailing and wholesaling in 1920, 57.6 percent were employers or self-employed and 42.4 percent were employees. This ratio indicates that retailing and wholesaling were carried out principally by working proprietors and members of their families. It is also clear that employment in manufacturing was still small in 1920. The proportion of employers to employees was 24 percent to 76 percent. (In table 2 all working proprietors are counted as small business owners.)

The 1960 census classified the employed population under four headings: employer, worker on own account, family worker, and employee. In agriculture, work is carried out almost entirely by self-employed workers and members of their families. Thirty-six percent of the agricultural labor force was composed of self-employed heads of families (worker on own account) and 58 percent were family workers.[15] There is no major change in employment in agriculture in this respect in spite of great technological changes in agriculture itself and in economic conditions affecting it.

In manufacturing and construction, the proportion of self-employed workmen (worker on own account) and family workers showed a significant decrease by 1960. Although about 12 percent of the remaining self-employed and family workers were in this group, the predominant employment was in large and expanding industrial enterprises.

In the wholesale and retail trades, 23 percent of the total were still workers on own account and 18 percent were family workers. By 1960 a few firms had become gigantic, and there had been considerable growth in the average size of firms. However, it is clear

---

[14]The 1920 figures are from Bureau of Statistics, Imperial Cabinet, *Shokugyō: Kokusei Chōsa Hōkoku*, Vol. II (Occupations: 1920 National Census Report, 1929), pp. 40–41.
[15]*JSY*, 1961, p. 56.

that in present-day Japan wholesaling and retailing are in considerable part still carried out by the working proprietor and members of his family.

Japan in 1883 was not an industrialized nation; more than three-fourths of its people were in agriculture, and labor specialization was not highly developed. By 1920 the occupational structure had shifted along the lines of industrialization. The agrarian population had decreased significantly, and the number of people who were business owners or managers, white collar workers, technicians, or laborers had markedly increased. Although the average business and industrial firm was small, Japan had gradually developed large enterprises in manufacturing and the service industries.[16] By 1960 Japan had become highly industrialized, with large organizations in business and industry. Correspondingly, clerical, fiscal, and administrative positions became abundant and are now the major occupations in large business and industrial organizations. These positions have increased vastly in recent years both absolutely and in relation to other occupations.

When studies of occupational shifts are compared with studies of occupational prestige,[17] there can be no doubt that the expanding occupations are on the whole those of higher prestige, whereas the contracting occupations are on the whole those of lower prestige. In general the increases in the categories of officials, managers, professional men, and white collar workers are much larger than among other groups. The large increase in the number of persons in high positions in the industrial hierarchy is, of course, due to rapid economic expansion and the development of large organizations and bureaucratic administrations.

---

[16]The growth of factory industry in Japan (1909–1938) is described in detail in Lockwood, pp. 100–150.

[17]A study of occupational ranking reports that professional men and administrators enjoy the highest prestige in present-day Japanese society. See Nihon Shakai Gakkai Chōsa Iinkai, *Nihon Shakai no Kaisōteki Kōzō* (Hierarchical Structure of Japanese Society) (Tokyo: Yūhikaku, 1958), pp. 12–17. International comparisons of occupational prestige among industrialized nations indicate that the social ranking of various occupations in Japanese society is similar to that in other industrialized nations. See Inkeles, Alex and Rossi, Peter H., "National Comparisons of Occupational Prestige," *American Journal of Sociology* 61 (Jan. 1956), pp. 329–39.

Chapter 2

OCCUPATIONAL ORIGINS OF
THE BUSINESS LEADERS OF 1960

Age and Time Factors

Who are the present Japanese business leaders included in this study? Their median age is 58.6 years. One percent are under 40 years of age and one percent are over 76. Slightly over three-fourths are between 51 and 65 years of age. Over one-third (36 percent) are between 56 and 60 years. The median age of American business leaders in 1952 was 53.7 years[1] and of British business leaders during the same year, 55.5 years.[2] The men occupying top management positions in the largest firms of Japan are thus older than their British and American counterparts by three and five years, respectively.

If we examine the Japanese business leaders of 1960 from a historical perspective, we see that most were born around the turn of the century. About 35 percent were born in the last decade of the nineteenth century, and the remaining 65 percent in the first decade of the twentieth. Thus, most were born from thirty to thirty-five years—one full generation—after the Meiji Restoration of 1868. They grew up during the Russo-Japanese War of 1905–06 and the First World War (1914–19) and began their business careers chiefly between 1915 and 1930.

Following Rostow's recent description of the stages of economic growth,[3] we may say that these men were born as Japan moved decisively toward industrialization. (Japan's "take-off" is placed

---

[1]Warner, W. Lloyd and Abegglen, James C., *Occupational Mobility in American Business and Industry* (Minneapolis; University of Minnesota Press, 1955), p. 135.
[2]Copeman, G. H., *Leaders in British Industry* (London: Gee & Company, 1955), p. 144.
[3]Rostow, pp. 4–16.

variously at 1878–1900 or 1900–1920.)[4] The men studied represent Japan's business leadership after Japan achieved technological maturity, and they appear one full generation later than their counterparts in the United States, in terms of national economic development.[5]

Occupation of Fathers of 1960 Business Leaders

After reviewing reports of empirical research on social mobility in various industrial countries, Lipset and Bendix conclude that "widespread social mobility has been a concomitant of industrialization and a basic characteristic of modern society. In every industrial country, a large proportion of the population have had to find occupations considerably different from those of their parents."[6] However, the same authors state that studies of the social origins of the business elite in the Western countries show that there is less intergenerational movement in occupational status among top executives in the business hierarchy than among men in lesser positions.[7]

In attempting to determine the patterns of movement of the business elite of Japan against the background of intergenerational mobility in occupations of the population as a whole, we sought answers to the following specific questions: Who are the business leaders of present-day Japan? What are their occupational origins? Who were their fathers and their grandfathers?

By comparing the proportions of business leaders of different occupational backgrounds with the proportions of such occupations in Japanese society as a whole, we are able to determine from which social classes Japanese business leaders are recruited, i.e., which occupations were overrepresented and underrepresented among leaders. It was also possible to get some indication of the effect of distinctions by social class and practices of inheritance.

---

[4]*Ibid.*, pp. 38–40.

[5]The rough symbolic dates for technological maturity are given by Rostow as 1900 for the United States and 1940 for Japan (*ibid.*, p. 59).

[6]Lipset, Seymour M. and Bendix, Reinhard, *Social Mobility in Industrial Society* (Berkeley and Los Angeles: University of California Press, 1959), p. 11.

[7]*Ibid.*, pp. 39–40.

Table 3. Occupation of Fathers of 1960 Business Leaders

Occupation	Number	Percentage
Unskilled or semiskilled workers	3	0.3
Skilled workers	10	1.0
Farmers (*jikosaku*)	65	6.7
Landlords (*jinushi*)	168	17.3
White collar workers (private business)	24	2.5
White collar workers (public service)	63	6.5
Owners of small businesses	210	21.6
Owners of large or medium businesses	113	11.5
Executives of large or medium businesses	105	10.5
Central government officials	42	4.3
Local government officials	54	5.5
Military officers	16	1.7
Professors and scholars	24	2.5
Doctors of medicine	23	2.5
Engineers	20	2.1
Lawyers	8	0.7
Priests	8	0.7
Other professions	11	1.2
Samurai	3	0.4
No occupation	4	0.5
Total	974	100.0

Did these keep members of socially elite families at the top, or did commercial competition produce an emphasis on individual achievement in the selection of business leaders?

Table 3 shows the occupations of fathers of the Japanese business leaders of 1960—their principal occupations at the peak of their working lives, when their sons were first embarking on their own careers. These have been grouped in twenty categories. (Of the total of 985 respondents, 11 did not answer the question concerning the occupation of their fathers.)

Only 0.3 percent of the business leaders are sons of unskilled or semiskilled workers, and only 1 percent are sons of skilled laborers. Twenty-four percent are sons of farmers, but the term *farmer* covers a broad range of meaning. About two-thirds of this category are sons of landlords, who did not themselves farm, and one-third are sons of owner-farmers and tenant farmers, who were generally much poorer than landlords.

Nine percent of the business elite are sons of white collar workers, the majority (6.5 percent) of whom were in public service. A much smaller number (2.5 percent) were employed by private enterprises. This kind of ratio is to be expected, since white collar work in public service was held in higher regard in Japanese society than employment in private firms.

Sons of men who owned small business concerns constitute 21.6 percent. An additional 11.5 percent are sons of owners of large and medium businesses, making the general category of sons of owners of business firms approximately one-third (33.1 percent) of the total. (As noted in chapter 1, "small business" means enterprises of very small scale, generally consisting only of the proprietor and members of his family.) If owners (11.5 percent) and executives (10.5 percent) of medium or large business concerns are regarded as approximate social equals, the total for this social category is 22 percent.

Sons of government officials and military officers account for 12 percent of the Japanese business leaders in 1960. Their fathers include 4.3 percent employed by the central government, 5.5 percent by local government, and 1.7 percent who were military officers.

Sons of professional men total 10 percent. Most of their fathers were college or university professors (2.5 percent), doctors of medicine (2.5 percent), or engineers (2.1 percent). Only a few were lawyers (0.7 percent) or priests (0.7 percent). A scattering of other professions constitutes 1.2 percent.

The remaining 0.9 percent are sons of samurai (0.4 percent) and men who had no occupation (0.5 percent). These are assumed to be families of high or fairly high social class who derived their livelihood from sources other than gainful employment.

Most of the occupational categories employed in this study are commonly used in describing social stratification in the United States and other Western countries. It is useful to apply this classification to the population of Japan, but the reader will be misled if he thinks the various occupations are the same in Japan and the West.

A generation ago, employment in Japan retained many characteristics of preindustrial times. Our questionnaire asked for the "principal occupation" of the father of the respondent. In some cases, where the respondent seemingly felt that a single answer was unsuitable, multiple responses were given. Table 4 gives detailed information on principal occupations and includes multiple occupations.

Table 4.   Detailed Occupation of Fathers of 1960 Business Leaders

Occupation of Father	Number	Detailed Occupation of Father	Number
Laborer: unskilled or semiskilled	3	Laborer (no other known occupation)	3
Laborer: skilled	10	Carpenter	3
		Garden designer	2
		Blacksmith	1
		Wax chandler	1
		Small boat operator	1
		Woodcarver	1
		Brush maker	1
Farmer	65	Tenant farmer or owner farmer (no other known occupation)	61
		Owner farmer and retail store owner	2
		Owner farmer and town mayor	1
		Owner farmer and fisherman	1
Landlord	163	Landlord	134
		Landlord and village or town mayor	16
		Landlord and *sake* or *shōyu* maker	6
		Landlord and retail store owner	4
		Landlord and textile manufacturing	3
		Landlord and lumbering	3
		Landlord and boat owner	1
		Landlord and medicine manufacturing	1
White collar worker (private business)	24	Company clerk	17
		Bank clerk	4
		Servant of noble family	2
		Bantō of *sake* maker	1
White collar worker (public office)	63	Clerk in public office	44
		Primary or high school teacher	16

Occupation of Father	Number	Detailed Occupation of Father	Number
		Draftsman in public office	3
Owner, small business	210	Retailer (clothing 8, food 6, jeweler 4, *sake* 3, other [e.g. coal, rice, charcoal, paper, ceramics, drugs], 27)	48
		Wholesaler (rice 8, textiles 8, general 3, others 3)	22
		Other wholesaler or retailer (type unknown)	24
		Service business	28
		Sake or *shōyu* maker	17
		Textile manufacturing	13
		Lumbering and construction	11
		Other small industry	21
		Owner of small business (type unknown)	26
Owner, large or medium business	113	Steel, machinery, chemical mfg.	25
		Trader (foreign and domestic)	16
		Banking and insurance	13
		Transportation and public utility	10
		Sake (4) and food manufacturing	11
		Textile and paper	9
		Other light industry	9
		Construction and lumbering	9
		Service industry	8
		Owner of large or medium business (type unknown)	3
Executive, large or medium business	105	Steel, machinery, chemical mfg.	14
		Trading	13
		Banking (24) and insurance	36
		Transportation and public utility	9
		Food industry	10
		Textile and paper	5
		Construction	7
		Service industry	5
		Executive of large or medium business (type unknown)	6
Government official (national)	42	Administrative branch:	
		Justice	8
		Railroad	7

Occupation of Father	Number	Detailed Occupation of Father	Number
		Home and colonial	5
		Treasury	4
		Foreign affairs	3
		Postal	3
		Agriculture and Commerce	2
		Imperial household	2
		Department or position unknown	4
		Legislative branch	4
Government official (local)	54	Principal of primary or middle school	20
		Mayor or senior staff in local office	17
		Postmaster	7
		Engineer in local office	2
		Local official (position unknown)	8
Military officer	16	General or admiral	8
		Colonel or major	5
		Captain or lieutenant	3
Profession	94	Professor or scholar	24
		Doctor of medicine	23
		Engineer	20
		Lawyer	8
		Buddhist priest	4
		Shinto priest	4
		Other professions	11
Other occupation	7	Samurai	3
		No occupation	4
Total	974		974

Of the thirteen respondents who stated that their fathers had been laborers, three gave no details. The fathers of the remaining ten were all skilled laborers in traditional arts and crafts. It appears likely that none of the three who are inadequately identified was employed as an industrial laborer.

Farmers consist of two groups. One of these is operating farmers, either owner-farmers or tenants. Only a few of this group had subsidiary employment. The second group, landlords, had substantial holdings of land and gained their livelihood from tenants' fees or by farming with hired or apprenticed workers. Members of this group tended more than operating farmers to have multiple employment and often held political offices or engaged in commerce, principally as owners of *sake* and *shōyu* factories.

With the beginning of industrialization, Japan established many local and national governmental bureaus and a system of public education. White collar workers in these offices and schools, and in the new manufacturing and service industries and financial institutions, soon constituted a large and important part of the labor force of Japan. They were soon given the name *sarari-man* (salaried man) that remains in use today. The white collar workers among the fathers of the 1960 business leaders were probably members of the first generation of this occupational specialty in Japan. Earlier employment in similar work was limited mostly to certain retainers of feudal lords and the *bantō* of merchant families.

In general, the small business owners represent traditional or early types of industrial firms, those that had existed before industrialization began and those established after Tokugawa restrictions on foreign trade had been lifted. Retailers and wholesalers of various commodities comprise about one-half of this group. Owners of small manufacturing firms are next in frequency, followed by owners of service industries.

Owners and executives of large or medium size businesses comprise the largest group of fathers, and their sons form the largest group of leaders in heavy industry. Sons of executives are best represented in finance. Men with other occupational backgrounds on the parental level are distributed widely among all categories of commerce and industry.

Sons of government officials and military officers compose 11.5 percent of the modern business leaders. Fathers who were officials of the national government were in all governmental branches, but were most commonly employed by the Ministry of Justice and the former Ministry of Railways. Officials of local governments include senior officials in public offices, postmasters, and principals of public schools. Among fathers who were military officers, those of high rank are best represented.

Professional men include college or university professors, medical doctors, engineers, lawyers, priests, and journalists. Sons of principals and teachers of public schools identified their fathers as officials and public servants, respectively, and we accordingly classified these occupations as clerks and officials in public service.

It is clear that not all occupational backgrounds are equally represented in top-level business positions. Sons of owners and executives of large or medium business concerns are represented in considerably greater proportion than men with other occupational backgrounds, and sons of laborers and farmers are few. The average age of the businessmen studied is about 59, and their average age at the time of first employment was about 22. The census statistics for 1920 are thus the most suitable for comparing the occupations of the fathers of the business leaders with national figures for adult males.

Detailed Analysis of 1920 Adult Male Occupational Structure

The distribution of the Japanese population by occupation in 1920 has already been briefly reviewed in connection with occupational trends from 1883 to 1960 (chapter 1, table 2). Table 5 shows the occupational distribution of employed adult males over age fourteen in 1920, and, because the statistics are limited to males, they show quite different proportions of various occupations than our earlier figures, which included females. Table 5 is not comparable with the earlier statistics for another reason. For purposes of comparison, we have reclassified the 1920 occupations into categories similar to those used in tables 3 and 4.

The census data for 1920 do not allow a breakdown by occupation into the number of categories employed in the questionnaire, and for this reason the comparison in the foregoing analysis is restricted to a more limited list of occupations. The first occupational group, government officials, was important in the analysis of occupational mobility. Central government officials are few in number but enjoy higher status than local government officials. Although status varies considerably from top to bottom ranks, government officials in general have superior social status on both national and local levels in Japanese society.

Table 5. Employed Adult Males Over Age 14 in 1920

Occupation		Thousands		Percent
Government officials[1]		62		.36
Central government officials	6		.04	
Military officers	17		.09	
Local public officials	12		.07	
Local officials, Post Office and National Railway	10		.06	
Principals of public schools	17		.10	
Executives of business firms[2] (approx.)		300		1.75
Professions[3]		225		1.32
Professors	7		.04	
Doctors of medicine	76		.45	
Lawyers	5		.03	
Priests	63		.37	
Writers, artists	49		.29	
Other professions	25		.14	
White collar workers[4]		1,348		7.89
Teachers in public schools	132		.78	
Clerks, civil service	332		1.94	
Clerks and sales workers in private business	884		5.17	
Small business owners[5]		2,249		13.17
Laborers		4,490		26.29
Farmers[6]		8,251		48.31
Landlords	1,243		7.25	
Farmers	7,008		41.06	
Unearned income only[7]		156		.91
Total		17,081		100.00%

Sources:
[1]Bureau of Statistics, Imperial Cabinet, *Shokugyō: Kokusei Chōsa Hōkoku*, Vol. II (Occupations: 1920 National Census Report, 1929). The figures are drawn from the most detailed breakdown (252 classifications) of occupations in the census (pp. 44–68).
[2]*JSY*, 1929.

Notes:
[1]"Central government officials" include 4,734 in the various branches of the central government and 1,399 of *chokunin* or *sōnin* rank in the National Railways and postal service, who are classified as transportation and communication officials in the census report (*JSY*, 1929, p. 398). Other officials (9,695) in the National Railway and postal service are classified as local officials (*Shokugyō: Kokusei Chōsa Hōkoku*, Vol. II, p. 63).
[2]The census does not give the number of executives of business firms. We estimated them on the following basis. There were 29,917 companies, of which three-fourths

were joint-stock corporations and the rest limited or unlimited partnerships (*JSY*, 1926, p. 207). We checked several yearbooks of companies for 1920 and found the number of directors in each company varying from 7 to 20 in the large companies and from 3 to 12 (mostly 5 to 9) in the smaller companies. The average appears to be about 7. However, in order to avoid underestimating the number of executives, we estimated 10 executives in each of the 29,917 companies. The number of executives was then deducted from the number of business owners or executives and those remaining were classified as small business owners. Others have estimated the number of executives in 1930 at 324,000 (Keizai Tōkei Kenkyūsho, ed., *Nihon Keizai Tōkei Shū* [Collected Economic Statistics for Japan] [Tokyo: Tōyō Keizai Shimpō Sha, 1960], p. 352). Our estimate of 300,000 executives in 1920 may be too high but is certainly not too low.

[3]The census report for 1920 does not separate professors in colleges or universities from teachers in primary, middle, or higher schools. The figure for professors is taken from *JSY*, 1923, p. 396.

[4]Among white collar workers, "clerks in public service" include clerks in the postal service (37,376), National Railways (24,468), and various central and local government offices (*Shokugyō: Kokusei Chōsa Hōkoku*, Vol. II, p. 63).

[5]Small business owners include all business owners and managers (*gyōshu*) except those in agriculture.

[6]We assume a proportion of 15 landlords to 85 operating farmers for our study on the following basis. We examined research reports concerning the status hierarchy of farmers in Japan, including both national surveys and individual case studies. A study of occupational mobility conducted by the Research Committee of the Japan Sociological Society in 1955 using a national population sample reports the following occupations for fathers of subjects studied: landlord, 7 percent; owner-farmer, 74 percent; tenant, 28 percent; unknown, 1 percent (Nihon Shakai Gakkai Chōsa Iinkai, *Nihon Shakai No Kaisōteki Kōzō* [Hierarchical Structure of Japanese Society] [Tokyo: Yūhikaku, 1958], p. 120). The sampling methods in this study seem not to have been entirely satisfactory due to overrepresentation of the urban white collar population and underrepresentation of laborers and farmers (*ibid.*, p. 86), but this 7 to 93 ratio helps support the view that the 15 to 85 ratio is a conservative estimate of the proportion of owner-operators and tenant farmers a generation ago.

A village study in Honshū reported by Furushima, Toshio, *Kisei Jinushi no Seisei to Tenkai* (Development of Parasitical Landowners) (Tokyo: Iwanami Shoten, 1952) indicates that 11 percent of the farmers in the community, consisting of 179 to 201 farm households during the period from 1903 to 1921, were owner-operators who owned 2 or more hectares, and the rest were owners with less than 2 hectares, tenants, or farm laborers. This study of class structure in a village community was conducted in Kugamura, Otokuni district, Kyoto Prefecture, in central Japan (*ibid.*, pp. 120–1). Farm households owning more than 3 hectares of land represented 10.3 percent of the total number of farm households in 1920 (*Meiji Taishō Kokusei Sōran* [General Statistics for the Meiji and Taishō Periods] [Tokyo: Tōyō Keizai Shimpō Sha, 1927], p. 508). If we define landlords as owners of more than 3 hectares, the proportion of landlords to operating farm is 1 to 10. We received expert advice on this problem from Professor Fukutake Tadashi. Reviewing table 4, Detailed Occupation of Father of 1960 Business Leaders, he commented that "the men who identified their fathers' occupations as 'landlord' come from families that held high social status in rural Japan, and with their families probably represented about 5 percent of the farm population."

[7]The total number of people in the census whose livelihood came from unearned income is 156,000 or 91 percent of the total number of employed adult males. One-fourth were landlords living on tenants' fees, one-fifth depended on income from investments in stocks, and the others lived on various types of pensions.

The second occupational group, executives of business firms, includes the fathers of more of the 1960 business leaders than any other. Unfortunately, the census data on occupations do not make possible an accurate separation of owners of small businesses from owners or executives of large or medium businesses, and it was necessary for us to make an estimate. In 1920 the total number of corporative enterprises was 29,917.[8] Studies indicate that 10 executives represent an average for 1 company. We assumed, then, that the number of owners or executives of large or medium businesses in the population in 1920 was approximately 300,000. (Additional details on this estimate are stated in note 2 to table 5.) This estimate is the basis for proportions employed in the table.

We have also separated professors in colleges and universities from teachers in primary, middle, or higher schools, classifying professors as professional men and teachers as white collar workers. As previously stated, school principals have been classified as local public officials.

The 1920 census did not divide laborers into skilled, semiskilled, and unskilled. Since almost one half of the employed adult males of 1920 were farmers and a substantial proportion of the 1960 business leaders were sons of "farmers," it was important to distinguish landlords from other farmers, who stand much below landlords in wealth and prestige. Various types of data providing a basis for estimating the ratio of landlords to operating farmers were examined (see note 6 to table 5). These studies indicate that landlords represented between 5 and 15 percent of the total number of farmers during 1920. We choose the higher figure but believe nevertheless that it is a conservative estimate.

The occupational distribution of the 1920 adult male population becomes more meaningful when it is condensed into large categories. Government officials, owners or executives of large or medium business and professionals, who are of high and approximately equal status in Japanese society, comprised 3.4 percent of the total in 1920. Owners of small business and white collar workers—the middle class—represented 21 percent. Laborers and operating farmers—the working class—represented 67 percent. About

---

[8]*JSY*, 1925, p. 207.

7 percent of the landlords may be assigned to either the upper or the middle class.

Vertical Mobility in Japanese Business Leadership

Table 6 presents data contrasting the occupational distribution in 1920 of the adult male population of Japan with that of the fathers of the 1960 business leaders. Comparison of the first and second columns shows that less than 1 percent (.36 percent) of the 1920 adult male population were government officials, but 11.5 percent of the 1960 business leaders are the sons of government officials. Only 1.8 percent of the 1920 adult males were business owners or executives of large or medium business firms, whereas 22 percent of the 1960 business leaders are sons of business owners or executives of large business firms. Although 26 percent of the 1920 adult males were laborers, only 1 percent of the 1960 Japanese business leaders are sons of laborers.

If the movement of the subjects of our study into their positions had been uninfluenced by the occupational positions of their fathers, the proportions shown in the first and second columns of table 6 would be the same, and the ratio between the occupation distribution in the whole population and that of the fathers of 1960 business leaders would be 1. The actual ratio for each occupational group is presented in the third column of table 6, expressed in proportion to one hundred population.

Government officials are by far the most overrepresented. Officials of the central government stand highest, with a ratio of 10,750 to 100. Local government officials are next. Military officers stand lowest in this occupational category. This circumstance reflects partly the difference in social status among the three official groups.

Owners or executives of large or medium business concerns are in second position, and it is possible that inheritance of business ownership or top executive positions may have played an important part in determining the careers of their sons. We shall later examine this question more closely.

Table 6. Occupational Mobility and Business Leadership in Japan: Occupation of Fathers of 1960 Japanese Business Leaders and of 1920 Adult Employed Males

Occupation	Fathers of 1960 Japanese Business Leaders	Japan's Population 1920 Adult Employed Males	Ratio of Leaders' Fathers to Population (1 = 100)
Government officials	11.5%	.36%	3,194
Central government officials	4.3	.04	10,750
Local officials	5.5	.23	2,391
Military officers	1.7	.09	1,889
Owners or managers, large or medium businesses	22.0	1.75	1,257
Professional men	9.7	1.32	735
Professors	2.5	.04	6,250
Lawyers	.7	.03	2,333
Doctors of medicine	2.5	.45	556
Priests	.7	.37	189
Engineers and others	3.3	.43	767
Small business owners	21.6	13.17	164
White collar workers	9.0	7.89	114
Teachers	1.7	.78	218
Clerks in public office	4.8	1.94	247
Clerks and sales workers in private businesses	2.5	5.17	48
Laborers	1.3	26.29	5
Farmers	24.0	48.31	49
Landlords	17.3	7.25	238
Operating farmers	6.7	41.06	16
Other occupations	.9	.91	100
Total	100.0	100.00	100

Sons of professional men stand third in rank and constitute 9.7 percent of the 1960 business leaders, whereas only 1.32 percent of the total population in 1920 were in the professions. The ratio is 735. Sons of college professors and lawyers are extremely well represented among the business leaders. Sons of doctors, engineers and other professions are moderately well represented. Sons of priests are least well represented.

Two additional occupational groups of the paternal generation produced business leaders in proportions somewhat higher than might be expected. Owners of small business firms stand fourth in rank but much below the first three. Thirteen percent of the 1920 population and 21.6 percent of the fathers of the business leaders of 1960 were in this occupation. The ratio is 164.

Sons of white collar workers stand fifth in order. Nine percent of the business leaders are sons of white collar workers, as against 7.89 percent white collar workers in the national population in 1920. The ratio (114) is only slightly above the average expectation. A sharp difference in frequency is observable among white collar workers according to specific occupations. Sons of teachers and clerks in public offices are much better represented than sons of clerks and salespeople in private business, whose ratio is below the average expectation.

It is clear that movement to business leadership is limited for sons of farmers and manual workers of all kinds and is especially uncommon for sons of laborers. For sons of small business owners and white collar workers, the rate of movement into these positions is a little greater than random chance would allow. For sons of men of upper status, chances of assuming leadership are markedly high. In spite of the great increase in top executive positions that has accompanied rapid industrialization, big business firms in Japan have tended to recruit their top executive force principally from a narrow social circle.

Only 24 percent of the 1960 business leaders are sons of farmers, who constituted 48 percent of the 1920 population. The ratio is thus one-half that expected. However, if we look at landlords and operating farmers separately, we see that the former more than doubles the expected rate, but the latter is far below expectation.

It is striking that sons of laborers compose only 1.3 percent of the 1960 business leaders, whereas more than one-quarter (26.3 percent) of the population in 1920 were laborers. The ratio is 26:1 or 5 per 100 and this occupational group is one least likely to produce business leaders.

The statistics leave no doubt that the 1960 business elite was composed chiefly of the sons of men of relatively high occupational status: government officials, business men, and professional men. It is clear that birth into a family in the business and professional echelons enormously increases the probability of a man's subsequently holding a leadership position in business.

It is interesting to speculate on the social implications of these proportions. The occupational categories are too general and crude to permit precise, graded assignments to social classes, but an approximation may be useful. Table 7 presents such an approximation, assuming that there is substantial reality underlying the ranks in which the several occupations are placed in the table.

The upper and upper-middle ranks of Japanese society appear to supply some three-fifths of the business leadership, while accounting for perhaps one-tenth of the adult population. The lower-middle ranks, presumably largely urban, are the source of about one-third of the business leaders and are represented in leadership in proportions slightly greater than their proportions in the population. The lower-ranked occupations, while accounting for slightly over two-thirds of the population, account for less than one-tenth of the business leaders.

Table 7.   Class Origin of Business Leadership

Social Rank	Occupation of Father	1960 Business Leaders	1920 Total Population
I	Big businessmen, government officials, professional men, and landlords	61%	11%
II	White collar workers and owners of small businesses	31	21
III	Laborers, operating farmers, and other laboring occupations	8	68
	Total	100%	100%

Family Influence on Business Leadership

An additional measure of occupational inheritance is available. Relations within the immediate family sometimes decisively influence the careers of business leaders. The influence of the family is felt not only in their choice of occupations but in the development and advancement of careers after the choice is made.

Nine percent of the men studied stated that they are in the same company as were their fathers. Of the 113 sons whose fathers were owners of large or medium business concerns, 45 percent are in their father's company. Among the 105 sons of executives of large or medium business firms, 19 percent are in the same companies as their fathers were. However, only 1 percent of sons whose fathers were in other occupations are in the same concerns as their fathers. For men whose fathers were not company owners or executives, there seems to be no favorable familial influence of the kind in question leading to business leadership. However, for the sons of owners of large or medium business firms, inheritance of positions of business leadership is notable. For the sons of executives in large or medium businesses, the influence of the father's position works favorably toward achieving positions of leadership in the companies with which their fathers were associated. We have also found that among 113 sons of owners of large or medium business concerns, 56 percent hold the positions of president or chairman of the board of directors, and 44 percent are vice presidents or senior managing directors. This indicates that inheritance is more common in chief executive positions than in other executive positions. It should also be noted that men who began their careers in the companies of which their fathers were owners or executives took less time than other men to reach executive positions. This is a subject we shall discuss in greater detail in ch. 5.

From the foregoing data on the occupations of the fathers of the 1960 business leaders, we have learned that there are substantial differences in what we may call the productivity ratio of the various occupational backgrounds from which the men spring. Most outstanding is the very high representation of sons of government officials and owners or executives of large or medium business concerns and the very low representation of sons of farmers. Now let us ask if there is any evidence that Japanese business leaders tend to be recruited more and more from big business background. Is there any tendency toward an increase or decrease of business executives whose fathers were professional men or white collar workers, groups that have increased in number and proportion in the total working population in recent decades? In attempting to answer these questions, it is useful to divide the executives into age groups and examine differences in their backgrounds as an indication of possible changes in mobility rates over time. This procedure is unreliable as a measure of long-term changes,[9] but we are concerned with only a relatively short span of time.

As we have noted, the average age of the 1960 business elite is 58.6 years. We have classified the men into three age groups. Table 8 shows the distribution of these groups according to the occupations of their fathers. Men under 61 years of age whose fathers were owners or executives of large business concerns, government officials, or professional men are overrepresented, and men of other occupational backgrounds in this age group are under-

Table 8. Distribution of 1960 Business Leaders by Age Group and Occupation of Fathers

Occupation of Fathers	Age of Sons in 1960			
	55 or Under	56–60	61 or Over	Total
Owner, large business	17%	9%	11%	11.5
Executive, large business	16	11	7	10.5
Government official	12	12	10	11
Professional man	8	14	7	10
White collar worker	9	9	9	9
Owner, small business	20	21	23	22
Laborer	2	1	1	1
Farmer	16	23	30	24
Other occupations	0	0	2	1
Total percent	100	100	100	100%
Number of individuals	271	347	356	974

[9]Lipset and Bendix, p. 174; Warner and Abeglen, p. 130.

represented. Among men 61 years of age or older, those whose fathers were landlords or farmers are most highly overrepresented, followed by men whose fathers were owners of small business firms.

These differences and others that may be noted among the age groups are, no doubt, the results of at least two factors working together. First, sons of owners or executives of large business firms reach important positions in business more rapidly than others do and thus are more strongly represented among the younger men of our sample. The sons of owners of small business concerns and of white collar workers apparently suffer some disadvantages in reaching positions of business leadership at early ages. The sons of farmers require a still longer time to reach important positions, and for this reason, few men of this occupational background appear in our youngest category. It is clear from these data that the occupational background of the business leaders exerts influence selectively. Negative selective factors are strongest for men whose occupational background on the parental level is farming, and relatively slight negative selection applies to men from middle-class urban backgrounds.

We may also recall that changes in the proportions of the various occupational groups during the last several decades include significant increases in managerial, professional, and white collar groups. These shifts that reflect increasing urbanization and industrialization certainly contributed toward the overrepresentation of men with managerial backgrounds and the underrepresentation of men with farming backgrounds, especially in the youngest age group. White collar workers fall in between these two extremes. From 1920 to 1960 white collar workers increased from 5 percent to 18 percent of the total working population. The present age of business leaders from the white collar groups is very close to the average for all business leaders.

Comparison by age groups thus does not reveal any clear trend toward decreased mobility for men with backgrounds of low social prestige. Only intergenerational comparisons of mobility rates to leadership positions can demonstrate increasing or decreasing net mobility rates. Conversely, it must be said that these data lend little or no support to the view that vertical mobility in Japan has been or is increasing.

Occupational Mobility from Paternal Grandfathers to Fathers of the 1960 Business Leaders

To understand executive recruitment in Japanese business and industry, particularly the roles of inheritance, family influence, and individual achievement, examination of occupational movement in one generation is inadequate. Inheritance of a business enterprise and the influence of familial connections may, of course, extend over many generations. Our discussion thus far has covered the occupations of two generations, father and son. Including the grandparental generation should allow more assured inferences concerning occupational mobility. Our investigations here are fortuitously aided by the circumstances of Japanese history; the span of time covered by three generations embraces the whole period of the industrialization of Japan. Grandfathers of present business leaders were generally born around 1850, just before the American fleet under Commodore Perry visited Japan. The grandfathers began their careers during the time of the downfall of the Tokugawa regime and the beginning of industrialization.

The occupational distribution for the three generations through the male line only is given in table 9. This does not tell us how many of the business leaders had fathers and grandfathers in the same occupations but does reveal changes in over-all distribution by occupation for these two generations.

The differences shown in the table are, on the whole, in accord with expectations. As a result of the industrialization taking place during the period covered, it was to be expected that a smaller proportion of farmers would be found among fathers than among grandfathers. The low rate of farmers supplying business leadership in 1960 was noted earlier in our discussion of parental occupations, but when seen over a period of three generations, the role of the farm background in business mobility assumes a different significance. The movement off the farm into urban occupations takes place in the preceding generation; it is the grandfather who was a farmer, while the father moved into an urban occupation, and the son moved upward into business leadership. Almost one-half (48 percent) of the paternal grandfathers of the present business elite were farmers and almost one-quarter (24 percent) of the fathers were farmers.

Table 9.   Distribution of Occupation of Paternal Grandfathers and Fathers of the 1960 Business Leaders

Occupation	Paternal Grandfather	Father
Laborer	1.1%	1.3%
Farmer	14.9	6.7
Landlord	33.4	17.3
White collar worker		
(Private business)	.2	2.5
(Public office)	1.8	6.5
Owner, small business	17.5	21.6
Owner, large business	5.5	11.5
Executive, large business	2.2	10.5
Government official		
(National)	1.6	4.3
(Local)	1.5	5.5
(Military)	1.1	1.7
Professional		
(Professor)	.9	2.5
(Doctor of medicine)	2.8	2.5
(Priest)	1.7	.7
(Other)	.7	4.0
Samurai	13.1	.9
Total percent	100%	100%
Total individuals*	857	974

*Among the 985 respondents, 128 failed to state occupations of their grandfathers and 11 failed to state occupations of their fathers.

A category that shows an interesting pattern is that of samurai. The warrior class was abolished at the beginning of the Meiji era (1872). About 13 percent of the grandfathers were identified as being samurai; but only about 1 percent of the fathers, most of whom came to maturity in the early Meiji era, were so identified. However, 31.5 percent of the business leaders identified themselves as being of "samurai background." The warrior class of the late Tokugawa period thus assumes great importance as a source of modern business leaders. We have set aside for separate discussion the question of the relationship between social status in feudal times and subsequent social mobility.

Nearly all the remaining occupational categories show increases from the grandfather's generation to that of the father in percentages. The following occupations show substantial increases in the proportions of fathers over those of grandfathers: executives of large or medium business firms, 10.5 : 2.2 percent; white collar workers, 9.0 : 2.0 percent; government officials, 11.5 : 5.1 percent; owners of large or medium business firms, 11.5 : 5.5 percent; professional men, 9.7 : 5.3 percent; and owners of small business firms, 21.6 : 17.5 percent. It should be noted that the laboring class, which greatly increased in the total population during the period from 1883 to 1960, did fail to participate in this general upward mobility in the three generations.

Two general trends may be noted. First, table 9 makes it clear that there was from one generation to another a good deal of mobility into higher occupational groups. At the same time, there is a major movement from the farm into urban occupations. The occupational distribution of the grandfathers of present business leaders will next be compared with the total Japanese adult population employed in 1883. (See chapter 1, table 2.) It is reasonable to assume that grandfathers of the present business leaders, whose average age is about fifty-nine years, were generally at the height of their careers around 1883. The statistics for that year include both males and females and are therefore not closely comparable with the later statistics. They serve, however, to show general trends of overrepresentation and underrepresentation of certain occupational groups.

In 1883, government officials and professional men composed only 1 percent of the total, but they are represented among the grandfathers of the present business leaders at a significantly higher ratio. Business owners or managers, white collar workers, and landlords were also represented among grandfathers in a substantially greater proportion. Laborers and operating farmers were significantly underrepresented. These ratios are similar to those we have seen in the fathers' generation.

To pursue the issue of intergenerational mobility, it is useful to follow the trend of movement of each occupational group through the three generations. We shall first consider occupational mobility from paternal grandfather to father of our respondents, i.e., the cases in which the fathers followed occupations different from those of the grandfathers. There is a strong tendency toward occupational continuity from grandfather to father of the present Japanese business leaders (44.6 percent), but a still stronger tendency toward occupational change (55.4 percent) is evident. Landlords and farmers together compose 48 percent of the grandfathers, but only 24 percent of fathers. In the course of industrialization, how did these men move from farm to city? One-third of the present business elite are of samurai origin. What were the transitional occupations through which the grandsons of samurai were able to move into the ranks of the business elite? In short, how were big business executives formed in Japan in the past two or three generations?

In table 10 we present a comparison of the occupations of fathers and grandfathers showing the occupational distribution of grandfathers for each occupational category of fathers. For the purpose of describing the phenomena of intergenerational movement of occupation for these two generations, the occupations of the grandfathers, listed across the top of the table, may be regarded as the classes of origin, and the occupations of the fathers, listed down the left hand side, as the new occupations. Let us now consider the phenomena of interoccupational movement as they have occurred in each of the ten occupations of origin listed in the table.

Laborer: About 56 percent of the sons of laborers followed occupations different from those of their fathers. The movements were into the categories of white collar worker, owner of small business firm, executive of large business firm, government official, and the professions, but not to farmer, landlord, and owner of large business firm. Unfortunately, the number of persons in the laborer category in our sample is small and further details of vertical occupational mobility from this occupation are not clear. However, it should be noted that very few men whose fathers were laborers are among the business elite.

Farmer and Landlord: In the course of industrialization there was extensive movement away from farming. One-third (33.4 per-

Table 10. Comparison of Fathers' and Grandfathers' Occupation

Occupation of Father	Occupation of Paternal Grandfather										% of Respondents' Fathers in Occupational Group *
	Laborer	Farmer	Landlord	White Collar Worker	Owner, Small Business	Owner, Large Business	Ex-ecutive, Large Business	Government Official	Professions	Samurai	
Laborer	44.5%	1.6%	0.7%	0%	0.7%	0%	0%	0%	0%	0%	1.1%
Farmer	0	43.8	0.4	0	0	0	0	2.8	1.9	0.9	7.0
Landlord	0	3.9	48.3	0	0.7	2.1	5.3	2.8	9.4	2.7	18.1
White collar worker	11.1	7.8	7.3	41.1	6.0	2.1	10.5	11.1	9.4	16.9	9.2
Owner, small business	11.1	21.8	10.8	11.8	60.7	6.4	10.5	0	3.8	14.4	20.5
Owner, large business	0	3.1	8.4	11.8	9.3	80.9	0	11.1	9.4	4.5	11.2
Executive, large business	11.1	3.9	7.3	17.6	7.3	8.5	36.8	33.3	7.5	21.4	10.7
Government official	11.1	8.6	11.5	11.8	8.0	0	21.1	30.6	11.4	17.8	11.7
Professions	11.1	4.7	5.3	5.9	6.6	0	15.8	8.3	47.2	16.9	9.7
Samurai	0	0.8	0	0	0.7	0	0	0	0	4.5	0.8
Total	100.0	100.0	100.0	100.0	100.0	100.0	100.0	100.0	100.0	100.0	100.0
Number of respondents in occupational group	9	128	286	17	150	47	19	36	53	112	857

*(See footnote, table 9)

cent) of the paternal grandfathers of our respondents were land-lords, but in the parental generation men in this occupation dropped by about one-half (to 13.7 percent). The greatest move-ment was to positions as government officials (11.5 percent) and owners of small business firms (10.8 percent). Sons of landlords moved into all other urban upper and middle class occupations. Only a negligible number (1.6 percent) moved socially downward to the occupations of laborer and operating farmer.

The general pattern of movement of operating farmers is similar to that of landlords, but farming plays a less important role in the occupational backgrounds of our respondents. Movement upward from farming is principally into the urban middle class occupa-tions of owners of small business firms and white collar worker. A smaller proportion moved to positions as executive of large busi-ness firms and government officials. There is little movement from other occupations to farmer and landlord.

White collar worker: An important characteristic of the move-ment toward business leadership is transitional employment as white collar worker. More than one-half (53 percent) of the sons of white collar workers (among the fathers of the business leaders) be-came owners or executives of business concerns (small or large) or government officials. The associations and traditions of white collar employment are more closely allied to business and civil service than to the professions, and it seems natural that the sons of white collar workers should turn their ambitions toward busi-ness. The proportion of fathers with this occupational background who were executives of large size business firms is 17.6 percent, and this occupation is the one most frequently entered by the sons of white collar workers who have moved upward occupationally. It appears also that a white collar background had considerable importance as a steppingstone to the categories of owner of large business and government official.

Which occupations on the grandparental level supplied the white collar fathers of our respondents? About 41 percent were sons of white collar workers. The other principal contributing occupations were samurai, government official, laborer, executive of a large business firm and the professions. White collar workers were drawn in small numbers from all of the remaining occu-pational categories.

Owner, small business: Although a majority of the fathers who were owners of small business firms remained in the occupations of their grandfathers, about 40 percent of the sons of small business owners (of the parental generation) entered occupations different from those of their fathers. Most of this group moved up the occupational hierarchy. A total of 31.2 percent moved upward to positions as owners or executives of large business concerns, government officials, or professional men. A small part (6 percent) of the group became white collar workers and remained in approximately the same social status as their fathers. Movement to a socially inferior occupation was rare.

Movement away from ownership of small business firms is comparatively small; that is, the majority of the fathers who were owners of small business firms (60.7 percent) were sons of men (the grandfathers of our table) who were in the same occupations. It is interesting to note that among the occupational categories from which fathers who were owners of small business firms were drawn (i.e., those whose fathers were not also owners of small business firms), farming is the most important.

Owner, large business: Vertical mobility of this group is small, and, since this class represents the social apex, such movement as occurred is downward. About 81 percent of the fathers who were in this occupational class remained in the same occupation as their fathers. Almost 9 percent moved to positions as executives of large business firms. About 10 percent moved socially downward, principally to positions as owners of small business firms (6.4 percent). A small number (2.1 percent each) became white collar workers or landlords.

Owners of large business concerns among paternal grandfathers of the present business leaders total 47, or 5.5 percent of the respondents. Owners of large business concerns among fathers of the present business leaders increased greatly to total 96, or 11.2 percent. Occupations on the grandparental level from which the increased number were drawn are varied, and no pattern beyond variability is evident.

Executive, large business: Sons of executives of large business firms tended to move away from the occupations of their fathers. However, most of them remained in the urban upper-middle class. Among those who moved, the largest percentage went to positions as government officials (21.1 percent) and into the professions (15.8 percent). It should be noted that the occupational category of business executive, like that of white collar worker, has been a springboard for occupational mobility and more important in this respect than white collar employment.

Which occupations on the grandparental level supplied the executives of large business concerns among the fathers? About 37 percent of the fathers were sons of executives of large business concerns. The remaining occupations from which executives of large business firms were drawn in proportions larger than normal expectation were government official, samurai and white collar worker. The other contributing occupations in descending order of importance were laborer, owner of a large business firm, the professions, landlord, and farmer.

Government official: The striking feature of this occupational category is the low degree (30.6 percent) of occupational transmission and the significant vertical mobility toward important executive positions. Thirty-three percent moved to positions as executives of large business firms, a rate greater than that of occupational transmission; 11.1 percent moved to positions as owners of large business firms; and 8.3 percent went into the professions. Thus, the occupational category of government official has played a key role as a transitional occupation over the generations of our investigation. What occupational groups were the government officials on the parental level drawn from? The most important categories are executive of a large business concern, samurai, white collar worker, landlord and the professions.

Professions: Nearly one-half (47.2 percent) of the second generation men whose fathers were professional men were also grandsons of professional men. Men who moved occupationally went into a variety of occupations. Much of the vertical movement (28.3 percent) was to occupations of higher prestige as owners or executives of large business firms and government officials, but the 24.5 percent who were landlords, farmers, white collar workers, or owners of small business firms had moved down the occupational ladder.

What occupations on the grandparental level supplied the professional men among the fathers? Many, as we have noted, had fathers in the professions. The remainder stem from various occupational backgrounds, of which the two most important are samurai and executive of a large business firm.

Samurai: We have already noted that 31.5 percent of the modern business leaders stated that they were of samurai descent. Following the abolition of the samurai class in 1872, the erstwhile samurai were forced to move to new occupations, and this movement occurred mainly during the lifetimes of the grandfathers of our respondents. Only 13.1 percent of the grandfathers and 0.9 percent of the fathers were samurai, but almost one-third of the business leaders came from samurai backgrounds. Data presented in table 9 do not show the occupational movements of the grandparental generation away from occupations of the great-grandparental generation. Because the samurai background is of such apparent importance as an influencing factor in the selection of the modern business leaders, however, we shall give this subject separate and detailed discussion. We shall note now that the principal movement from positions as samurai in the generation from grandfather to father was to positions as executives of large business firms, government officials, professional men, owners of small business firms, and white collar workers. Only a small proportion moved into positions near the bottom of the social scale as operating farmers, and none became laborers.

Social Status and Mobility in Feudal Times

During the Tokugawa period (1603–1867), the samurai were military, administrative, and intellectual leaders with status inferior only to that of the rulers whom they served. Economic activities were carried out entirely by commoners. How did they adapt to the industrializing society after the samurai class, as such, was abolished in 1872? Joseph A. Schumpeter comments on the tendency of classes to perpetuate themselves: "Classes, once they have come into being, harden in their mold and perpetuate themselves, even when the social conditions that created them have disappeared."[10]

The samurai class could not, of course, perpetuate itself as samurai, but the question is open as to whether or to what extent its members retained high social status. The role of ex-samurai in the recruitment of Japanese business leaders is a debatable one and is not settled.[11] We shall try to answer this question from our data by seeking answers to several specific, lesser questions. Did ex-samurai turn toward business at the beginning of the industrial period? Did sons of samurai often become owners or executives of business and industrial firms? What occupations do men with samurai backgrounds tend to follow?

At the beginning of the Meiji era, the Japanese nobility, consisting of imperial court families and ex-feudal lords, numbered 470 families and 2,675 individuals—less than one-tenth of 1 percent of the total population of 7,000,000 families and 33 million individuals.[12] Below this class stood the various subclasses of samurai, numbering 426,000 families and 1,900,000 persons. Since the samurai made up about 6 percent of the total population of the time, it might be expected that about one out of twenty people in present-day Japan can trace his descent to a Tokugawa samurai or a member of the nobility. However, the incidence of men with samurai backgrounds (31.5 percent) among the business leaders is five to six times greater than their distribution in the total population.

These data suggest that despite the loss of hereditary high status and other extensive social changes the descendants of the social

---

[10]Schumpeter, Joseph A., *Imperialism and Social Class*, tr. by Heintz Norden (New York: Augustus M. Kelley, Inc., 1951), p. 145.
[11]Kanno Wataro emphasizes the leading role of ex-samurai in establishing cooperative enterprises in the early Meiji period; see his *Nihon Kaisha Kigyō Hassei-shi no Kenkyū* (Study of the Origins of Japanese Company Enterprises) (Tokyo: Iwanami Shoten, 1931). Tsuchiya Takao also writes of the dominance of samurai and quasi-samurai (*jun-bushi*, which includes *ashigaru*, *gōshi* and village officials) among early Japanese managerial personnel; see his *Nihon Shihonshugi no Keieishi-teki Kenkyū* (Study of the Managerial History of Japanese Capitalism) (Tokyo: Misuzu Shoten, 1954). Fujita Gorō, however, points out the substantial role of rich farmers in the development of the cotton and silk manufacturing industries; see his *Nihon Kindai Sangyō no Seisei* (The Development of Modern Japanese Industry) (Tokyo: Yūhikaku, 1948).
[12]These figures are adopted from the original census report of 1872, *Dajōkan Kosekiryō*, from the Bureau of Statistics, Office of the Prime Minister.

elite of Tokugawa times have suffered no revolutionary change in social position. At least a substantial part of the descendants of that elite are in all probability included among the elite of today. It is not, of course, maintained that all the families who held elite hereditary status in pre-Meiji Japan were wealthy or powerful. Many families of noble or samurai rank suffered a considerable decline, especially toward the end of the feudal regime. However, these classes are clearly an important source of modern business leaders.

The foregoing statements are not intended to imply that sons of samurai moved directly to positions of business leadership. Like others we have already discussed, they could arrive at positions of business leadership through various occupational steps taken by their forebears. What occupational positions did they move through during the generations of the grandfather and father? From our data, it is possible to see the steps that were taken and to determine to what extent traditional high status persisted in the modern industrialized society among the subjects of our study. As shown in table 11, there can be little doubt that there was a strong tendency toward entering occupations that conferred high social status, although this was not necessarily done in one generation.

Of the military officers among the grandfathers of the modern business leaders, 89 percent were of samurai or noble origin. In contrast, only 9 percent of the grandfathers who were owners of small business firms were of elite background. Although there is some movement in the grandparental generation to positions of still lower prestige than ownership of small business concerns, a marked trend is evident toward socially favored occupations as military officers, government officials, professional men, and managers of large business firms. Few turned to the occupations that imply ownership of extensive property, i.e., owner of a large business concern and landlord. A moderate number were clerks, an occupation that conferred no high prestige, but which, as we have noted, served as an important transitional step through the generations.

Among the fathers, a shift is apparent toward occupations in the commercial world, and this trend includes an increased number of owners of large business concerns. An overall view taking us down to the modern business leaders shows a pronounced tendency toward maintenance of high social status.

Table 11. Descendants of Nobles and Samurai, as Percentage of Occupational Groups

Occupation	Percent Claiming Noble or Samurai Descent	
	Among first generation* (Grandfathers)	Among second generation** (Fathers)
Military officer	89%	50%
Government official	70	53
Clerk in public office	71	48
Professional man	53	51
Executive, large business	50	48
Owner, large business	21	39
Owner, small business	9	20
Clerk in private business	0	54
Laborer	20	8
Landlord	15	12
Farmer	12	12

*Grandfathers of the 303 business leaders of 1960 who claim descent from nobles or samurai.
**Fathers of these 303.

Chapter 3

COMPARISONS OF ELITE MOBILITY

General Vertical Mobility in Japan

Thus far, we have analyzed the occupational mobility of Japanese business leaders against the background of the total Japanese population. Now we will examine the data further in contrasting elite mobility with general occupational mobility in Japanese society. A research committee of the Japanese Sociological Society conducted a sample survey on social stratification and mobility in Japan in 1955.[1] Their survey gives us comparable data on the extent to which Japanese society, as a whole, has occupational succession and mobility from generation to generation. With this information, we can determine more accurately the pattern of occupational mobility of Japanese business leaders.

Table 12 compares the distribution of occupations of grandfathers, fathers, and subjects of the 1955 sample survey and of the 1960 Japanese business leaders.

In contrast to the steady decrease in farm population, laborers, white collar workers and professionals have greatly increased in proportion. Sales workers have also increased. But the managerial population of the 1955 generation had not increased as much as expected. It may be due to the fact that the 1955 sample included younger men who had not yet attained managerial positions. It is clear that the shifts in occupational distribution over three generations were due to economic growth and the urbanization and

---

[1] It should be noted that the sampling employed by the committee deviates from the occupational distribution of the 1955 census; it overrepresents professional, managerial, white collar workers and farmers, and underrepresents laborers. See Nihon Shakai Gakkai Chōsa Iinkai, *Nihon Shakai no Kaisōteki Kōzō*, p. 160, and *JSY*, 1959, p. 34.

industrialization of the Japanese society. It should be pointed out that the general occupational mobility caused by economic advancement of a given society should not be counted as net occupational mobility.[2]

Regarding elite mobility, in contrast to general occupational

Table 12.   Occupational Change in Three Generations in Total 1955 Population and 1960 Business Leaders

Occupation	Sample of 1955 Total Population			1960 Business Leaders		
	Grand-father	Father	Present generation in 1955	Grand-father	Father	Business leader, 1960
Professional	3%	4%	7%	6%	10%	—
Managerial	4	7	5	12	34	100%
White collar worker	2	4	12	2	9	—
Owner, small business or sales worker	8	11	13	18	21	—
Laborer	12	20	26	1	1	—
Farmer	71	54	37	48	24	—
Other (including samurai)	—	—	—	13	1	—
Total	100	100	100	100	100	100
Number	1,765	1,866	1,866	857	974	985

Nihon Shakai Gakkai Chōsa Iinkai, *Nihon Shakai no Kaisōteki Kōzō* (Hierarchical Structure of Japanese Society) (Tokyo: Yūhikaku, 1958), pp. 160, 163.

---

[2]On this point, Nelson N. Foote and Paul K. Hatt comment that: "If everyone moves upward by some absolute standard, none moves by the invidious standard. It should thus be clear that social mobility and economic advancement occur independently. Nevertheless, many studies of social mobility arrive at their conclusions simply by comparing the occupations of sons with the occupations of their fathers without subtracting the influence of the flow of labor into the more advanced occupations." Foote, Nelson N. and Hatt, Paul K., "Social Mobility and Economic Advancement," *American Economic Review,* Vol. 43 (May 1953), p. 370.

mobility, some characteristics stand out. First, the grandfathers of the 1960 business leaders were overrepresented in positions of high social status. This means that the second generation—the business leaders' fathers—started their careers with substantially higher positions than average people. The overrepresented occupations among the grandfathers of the 1960 business leaders in comparison to those of the 1955 total population were those of professional, managerial, small shop owner, salesman and samurai. The underrepresented occupations were laborer and farmer. White collar workers were evenly represented and were not developed during the generation of grandfathers.

Second, the distribution of occupations of fathers among present business leaders substantially moved from that of the total Japanese population toward more concentration in urban upper or middle class occupations. The distribution of occupations of fathers in the sample survey had also shifted from the grandfathers' generation in the same direction, but elite mobility reveals an acceleration of this tendency. One-third of the present business leaders had achieved managerial positions in the generation of fathers, and they remained in the same occupational status as their fathers.

Third, the present business leaders hold top positions in the largest firms in Japan. Conspicuous mobility on the part of business leaders as against occupational mobility in the sample survey has been taking place in the generation of the business leaders. Two-thirds of the business leaders, who were not in managerial occupations in the father's generation, moved up to business leadership from various non-managerial occupations.

In summary, high ascriptive status of grandfathers and fathers is related to career success in business. Yet, the mobility of the two-thirds of the present business leaders who are drawn from urban middle class or rural backgrounds indicates that the principle of individual achievement was strongly operating in their advancement toward the business hierarchy in Japan.

Next, we will examine occupational succession and mobility from grandfathers to fathers and the present generation in the 1955 sample survey. What patterns of mobility were found in the general shift to urban occupations? What proportion in each occupational group remained in the same occupation as their father?

General Mobility vs. Elite Mobility—Grandfather to Father

The 1955 sample survey indicates that 65 percent of the second generation remained in the same occupation as their fathers, the first generation. Farmers and laborers were the highest in occupational transmission, and the white collar group the lowest. The proportion of occupational transmission among managerial, professional and small shop owners is 45 to 46 percent. More than one-half of the sons (the fathers of the present generation) found occupations different from the preceding generation. A somewhat larger proportion of downward mobility from grandfather to father in higher and middle class occupation is compensated for by upward mobility among the farmers and laborers.

Elite mobility from grandfather to father indicates a lower occupational transmission (45 percent) than among the whole population (65 percent), as shown in table 13. Thus, there was higher vertical mobility in the elite group in contrast to higher transmission in the total society. There is also a striking contrast between elite mobility and general mobility. In the latter, the proportion that remained in the same occupation as the preceding generation is largest among farmers and laborers, but in elite mobility, the proportion is lower in these occupations. Among the elite in general, sons with higher occupational backgrounds showed a strong tendency to remain in their fathers' occupations, whereas men in lower occupations showed a definite tendency toward upward movement.

General Mobility vs. Elite Mobility—Father to Son

The 1955 sample survey indicates that occupational stability in the third generation is less than in the second generation. This confirms the thesis that intergenerational occupational mobility increases with the advancement of industrialization. The total amount of occupational transmission from second to third generation in the 1955 sample survey is 48 percent in contrast to 65 percent from first to second generation.[3]

In the third generation, many sons of farmers became laborers (17 percent) or entered white collar and sales groups (15 percent), or professional and managerial groups (7 percent). The rest (61 percent) remained farmers. The movement toward industrial jobs and higher urban occupations is notable. For laborers, most out-mobility was toward white collar occupations, professional and managerial posts, and less toward farmers.

For white collar and sales groups, vertical mobility increased. More than one-half (53 percent) remained in the same occupational levels as their fathers, but 15 percent moved up and 32 percent moved down, either to laborer groups (21 percent) or farmer groups (11 percent). In general, there was fairly extensive vertical mobility in these groups. For the white collar occupation alone, out-mobility was predominant.

For the combined category of professional and managerial, intergenerational stability (38 percent) was comparatively low

Table 13. Occupational Stability from Paternal Grandfather to Father

	Father in Same Occupation as His Father	
Occupation	1955 Sample Survey	1960 Business Leader
Laborer	62%	45%
White collar worker	19	41
Owner, small business or sales worker	6	61
Manager, officer, and owner of large business	45	55
Professional man	46	47
Farmer	71	47
Others	—	5
All occupations	65%	45%
Number of individuals	1,765	857

[3]Nihon Shakai Gakkai Chōsa Iinkai, p. 160.

and out-mobility (62 percent), comparatively high: downward mobility to white collar and sales worker was especially notable (35 percent), with a substantial proportion moving downward to become laborers and farmers (27 percent). Professional men showed a relatively high degree of occupational stability (44 percent), but the managerial group a low degree (16 percent).

In contrast to general occupational mobility in the third generation in society as a whole, elite mobility to business leadership may be summarized as follows: there is no downward mobility for the elite group. One-third of the 1960 business leaders were sons of men in managerial status. The other two-thirds came from occupational backgrounds other than managerial.

There is another way to illustrate the conspicuous mobility of the business elite in contrast to mobility in the society as a whole. In the sample survey of 1955, the managerial group in the third generation is 5 percent of the total sample. The distribution of occupations of fathers of the managerial group shows managerial 23 percent, farmer 35 percent, white collar or sales group 23 percent, laborer 14 percent, and professional 5 percent. In comparing this distribution to that of occupations of fathers of the 1960 business leaders, several characteristics stand out. First, the proportion of third-generation men in managerial positions whose fathers were also in the managerial group is smaller in the sample survey (23 percent) than in the business elite survey (34 percent). Second, occupational movement of sons of professional men, white collar workers and sales workers to managerial positions is rather low (28 percent) in the 1955 sample but high (40 percent) among the business leaders. Third, almost half (49 percent) of the men in managerial positions in the 1955 survey were sons of laborers or farmers, in comparison with only one-quarter (25 percent) of the 1960 business leaders. In general, men in managerial positions in the sample survey are drawn more from the lower classes than was the case with the 1960 business leaders.

The differences in recruitment of the two groups are due to disparity in composition of the groups. The 1960 business leaders occupied the top positions in the largest firms in Japan, whereas the managerial group in the sample survey included both major and minor executives in private business as well as in public offices.

More managerial men in the society as a whole are recruited from lower occupational groups in the society than is true for the 1960 business elite.

On the average, the rate of occupational transmission for villages (53 percent) is twice that of metropolitan areas (26 percent). There is an extremely high rate of stability among farmers, but even in villages, occupational transmission rates for occupational groups other than farmers are not low. In metropolitan areas occupational stability is low in almost every occupational group. In general, professional men and small shop owners show more occupational transmission; managerial men and white collar workers show less, and laborers, somewhat more occupational stability.

More recently, a sample survey[4] in Japan's largest metropolitan community, Tokyo, revealed that occupational mobility in Tokyo has increased substantially in recent years. The author reported his findings as follows:

> The rate of intergenerational occupational mobility is quite high. . . . The rate of occupational succession is very low; only 15% of the total are now engaged in the same occupations as their fathers. As regards in- and out-mobility, in accordance with occupational classification, every occupational category except agriculture has in- and out-mobility of more than 50% . . . We may conclude that the total rate of intergenerational mobility is extraordinarily high.[5]

Of course, the process of urbanization is much farther advanced in Tokyo than elsewhere in Japan. No doubt, the growth of large firms there provides maximum opportunity for occupational mobility. This movement is also supported by the desire for social advancement. Rural youths long for city life, and sons of industrial workers long to become white collar workers. For the vast majority of Japanese the life of the salary man of the emerging middle class represents as high a standard as they aspire for.[6]

[4]Tominaga Ken'ichi, "Occupational Mobility in Japanese Society: Analysis of Labor Market in Japan," *The Journal of Economic Behavior*, II:1 (April, 1962), p. 17. This is a survey of a sample of 2,000 adult males over twenty years of age (as of 1960) in Tokyo, of which 1,227 gave complete responses.
[5]*Ibid.*, pp. 16–7.
[6]Vogel, Ezra F., *Japan's New Middle Class* (Berkeley and Los Angeles: University of California Press, 1963), p. 9.

General occupational mobility in Japan should be viewed in comparison with other industrialized countries. Lipset and Bendix examined rates of occupational mobility in various countries and concluded that:

All the countries studied are characterized by a high degree of mobility. From one generation to another, a quarter to a third of the non-farm population moves from the working class to the middle class, or vice-versa. Second, there is, among the first six countries, a high degree of similarity in this total mobility rate. The total range is between 23 and 31%, and five of the six countries (United States, Germany, Sweden, Japan, France) range between 27 and 31%. Such narrow differences lead quickly to one interpretation: total mobility rates in these countries are practically the same.[7]

Japan follows the general pattern of occupational mobility in industrialized societies. This nation, which has achieved high industrialization only in the last two or three generations, inevitably has higher rates of occupational mobility as a necessity in the rapid transformation of preindustrial population into industrialized population. Japanese society has a high degree of upward vertical mobility from fathers in the middle class, farmers, and laborers, to sons in professional and managerial occupation. Also it has a high degree of downward mobility from professional and managerial fathers to sons in other occupations including manual labor. However, it has a low degree of movement by laborers into non-manual occupations.[8] Farmers in Japan have the highest rate of continuity of occupation from father to son, although they also move out to the other occupations most frequently in absolute number. In conclusion, the following features are somewhat exceptional in occupational mobility in Japan, as indicated by R. P. Dore: "For a society as generally mobile, the proportion of non-agricultural laborers' sons who move up the prestige scale seems to be low. Conversely, the proportions of farmers' sons who move into non-manual occupations seems to be unusually high."[9]

[7]Lipset and Bendix, p. 25.
[8]Miller, S. M., "Comparative Social Mobility," Current Sociology, IX:1 (1960), p. 56.
[9]Dore, R. P., "Mobility, Equality, and Individuation in Modern Japan," in Aspects of Social Change in Modern Japan, edited by R. P. Dore (Princeton: Princeton University Press, 1967), p. 116.

The pattern of mobility of the 1960 business elite generally resembles the pattern found in the population at large. For sons of laborers it was almost impossible to achieve positions of business leadership; only 1 percent of the business leaders had grandfathers or fathers who were laborers. On the contrary, sons of farmers enjoyed a better chance of climbing higher in the prestige hierarchy of industrial society. Almost half (48 percent) of the present business elite were grandsons of farmers, and almost a quarter (24 percent) were sons of farmers. Despite the distinct overrepresentation of samurai decendants (32 percent) in the 1960 business leaders, social mobility to business leadership was substantial. For Japan the business class was a new social class, not closely related to traditional merchants. Men in any social class had opportunities to achieve positions of business leadership although laborers and tenant farmers did not often do so. Insofar as elite mobility in business is concerned, Japan was not a closed society in which prestige positions were monopolized by one class, but an open and fluid society with a high degree of mobility.

International Comparison of Social Origins and Mobility in Business Leadership

Current studies of social mobility give special attention to movement of elites in comparative terms. They include studies of social origins and careers of political, intellectual as well as business elites in various countries. The social origins and mobility of business leaders in various countries are the most carefully studied sectors. We shall examine the research results of occupational origins and mobility in comparison to those of other countries studied.

A broad perspective of this issue is provided by a recent survey of mobility in industrial societies:

A number of studies of the social origin of the business elite have also been completed in the past few years. We know of such studies for Germany, Great Britain, the Netherlands, Sweden, Switzerland and the United States. They vary in the methods of collecting data, in the classification employed for describing the social background of the elite, and above all in the definition of the elite. But despite much methodological uncertainty, some conclusions stand out. Approximately 60% of the samples of the business elite in Britain, the Netherlands, Sweden, and the United States have businessmen as fathers, of whom about 15% are small businessmen. The Swiss data indicate that about 50% had fathers in business. Between 10 and 15% of these groups have manual-working class or lower-white-collar origins. There is, however, a variation among countries in the proportion of business leaders who come from rural backgrounds, which corresponds to the importance of agriculture in the national economy.[10]

The corresponding figures on the Japanese business elite are not always similar to those cited in this review of studies in the West. Compared with 60 percent of all business leaders being sons of businessmen and about 15 percent of these being sons of small businessmen, in Japan the corresponding proportions are 44 percent and 22 percent, respectively. While this review finds that 10 to 15 percent of Western business leaders are sons of laborers or white collar workers, the proportion in Japan is 10 percent.

These comparisons of the Japanese data with that of other countries then suggest somewhat different rates of recruitment of business leaders from the several occupational backgrounds, with the marked exception of the very limited access of Japan's manual workers to business leadership. These comparisons are not helpful, however, in terms of rates of mobility since they do not consider differences in distribution of the total population by occupational background.

Comparison with the United States: Table 14 presents some comparative data on the recruitment of men in the top business positions in Japan and the United States. The Japanese data are those for fathers of the business leaders in this study and for the 1920 adult male employed population. The data for the American business leaders are those for fathers of 7,500 executives of the largest firms in the United States in 1952.[11] The population data of the United States in the table are for the distribution by occupation of adult males in the census of 1920, the nearest equivalent to the

[10]Lipset and Bendix, p. 40.
[11]Warner and Abegglen, p. 152.

population of which the fathers of the U.S. business leaders were a part.

Table 14. Mobility in Business Leadership in Japan and the United States*

Occupation	Fathers of Business Leaders		1920 Population		Mobility Rates	
	1960 Japan	1952 U.S.	Japan	U.S.	Japan	U.S.
Government official	11.5%	2%	0.4%	1%	3,149	200
Professional	10	14	1.3	4	769	350
Executive or owner, large business	22	31	1.7	4	1,294	775
Owner, small business	21.5	18	13.2	5	166	360
White collar worker	9	11	7.9	12	114	92
Farmer	24	9	48.3	27	49	33
Laborer	1	15	26.3	47	4	32
Other occupation	1	—	0.9	—	111	—
Total	100.0%	100%	100.0%	100%		

*The U.S. data are from Warner, W. Lloyd and Abegglen, James C., *Occupational Mobility in American Business and Industry* (Minneapolis: University of Minnesota Press, 1955), p. 40.

First, Japan and the United States differ markedly in the number of modern business leaders who are sons of government officials. A far higher proportion of business leaders are sons of government officials and military officers in Japan (11.5 percent) than in the United States (2 percent). The proportion of sons of professional men who are in top business positions is somewhat smaller in Japan (10 percent) than in the U.S. (14 percent). The proportion of sons of executives or owners of large businesses is considerably smaller in Japan (22 percent) than in the U.S. (31 percent), whereas the proportion of sons of owners of small businesses is slightly larger in Japan (21.5 percent) than in the U.S. (18 percent). The proportion of sons of white collar workers is approximately the same in both countries—about one-tenth of the total. Less than 10 percent of the U.S. business leaders are sons of farmers, compared with almost one-quarter of the Japanese group (24 percent). Only 1 per cent of sons of laborers have reached a top level business position in Japan, whereas in the U.S., 15 percent of the sons of laborers have reached the same position.

In order to understand the significance of these differences and similarities, the distribution of the total employed population must be compared with the occupational origins of the business leaders. In examining the 1920 employed adult male population in the two countries, the stage of economic development measured by the occupational distribution must also be taken into account. In the United States, 49 percent of the total work force in 1880 were farmers.[12] In Japan, 48 percent of the total work force in 1920 were farmers. This means that the occupational structure of Japan is behind the United States by about forty years, or more than one generation. The later industrialization in Japan is also shown in the proportion of professional men, managers, white collar workers, and laborers. The United States had these industrial and business occupations in much larger proportions than Japan did. It should be noted that Japan had a larger proportion of small business owners than the United States, because of the prevalence in Japan of working proprietors, who are classified here as small business owners.

Despite the statistical hazards involved in undertaking such international comparisons, some points of substantial difference appear in comparative mobility rates. First, while men from backgrounds of government officialdom, the professions, and big business are fewer in Japan than in the United States, the proportion of business leaders from such backgrounds is substantially greater. Sons of government officials, professionals and big businessmen have an advantage in access to top level positions in the United States and occupy 2 to 8 times their proportionate share of top business positions. However, this advantage increases to 32 in the Japanese case.

Conversely, while few sons of laborers reach the upper level of the United States business hierarchy, only one-third as many as might under conditions of "equal opportunity," this study of Ja-

12Clark, 2nd ed., p. 404.

pan's business leaders shows almost an exclusion of sons of laborers from Japan's business elite. It cannot be maintained that the
U.S. proportion is high; still, mobility to the very top of the business hierarchy is possible in the United States for men from working class backgrounds.

Farmers' sons who become business leaders are more numerous
in Japan than in the United States, reflecting the relative weight
of agriculture in the national economies of both countries. In
mobility ratio, sons of farmers had a disadvantage in achieving top
positions in the business hierarchy.

Comparison with the United Kingdom: The social origins and careers of more than one thousand directors of large British public
companies were studied by G. H. Copeman in 1952.[13] The distribution of occupations of fathers of British directors is shown in the
first column of table 15. An extremely high proportion of the British directors were sons of professional men and high administrators
(non-business). More than one-fifth were directors in the same
firm as their fathers (22 percent). Sons of directors of other firms
were 10 percent of the total. Sons of owners of small business were
almost one-fifth (19 percent) of the total. Together with directors
and owners of small businesses, 51 percent of the British business
leaders were drawn from business backgrounds. Sons of landlords and farmers totalled 5 percent, divided evenly between the
two groups. The "others" category includes those who were
"neither professional nor executive" (10 percent) and "business
executive [but] not a director" (8 percent). They presumably include white collar workers and laborer.

As a highly advanced industrial nation, Britain has a large proportion of professional men, non-business administrators, and
business directors. A sample survey of social mobility in Britain in
1949 showed 3.7 percent of fathers' occupations were professional and administrative (non-business) and 4.3 percent were
executives.[14] These figures provide the proportion of high occupational classes in Britain a generation ago. It appears that these

[13]Copeman, G. H., *Leaders of British Industry* (London: Gee and Company, Ltd., 1955),
pp. 94–8.
[14]Glass, D. V., *Social Mobility in Britain* (London: Routledge and Kegan Paul, Ltd.,
1954), p. 183.

two higher occupational classes in Britain supply business leaders 7 to 8 times more often than the expected 1 to 1 ratio. The proportion of landlords and farmers in the total population of Britain is the lowest among industrialized countries. It was about 7 percent of the labor force in the 1930s,[15] and fewer business leaders came from landlord or farmer families than in Japan and the United States. Although we have no comparable figures for other occupational categories, it is reasonable to assume that sons of owners of small businesses are also underrepresented among British business leaders. The "other" category in the United Kingdom includes 10 percent "neither professional nor executive" and 8 percent "business executive not a director." Some of these men definitely belong to the upper-middle class in British society. Of the 1952 British business leaders, Copeman stated that "somewhere around 10% of the seats at the board table may have gone to persons who came from the lower middle class or the working class."[16]

From this examination of social origins of British business leaders, it is clear that sons of men in the upper class (including professional men, non-business administrators, and directors in business firms) comprised 58 percent of the directors in the chosen sample. They started their careers with the advantage of having business connections in the family or at least the indirect advantage of higher social status. The overrepresentation of the upper classes is characteristic of business leaders not only in the United Kingdom but also in Japan and the United States, as already indicated.

A comparison of the occupations of fathers of business leaders in the United Kingdom, the United States, and Japan is shown in table 15. Similarities and differences in proportion of different occupations in recruitment of business leaders are evident. The proportion of sons of professional men and administrators among business leaders is highest in the United Kingdom. Although there is no differentiation between professional worker and administrator in the British survey, it is clear that both professional men and

---

[15]In 1931, the farm population was 7 percent of the total labor force in England and Wales. See Clark, 3rd ed., p. 507.
[16]Copeman, p. 96.

government officials enjoy high prestige in British society. Discrepancies in proportion between professional men and government officials in the United States and Japan are sizable. This presumably reflects differences in prestige of these occupations in the two countries.

Table 15. Comparison of Fathers' Occupation of Business Leaders: United Kingdom, United States and Japan*

Occupation of Father	United Kingdom	United States	Japan
Professional man	26%	14%	10%
Administrator (non-business)		2	11.5
Executive or director	32	31	22
(father and son in same firm)	(22)	(9.5)	(9)
Owner, small business	19	18	21.5
Landlord and farmer	5	9	24
Others (including white collar worker and laborer)	18	26	11
Total percent	100%	100%	100%
Total number of individuals	1,045	8,300	985

*Data for the United Kingdom are drawn from Copeman, p. 95. Data for American business leaders are from Warner and Abegglen, p. 38. Data for Japan are based on the present study of 1960 Japanese business leaders.

Sons of executives or directors are most numerous among business leaders in all three countries studied, but the proportion is different in Japan. Almost one-third of the business leaders are sons of executives or directors in Britain (32 percent) and the United States (31 percent), but less than one-fourth in Japan (22 percent). One explanation of this difference is that the United Kingdom and the United States, which represent the most advanced industrial countries, had a larger proportion of executives a generation ago than Japan. The structural difference caused by the extent of industrialization is adequate to explain the similarity between the United Kingdom and the United States and the difference between these two countries and Japan.

It is worth noting that the proportion of business leaders who are in the same firm as their fathers is highest in the United Kingdom, whereas the proportion in the United States is about the same as in Japan. This is the area in which cultural differences are important in determining succession to executive positions. Inheritance of executive positions in large business firms is now usually criticized as nepotism, but has been traditional in every society in the past. Moreover, the ownership of a business in modern capitalist societies is strongly associated with inheritance. It appears that family influence in selecting directors is still an important factor in large public companies in British industry. Nearly a quarter (22 percent) of the business leaders were sons of men who had been directors in the same firm. More than one-half of this group (12 percent out of 22 percent) were in fact from families in which three successive generations served as directors in the same firm.[17] Thus it is evident that British industry still often follows hereditary principles in choosing top executives. This practice of limiting the selection of executives to members of certain families is less noticeable in the United States and Japan.

Sons of small business owners in the three countries comprise around one-fifth of the total business leadership. The proportion of small business owners is somewhat larger in Japan than in the United States and United Kingdom. This may be due to the fact that small business firms were more common in Japan than in the United States and the United Kingdom a generation ago.

The proportion of sons of farmers among business leaders is lowest in the United Kingdom (5 percent) and largest in Japan (24 percent). The proportion for the United States is 9 percent. No doubt these figures are related to the extent of industrialization of each country. Almost one-half the population (48 percent) were farmers a generation ago in Japan, whereas a little over a quarter of the population (27 percent) were farmers a generation ago in the United States. In the United Kingdom the proportion was even less than in the United States.

The above explanation is not sufficient to understand the reasons for the large proportion of farm backgrounds among the 1960 business leaders in Japan. Thomas C. Smith concluded that "landlords are not necessarily enemies of industrialization . . . Japa-

---

[17]*Ibid.*, p. 97.

nese landlords contributed much to the creation of a modern business class."[18] Kazushi Ohkawa and Henry Rosovsky found some special relationships between agriculture and industry in Japan: "Revolutionary progress in Japanese agriculture occurred not before but side by side with industrialization. This was not the typical European sequence. The concurrent and rapid changes in Japanese agriculture and industry suggest to us the possibilities of a peculiar and interesting model of economic growth."[19]

There are difficulties in comparing other occupational categories, which broadly include white collar workers and various levels of laborers. Here again, both structural and cultural determinants in producing business leaders are observable. The working class in Britain was about 75 percent of the total population in the 1910s.[20] The combined proportion of white collar workers and laborers in the United States was almost 60 percent in 1920,[21] although only one-third of the total population in Japan. The variations in proportion of business leaders from the working class should be attributed partly to cultural differences. It is clear that sons of lower occupational groups in the United States have a much greater chance of achieving top positions in the business hierarchy than do those in the United Kingdom. The lower representation of business leaders from this background in Japan was due to the fact that industrialization did not start as early.

None of the three countries has a monopolistic class that occupies a majority of the positions of business leadership. About One-third to one-fourth of the business leaders remained in the same occupation as their fathers. The rest of the positions were occupied by sons of men in other occupations. It appears that industrially mature countries like the United Kingdom and United States, as well as rapidly industrializing Japan, have a high degree of social mobility in recruiting for vacancies and newly added positions of business leadership.

---

[18]Smith, Thomas C., "Landlords' Sons in the Business Elite," *Economic Development and Cultural Change*, IX:1, Part II (Oct. 1960), p. 107.
[19]Ohkawa, Kazushi and Rosovsky, Henry, "The Role of Agriculture in Modern Japanese Economic Development," *Economic Development and Cultural Change*, IX:1, Part II (Oct. 1960), p. 66.
[20]Erickson, Charlotte, *British Industrialists* (London: Cambridge University Press, 1959), pp. 233–5.
[21]Warner and Abegglen, p. 40.

Chapter 4

EDUCATION OF JAPAN'S BUSINESS LEADERS

Level of Formal Education

The importance of higher formal education is strongly emphasized in professional and business careers in Japanese society. The
Japanese business leaders studied here had received their education about thirty to forty years ago, in which period chances for
higher education were few for sons of the lower classes. In the examination of their educational backgrounds, we want first to know
to what extent the level of formal education of the business leaders
was related to their achievement in executive positions.

A comparison of the proportion of the 1960 business leaders at
each level of educational advancement would provide a crude
answer to the question.

Table 16 compares the education levels of the 1960 business
elite and the general population of comparable age. In order to
read the table accurately, some notes on the Japanese educational
system are useful. Before the Second World War six years of primary school were compulsory. Beyond the primary school a four-
or five-year middle school course was set up as preparation for
three years of higher education in specialist schools *(senmongakkō)*
or university preparatory schools. The middle school also included
vocational training for commercial, industrial, and agricultural
activities. Those who completed middle school or vocational
training at the middle school level are classified as middle school
graduates. Three to four years of specialist school courses were
established for professional training for business, engineering,
and other industrial arts. Three years at a preparatory school
(equivalent to the specialist school) was usually required for
admission to a college or university.

An overwhelming majority of the 1960 business leaders received higher education in specialist schools or universities (91 percent). Over two-thirds graduated from universities (68 percent), but only a few took advanced graduate study (2 percent). Only 9 percent went no further than middle school. Only 3 percent did not go beyond the compulsory primary school. The top level of Japan's business world is a homogeneous group in terms of educational attainment. Moreover, as shown in table 16, they had substantially more education than most men their age. Only 7 percent of all males of comparable age had specialist school or university training.

Table 16. Level of Education: 1960 Business Leaders (Percent)

Highest Level of Education	Sample of Total Japan 50–69 years old*	1960 Business Elite
Primary school graduate or less	83%	3%
Middle school graduate	10	6
Specialist school graduate	7	23
University graduate		66
Graduate school	**	2
Total	100	100
Number	277	985

*Adapted from Nihon Shakaigaku Chōsa Iinkai, *Nihon Shakai no Kaisōteki Kōzō* (Hierarchical Structure of Japanese Society), (Tokyo: Yūhikaku, 1958), p. 187.
**Less than 1 percent

Higher education and success in a business career are closely associated in Japanese society. The contrast between the high proportion of specialist school or university graduates among the elite and the low proportion in the general population is striking. It is safe to conclude that graduation from a specialist school or university is almost a prerequisite for achieving business leadership in present-day Japan.

Comparison of older and younger men in our sample with reference to the highest stage of schooling completed, as shown in table 17, indicates that the proportion of university graduates has increased with time. All respondents under forty years of age were university graduates. Post-graduate study is increasing among Japanese business elite in the younger age group, but is still uncommon. While a university diploma is almost essential to attaining leadership positions, it appears that graduate work is not considered very important for business careers. Business leaders with only a specialist school degree are decreasing, as are men with only middle school or primary school education. If these trends persist, it is clear that the Japanese business leaders will be virtually all university graduates within a few decades. (The educational reform after the Second World War elevated most of the former specialist schools to college rank. Specialist school graduates among business leaders will therefore disappear in time.)

Table 17.   Education and Present Age of Japanese Business Leaders

Highest Level of Education	Under 40	Present Age			Over 71	Entire sample
		41–50	51–60	61–70		
Less than primary school	0	1	2	4	10	3
Middle school	0	4	5	6	16	6
Specialist school	0	14	21	29	30	23
University	91	77	70	60	44	66
Graduate school	9	4	2	1	0	2
Total	100	100	100	100	100	100
Number	11	70	542	319	43	985

It should be noted that the motivation to complete a school course was so strong among future business leaders (as well as the general population) in Japan that few men failed to finish a given school level in our sample. Obviously, both students and their families were quite aware of the importance of educational achievement in maintaining their higher ascribed status as well as in achieving an even higher status in the society. Most of the business elite came from higher educational institutions, but differences in education require further examination.

Who Gets Educated?

While it is true that formal education provides a chance to achieve social mobility, the actual fact is that the higher the social class of a child, on the whole, the more and better education he gets, and the better his chances are, therefore, to maintain or improve his social position. Table 18 clearly indicates that educated men come from the higher occupational backgrounds in larger proportions than from other levels. Nearly four-fifths of the business leaders who were sons of professional men, government officials, owners or executives of large businesses had a university degree. Well over 90 percent of this group finished either a specialist school or a university course. Business leaders who were sons of landlords, white collar workers, or owners of small businesses had somewhat less education on the average. The inferiority of education among business leaders who were sons of laborers or farmers is marked. Of the latter, 25 to 30 percent achieved top positions in business with no more than a middle school education. In general the men with higher social origins get the most education, and the ones from the lower, the least.

Perhaps an even more important generalization about the education of business leaders is that among sons of every occupational group except laborers more had reached the level of university graduate than stopped at any other level of educational achievement. Researchers on American business leaders have said that "the men who achieve and advance themselves in business most often are the kind of men who achieve and advance themselves in school. Their ambitions drive them upward step by step to higher educational levels just as they push them upward in business."[1] This statement is equally true of Japanese business leaders.

The relationship between education and achievement in business will be further illuminated by contrasts with the general

---

[1]Warner and Abegglen, p. 99.

Table 18. Occupational Mobility and Education of 1960 Business Leaders

Occupation of Father	Less than Primary School	Middle School	Specialist School	College or University	Total	Number
Laborer	15%	15%	39%	31%	100%	13
Farmer	14	11	29	46	100	65
Landlord	4	8	27	61	100	168
White collar worker Owner, small business	3	6	28	63	100	297
Owner, executive of large business	1	5	16	78	100	218
Govt. official Professional man	0	2	20	78	100	206
All occupations in sample	3	6	23	68	100	967

population. A national sample survey on this subject is not available. However, a sample survey of the adult male population of Tokyo reports the amount of education received by the sons of men in different occupations. (It should be noted that the educational level of the Tokyo population is higher than that of the rest of Japan because it is the most urbanized and industrialized metropolitan center.) As shown in table 19, the statement that "the sons of men in higher occupations get the most education, and the sons of laborers and farmers, the least" is even truer here than in the elite sample. Sons of managers and professional men tend to get higher education and remain in or advance from their inherited social status, while sons of farmers or laborers mostly get less education.

The relation of a son's educational achievement to the occupation of his father can be summarized as follows. First, for the population as a whole the level of education is determined chiefly by the occupation of the father. A low proportion of sons from working class families get higher education, while a far greater proportion of sons from higher occupation families get higher education. Second, the educational level of the business elite is also

Table 19. Occupational Mobility and Education of 1955 Tokyo
Population

Occupation of Father	Less than 9th Grade Education	High School	College or University	Total	Number
Laborer	71%	17%	12%	100%	304
Farmer	68	23	9	100	243
Sales occupation and clerical	36	35	29	100	295
Managerial	23	33	44	100	168
Professional	16	27	57	100	82
All occupations in sample	50	26	24	100	1092

These figures are adopted from Nihon Shakai Gakkai Chōsa Iinkai, *Nihon Shakai
no Kaisōteki Kōzō* (Hierarchical Structure of Japanese Society), (Tokyo:
Yūhikaku, 1958), p. 198.

largely determined by the father's status, but the differences are
less marked than for the general population. The business elite
from each occupational origin uniformly show higher educational
attainment than that of the general population. The business elite
from lower class families mostly achieved their positions by getting a higher education. Considerable social mobility is possible in
Japan for those who get extensive education, but the opportunity
for higher education is largely predetermined by a given occupational status.

Education of Father

The educational attainment of the father is an important factor
in determining the educational achievement of the son. How much
education did the fathers of the 1960 business leaders get? Did
they get more education than the general population? How much
more education did the present business leaders get than their
fathers? Is the educational level of the father related to the education of the son? Table 20 provides answers to some of these

questions, by comparing the educational levels for the 1960 business leaders, their fathers, and an age group comparable to their fathers in the general population—the fathers of a sample of Japan's adult male population (twenty to sixty-nine years old) in 1955.

Business leaders' fathers with less than primary school education totalled 49 percent, in contrast to 89 percent in the population as a whole. The percentage who graduated from a specialist school or university was 28 percent among the business leaders' fathers, but only 4 percent in the general population. The proportion of middle school graduates among the business leaders' fathers was almost one-fourth, in contrast to 7 percent in the general population. On the whole, the educational level of the 1960 business leaders' fathers is markedly higher than that of the preceding generation. The percentage with less than middle school education was much lower, and the percentage who received specialist school or university education much higher for business leaders than for their fathers. Although these general figures tell us much about the differences in education of the fathers and sons, they do not answer the question about the extent to which the education of the father determines the amount of education given the son.

As we have already made clear, the Japanese business system places greatest weight on educational achievement in selection of top executives. Are the sons of educated fathers more likely to go to a specialist school or university? Are the sons of less uneducated men least likely to get a higher education? Table 21 provides the answers to these important questions. In general the sons of fathers trained in a specialist school or university were more likely to go to a specialist school or university than others; yet the important indication in this table is not this so much as the fact that the sons of men from all eductional levels—primary school, middle school, specialist school, or university—were highly represented at the specialist school and university levels. It is true that 98 percent of the business leaders with specialist school or university educated fathers were also specialist school or university educated; yet 88 percent of those whose fathers had no more than primary school education also advanced to specialist school or university study, as did 93 percent of those whose fathers had finished middle school.

Table 20.   Education of Father: 1960 Business Elite (Percent)

Level of Education	Comparable age group to father of 1960 business elite*	Father of 1960 Business Elite	1960 Business Leaders
Less than primary school	89	49	3
(temple school)		(4)	
Middle school	7	23	6
(domain or private			
school)		(6)	
Specialist school		11	23
University	4	17	68
Total	100	100	100
Number	1,896	838	985

*These figures are adapted from Nihon Shakai Gakkai Chōsa Iinkai, *Nihon Shakai no Kaisōteki Kōzō* (Hierarchical Structure of Japanese Society), (Tokyo: Yūhikaku, 1958), p. 196.

Table 21.   Education of 1960 Business Leaders and Their Fathers (Percent)

Highest level of education of business leaders	Education of Father			All business leaders
	Less than primary school	Middle school	Specialist school or university	
Less than primary school	5%	1%	1%	3%
Middle school	7	6	1	6
Specialist school or university	88	93	98	91
Total	100	100	100	100
Number	413	198	232	843

Only 1 percent of the men whose fathers had a specialist school education and 5 percent of those having fathers with low schooling had only a grammar school education; only 1 percent of those having specialist school educated fathers and 27 percent having fathers of low schooling went no farther than middle school. Clearly the education of the father is an important but not conclusive determinant of the son's education.

In Japanese business formal education is important for providing the opportunity for social mobility. The peculiar role of education in Japan's industrial achievement should be examined in comparison with similar data from other countries. This will be dealt with later in this chapter.

Higher Education of Business Leaders

Because of the important role of higher educational institutions in the recruitment of the business elite, it will be worthwhile to examine what specialist school or university they were educated in and what kind of education they received in these higher institutions. Table 22 presents the names of the schools attended and the major fields of study. The two columns at the extreme right show the percentage and number of men attending each school. The graduates of Tokyo University account for more than a third (36 percent) of the graduates among the present business leaders. Another imperial university, Kyoto, provided 11 percent. It should be noted that Tokyo University was about three times larger than Kyoto University in students graduated in 1922, which is when most of the business leaders completed their university courses. The overrepresentation of Tokyo University graduates is partly due to this.[2] Hitotsubashi University supplied 10 percent. Other colleges and universities include private and municipal universities and commercial and engineering specialist schools throughout Japan. They recruited 17 percent of the total.

The last line shows the percentage distribution of major fields of study. Majors in economics are most numerous (42 percent). Majors in engineering are next (27 percent), including mechanical engineering (7 percent), electrical engineering (7 percent), chemical engineering (4 percent), civil engineering or architecture

[2]More details of the enrollment of Japan's universities are given in "Trends of Education of Japan's Elite Groups," (chapter 8 of this book), pp. 159–190.

Table 22. Specialist School and University Attended and Major Subject Studied by Business Leaders

	Major Field of Study					
School	Eco-nomics	Engi-neering	Law and Govern-ment	Other Subjects	Percent of Total	Total Number
Tokyo University	18%	43%	65%	24%	36%	(325)
Kyoto University	9	15	13	4	11	(100)
Hitotsubashi University	24	0	0	0	10	(88)
Keiō University	14	0	6	3	7	(67)
Kobe University	13	0	0	0	6	(47)
Waseda University	5	6	3	3	5	(42)
Kyushu University	0	9	1	3	3	(26)
Tokyo Institute of Technology	0	9	0	0	2	(22)
Osaka University	0	9	0	0	2	(21)
Tōhoku University	0	4	2	0	1	(13)
Others	17	5	10	63	17	(151)
Total	100%	100%	100%	100%	100%	(902)
Number	373	238	211	80		902
Percentage by field of Study	42%	27%	24%	7%	100%	(902)

(4 percent), mining or meteorology (3 percent) and others (2 percent). Among majors in law and government, the former total 18 percent and the latter 6 percent. The others are scattered over various subjects in medicine, agriculture, and the arts and sciences.

Tokyo University graduates were most numerous in every field except economics. The predominance of Tokyo graduates in law or government and engineering is notable. However, it should be noted that the School of Law produced far more graduates than any other school in Tokyo University. From its founding in 1877 to 1923 the School of Law had 9,978 alumni, the Engineering School 5,372, the School of Economics 679.[3] (The small number of economics graduates is due to the fact that prior to 1919 the curriculum in economics at Tokyo University was a part of the Law Faculty.) The majors in engineering and economics are far more overrepresented in the business elite than appears in table 22. Keiō and Waseda University, the two largest private universities in Tokyo, share a substantial proportion of the business leaders who majored in economics. In the field of engineering, government-supported universities and colleges supplied all the leaders except for six from Waseda University. In the field of law and government, Tokyo and Kyoto had a near monopoly in training the present business leaders. It is important to note that different types of universities and colleges supplied substantially different proportions of the business leaders. The six imperial universities produced more than half (53 percent) of the 1960 business leaders. These are Tokyo, Kyoto, Kyushu, Tōhoku, Osaka, and Hokkaido. Other government-supported colleges including the former Tokyo College of Commerce (now Hitotsubashi University), and the Tokyo Institute of Technology, accounted for 28 percent of the 1960 business leaders with higher education. Private specialist schools and private universities such as Keiō and Waseda supplied the remaining 19 percent. It is quite clear that Japan's imperial universities were the most important source. Professional colleges under the support of the government were next most important. As a whole, private universities and specialist schools, other than Keiō and Waseda, played only a lesser role in the training of the top executives of the biggest firms in present-day Japan.

We have also examined the major fields of study of the 1960 business leaders by type of business and industry. The men who majored in economic subjects are overrepresented in the following sectors of business (in descending order of importance): trading, finance, service, food, and textiles. Those who majored in sciences and engineering more frequently appeared in construction, power or gas, and heavy manufacturing. The men who studied law and government tended to work in finance, transportation or communication, and services. Those who majored in subjects other than the above appear more frequently in food and services. It

---

[3]Ministry of Education, Mombushō-Nempo (*The Annual Report of the Ministry of Education*), 1924.

should be noted that men who majored in economics and law uniformly shared top executive positions in all types of business and industry. However, men who majored in sciences and engineering rarely appear in finance, trading, services, or food industries. The dominance of the university or specialist school graduates in economics and law or government is a major characteristic of 1960 Japanese business and industrial leaders.

We wish now to examine whether graduates of a particular university achieved leadership positions only in certain types of business or industry. Was there any specific pattern relating a university to a particular industry? Table 23 distributes business leaders by type of business and industry and by university attended. The proportion of specialist school or university graduates in each industry is shown in the extreme right column. Over or underrepresentation of a certain industry by a certain university should be read in comparison to the figures in this column.

Tokyo University graduates are overrepresented in mining, construction, steel, machinery and finance. They are underrepresented in textile, food, trading, and service. As a whole they are active in all sectors of business and industrial leadership. Kyoto University graduates are also well represented in every manufacturing and tertiary industry, although overrepresented only in public utilities. Osaka, Kyushu, and Tōhoku (which grew out of an engineering college), and the Tokyo Institute of Technology are clearly overrepresented in mining, construction and all manufacturing industries but are little represented in tertiary industries. Hitotsubashi and Kobe universities, the former a commercial college, are distinctly overrepresented in tertiary industries and are also well represented in all manufacturing industries. It is clear that while nearly all graduates of former engineering colleges achieved business leadership positions chiefly in manufacturing and not in tertiary industries, graduates of former commercial colleges achieved leadership positions not only in trading and finance, but also in manufacturing. The business system in selecting the top executives in Japan evidently places more emphasis on economic and business subjects in university training than on engineering. The two important private institutions, Keiō and Waseda, supplied leaders more in tertiary industries than in secondary industries.

Table 23. Distribution of Business Leaders by Type of Business or Industry and by University Attended

Type of Business or Industry	Tokyo University	Kyoto University	Osaka University Kyushu University, Tōhoku University Tōkyo Institute of Technology	Hitotsubashi University, Kobe University	Keiō University, Waseda University	Other	Total
Mining, construction	10%	6%	10%	8%	10%	4%	8%
Steel, machinery	24	24	30	12	14	28	22
Chemical, pharmaceuticals	13	11	26	13	13	6	13
Textile, food	14	16	22	18	21	26	19
Trading, service	6	5	1	17	14	13	9
Finance	20	14	2	19	17	7	15
Public utility	13	24	9	13	11	16	14
Total	100	100	100	100	100	100	100
Number	325	100	81	135	109	152	902

Foreign travel and study abroad will be examined next. Nearly all of the business leaders obtained their higher education in Japanese institutions; only 3 percent studied abroad. Despite the fact that Japan was most anxious to import Western sciences and technology, only a few successful businessmen studied abroad. However, the small proportion educated abroad does not imply that there were few foreign contacts among the Japanese business leaders. Ninety percent have traveled abroad, with an average of 2.5 trips per person. Two-thirds stayed abroad less than one year (one-third stayed less than three months); one-third stayed more than a year. If the frequency and duration of foreign travels of the business leaders are examined by business position, size of business, and type of business, no significant trend can be observed. It appears that foreign travel constitutes an important experience for a business career in present-day Japan but is not a determining or accelerating factor in achieving a leadership position in the business hierarchy.

Education and the Business System

Next we want to determine whether there is any evidence of a positive relationship between level of schooling and level of success achieved in business. To answer this, we first distribute the data on level of formal education of the 1960 business leaders by amount of capitalization of their respective companies, as shown in table 24.

The two outstanding features in the table are: first, the positive correlation between size of firm and proportion of university graduates, and second, the inverse correlation between size and the proportion of specialist school graduates and middle school or primary school graduates. The figures seem to indicate that the larger the scale of business enterprise, the greater is the extent to which its important executive and managerial positions are filled by university graduates.[4] There is a clear positive relation between

---

[4]Similar findings on American firms were reported in Taussig, F. W. and Joslyn, C. S., *American Business Leaders* (New York: MacMillan Co., 1932), pp. 182–3; and Warner and Abegglen, pp. 152–3.

the level of formal education and the degree of business achievement, when the latter is measured solely in terms of size of business.

Table 24. Education of 1960 Business Leaders, by Size of Firm:
Capitalization

Capitalization of Firm	Less than Middle School	Specialist School	College or University	Total	Number
More than 20 billion yen	0	7	93	100	41
More than 10 billion yen	8	14	78	100	71
More than 5 billion yen	5	24	71	100	119
More than 1 billion yen	10	26	64	100	716
All business leaders	9	23	68	100	947

Is this still true when business achievement is measured by level
of executive position? Table 25 suggests that there is no significant
correlation between business position and level of education. The
proportion of university graduates among chairmen and presidents
is neither appreciably larger nor appreciably smaller than among
subordinate executives such as vice presidents, *semmu torishimariyaku,* and other senior managing directors (*jōmu torishimariyaku*). This
same absence of consistent variation is also observed in the proportions of men who were not university graduates. No clearly
defined relation appears to exist between level of education and
the nature of the position held.

Marked differences are disclosed, however, when the proportion
of university graduates by position level is calculated separately
for each of the four sizes of business firms by capitalization. The
results of this calculation are presented in table 26. We are already
familiar with the figures appearing in the extreme right-hand
column of the table. They indicate that the proportion of university graduates tends to increase as the scale of business increases.

Table 25. Education and Position of 1960 Business Leaders

	Education				
Business Position	Less than Middle School	Specialist School	University	Total	Number
Chairman	15%	17%	68%	100%	59
President	10	26	64	100	263
Vice president	6	24	70	100	360
Senior managing director	10	22	68	100	303
All positions	9%	23%	68%	100%	985

The same tendency holds for each of the senior position levels also, except for a small discrepancy among presidents. It appears that as the scale of business expands, a university education comes to be requisite for top executive positions. In the smaller firms all levels of top executive positions have fewer university graduates.

When comparisons are made horizontally, instead of vertically, in table 26, are there any differences among the four groups of top executives by different size of business? In reading the table horizontally, we see that the proportion of university graduates decreases as the position level rises, in most instances. The percent for presidents is far below that for senior managing directors. We initially assumed that the more responsible the position to be filled, the greater would be the percentage who were university graduates. This relation does not hold true. The main reason for this is the time or age factor. The presidents (average age 62.4 years) are much older than senior managing directors (average age 55.9 years). As we have noted in table 17, the educational level is much higher for younger executives than for older ones. Presumably, the positions of subordinate directors tend to be filled more on the basis of formal education than the positions of chief executives.

In general the requirement of university graduation for all top executive positions is strong in the Japanese business system with relatively small differences in educational level by size of business. It is clear that Japanese business leaders holding different business

Table 26. Proportion of University Graduates Among Business Leaders Holding Specified Positions in Businesses of Specified Capitalization

Size of Business Capitalization	Chairman	President	Vice President	Senior Managing Director	All Positions
More than 20 billion yen	100	92	88	93	93
More than 10 billion yen	75	68	78	83	78
More than 5 billion yen	78	58	73	77	71
More than 1 billion yen	59	60	58	63	64
All Businesses	68	65	68	67	68

positions and employed in different sizes of business tend to consist of a highly homogeneous group in terms of formal educational attainment. In reviewing education of the business leaders and business system in Japan, we want to examine education in relation to type of business. In the relationship between education and the type of business, as given in table 27, business leaders with a university education were proportionately most numerous in public utilities and finance and least numerous in trading, food manufacturing, and services.

Higher education is evidently an important factor in recruiting top executives. How is this superior achievement of university graduates to be accounted for? Their higher education may be due to favorable environment, i.e., family social and economic status and influential connections. It is true that the higher education of business leaders is closely associated with high occupational status, as we have seen in chapter 3. However, this explanation is insufficient; not all business leaders are from favorable family backgrounds and not all high status families can send their sons to the best universities. Moreover, men for the highest positions in the largest operations are recruited less by direct inheritance and more from career men with the highest education, regardless of their social status backgrounds.

It seems improbable that favorable family status and influential connections alone should be responsible for the observed correlation between degree of formal education and degree of business achievement. Examination of the data on occupational origins discloses that the representation of the two most favored groups (sons of executives and owners of large businesses) shows little variation from the other groups in relation to size of business and speed of advancement.[5] We are led to believe that the large proportion of university graduates in the largest businesses reflects the influence of educational training as such, rather than that of environmental factors distinct from schooling.

Table 27. Education and Type of Business

Type of Business	Education of Business Leaders			
	University Graduate	Specialist School Graduate	Less Than Middle School	Total
Public Utility	84	16	0	100
Finance	78	14	8	100
Chemicals	76	21	3	100
Steel	76	21	3	100
Mining	76	18	6	100
Transportation & communication	73	21	6	100
Construction	72	16	12	100
Textile	68	30	2	100
Machinery	57	28	15	100
Service	52	22	26	100
Food	47	31	22	100
Trading	46	46	8	100
All Types of Business	68	23	9	100

The authors of *American Business Leaders* attributed the superior performance of college men in American business to the following:

Generally speaking, the individuals able to survive the process of educational selection to the point of graduating from a

[5]Education of the 1960 Japanese leaders in relation to their careers is treated in chapter 5.

college are superior in general ability to those leaving school at the lower stages. It is hardly surprising, then, that the college graduate makes a better showing in business than either the high school or the grammar school graduates. The same relation would, in all likelihood, hold true in any other vocation. College men do well in business for the same reason that they did well in school,—because they have industry and intelligence beyond the average.[6]

Japanese business leaders receive much more education than the average for the whole population. Positions of business leadership require more and more education. With continued growth Japanese business organizations have tended to establish bureaucratic hierarchies and institutionalize the careers of men in steps measured by schooling and seniority. A university education becomes most important in determining achievement in such an industrial bureaucratic career.

International Comparison of Education of Business Elite

. Some measure of our educational data on a comparative basis is possible through a comparison of the Japanese business leaders studied here with American and British business leaders. Is the educational level of the Japanese business leaders higher or lower than that of the American or British business leaders? What are special roles of education in occupational mobility of the Japanese business leaders in comparison to those of other countries? The bases for these comparisons are shown in table 28. The considerably higher level of formal education of the Japanese groups is apparent. Ninety-one percent of business leaders are specialist school or university graduates. Only 9 percent of the business leaders have achieved their positions of leadership with less than a middle school education. It seems no exaggeration to conclude that university graduation is now for all practical purposes prerequisite to advance to a top level position in Japan.

---

[6]Taussig and Joslyn, p. 188.

Table 28. Educational Level of Business Leaders: Japan, United States and United Kingdom

Level of Education	Japan 1960[1]	United States, 1952[2]	United Kingdom, 1952[3]
Primary school graduate or less	3%	4%	10%
Middle school or secondary school graduate	6	20	27
Specialist school graduate	23	—	—
Some college or university education*	—	19	27
College or university graduate	66	38	29
Graduate school	2	19	7
Total percent	100	100	100
Total individuals	985	8,300	1,243

Sources: 1. Japanese data are from our questionnaire study for 1960.
2. U.S. data are from Warner and Abegglen, pp. 95–114.
3. U.K. data are from Copeman, pp. 99–105.
*Some college education, without graduation

As a highly advanced industrial society, the American business world places great emphasis on formal education in recruiting top executives. However, almost a quarter (24 percent) of the 1952 business leaders attained the positions of business leadership with high school graduation or less. Attending college without graduation was not uncommon (19 percent) among the American business leaders. Among American business leaders who were university graduates (57 percent), one-third (19 percent) had some graduate training. It is clear that the American business community recognizes professional training in graduate school as an important qualification for executive positions. It appears that the American business leaders have more diversified backgrounds in formal education than the Japanese business leaders have, and that formal education is evaluated differently in the United States and Japan.

The role of formal education in recruitment of business leaders in Britain is still different from that of the United States and Japan.

Despite a high degree of industrial maturity, the British business community requires less formal education for executive positions than the other two countries do. Among British business leaders, 37 percent receive a secondary education or less. Those with some education after secondary school account for 27 percent. Thirty-six percent have university training, of which 7 percent had graduate work. The educational levels of the British business leaders differ even more widely than those of the American. It is evident that formal education alone is not a very important factor in determining the success of a business career in Britain.

A further perspective on the relationship between formal education and a business career in the United States as compared with Western Europe was offered in a summary statement on education and social mobility in industrial societies by Lipset and Bendix:

> In America a college education becomes an almost necessary requisite for a position of responsibility, and its completion is timed to coincide with becoming an adult. In Europe on the other hand, a university degree is considered necessary only for a professional career, fewer go to the university, and many begin their business careers without completing or even attending a university. Hence, it should not be surprising that American big businessmen have more schooling than their British colleagues and that the latter start work at a younger age than the Americans.[7]

It may however be of some surprise to find Japan still more committed to advanced education than the United States, which itself emphasizes a university degree for elite careers to a greater degree than does Western Europe. The rapid progress of Japanese business and industry in the recent period may be due to the fact that business executives who are university graduates are by training receptive to new ideas, new technology, and new management practices.

---

[7]Lipset and Bendix, p. 41.

Chapter 5

CAREER PATTERNS, MARRIAGE, AND GEOGRAPHICAL MOBILITY OF THE 1960 BUSINESS ELITE

Career Patterns

The great majority of Japanese business leaders of 1960 were conspicuously mobile. The question is, then, what was the general course of their occupational mobility after they began their occupational life? In this chapter, first, we describe the career patterns of the business leaders and then relate them to family occupational backgrounds and formal education.

It is a well-known fact that career patterns of Japanese industrial workers show a marked degree of occupational immobility. Employees tend to remain with one company until retirement. This mode of employment has been called *lifetime commitment*.[1] It is of interest to compare the career patterns of business leaders with those prevailing elsewhere in Japanese society. We shall first focus on movement from one firm to another. The extent of interfirm mobility among the men studied is shown in table 29.

About half the business leaders show no interfirm mobility in their occupational life: they were always employed by a single company, in which they worked their way upward to top executive positions. Men who have been employed by two firms represent 30 percent of the total, and men employed by three different firms, 19 percent. Only 3 percent have worked for more than three firms. Median interfirm movement is less than twice (1.8 times). Whether the move from one company to another took place before achieving an executive position or after is not known. Interfirm mobility is slightly more frequent among men who have attained the positions of chairman of the board of directors or company president than among men who are vice presidents or managing

---

[1]Abegglen, James C., *The Japanese Factory* (Glencoe, Illinois: The Free Press, 1958) pp. 11–46.

Table 29. Interfirm Mobility of 1960 Business Leaders

Number of Companies	Percentage of Business Leaders	Percentage of a Sample Survey
1	48	30
2	30	23
3	19	19
4	2	13
More than 5	1	15
Total	100	100
Number of individuals	977	1,227

directors. Presumably this circumstance reflects in part the fact that these chief executives are generally older and have had longer business careers than the others.

A study of interfirm mobility in Japan reports that a sample survey among adult males in Tokyo indicates an average incidence of 2.8 firms.[2] Subjects of this study have careers spanning thirty to forty years, comparable with the business leaders of the present study, and averaged 3.5 firms.[3] In general, interfirm mobility in Japan does not seem to provide the best opportunities for receiving training and acquiring the management skills necessary for top positions. Executives are thus preferably recruited from within the company. It should be noted that interfirm mobility among Japanese business leaders is markedly lower than among business leaders of the United States, where it is common to move from one company to another to take a better position.[4]

Interoccupational mobility among the business leaders has also been examined. Some men have had experience as government officials (7.5 percent), but only a very few have professional backgrounds (1.3 percent). The vast majority have been employed

[2]Tominaga Ken'ichi, "Occupational Mobility in Japanese Society: Analysis of Labor Market in Japan," *Journal of Economic Behavior*, II: 1, April 1962, Tokyo, p. 29.
[3]*Ibid.*, p. 32.
[4]Warner and Abegglen, p. 126.

only in the business world. Low interoccupational as well as low interfirm mobility are outstanding characteristics.

Leaders' Achievement Time and Occupational Backgrounds

The typical career of the 1960 business leaders may be inferred in rough outline from data on age and achievement time. The average age of the 1960 business elite is 58.6 years. The average business leader entered business at the age of 23.6 years and entered his present business firm 9.6 years later. He served this firm for 25.4 years. From the time of entering the business world, the average number of years required to attain high positions was 29.5 years. The typical business leader has held his position of eminence for 5.5 years.

As previously stated,[5] the profile of the typical career of the Japanese business leaders indicates that they represent an older group than their counterparts in the United States and the United Kingdom. The Japanese businessmen started their business careers rather late, owing to longer formal education and extra study before entering a college or university.[6] The majority of the men studied entered their present firms directly after graduation from school. However, movement to another firm sometimes occurred late in the career, and for this reason the average time of entrance into present business firms is rather late. It appears that attaining top executive positions requires many years of movement upward through a rigid hierarchy, a subject which we shall discuss later in this chapter.

Data on achievement time provide a measure of the effects of family occupational background, influential connections, and education upon the careers of the business leaders studied. An idea of the effect of occupational background may be gained from table 30. Four time factors are presented: average age on entering the

---

[5]See chapter 2.
[6]Extra study is often required to pass highly competitive university entrance examinations. Failure in the examinations quite often delays one's entry into a career, since the examinations are commonly taken again in successive years until passed.

business world; average age on assuming present position; average number of years in business before attaining a position of leadership; and average present age. These are given, according to the occupation of the father, in nine occupational groupings.

Sons of laborers entered the business world at an earlier age (22.2 years on the average) than men of any other occupational background. Sons of government officials entered business at an average age of 24.1 years. In general, it is clear that men from upper occupational backgrounds started their careers somewhat later than those from lower occupational backgrounds. However, differences of age at first entry into business employment among

Table 30.   Occupational Mobility and Speed of Career Rise

| | Business | Leaders | | |
Occupation of Father	Average Age on Entering Business World	Average Years to Achieve Position	Average Age at which Present Position Assumed	Average Present Age
Laborer	22.2	29.7	51.9	59.0
Farmer	22.9	31.4	54.3	60.5
Landlord	23.3	30.8	54.1	60.1
White collar worker	23.4	30.4	53.8	59.1
Owner, small business	23.3	30.8	54.1	59.0
Owner, large business	23.8	25.9	49.7	56.5
Executive, large business	23.9	27.2	51.1	56.3
Government official	24.1	29.8	53.9	58.4
Professional	23.8	29.5	53.3	58.4
All business leaders	23.6	29.5	53.1	58.6

the men from the various occupational backgrounds are small (1.9 years maximum). Regardless of their family occupational background, the majority of the business leaders have had specialist school or university education.

Column two of table 30 shows average years required to achieve the position presently held, from the time the men entered the business world. The length of career before attaining a top position is greatest for sons of farmers (31.4 years) and shortest for sons of owners of large business concerns (25.9 years). Apart from the advantages already noted in chapter 2 in terms of representation in business leadership, the time difference of some 5.5 years may be taken as an index of the advantage of birth into a socially and economically favored family, particularly one owning a firm.

Column three of table 30 shows the average age at which the subjects assumed their present positions. Sons of farmers attained their present positions at the highest average age (54.3 years), and sons of owners of large business firms at the youngest (49.7 years). The greatest average difference of age upon assuming present positions is thus 4.6 years, in contrast with a maximum difference in age upon entering employment of 1.9 years. It appears that the effect of the occupational status of fathers is substantial.

Present age, as given in column four of table 30, may be taken as a summary measure of time factors presented in the three preceding columns. The younger business leaders are principally sons of executives and owners of large firms; those who reached their positions later in life are principally sons of landlords and farmers. These two groups represent the extremes, and differences of age among the other groups are small. All groups are near the average of 58.6 years for the entire sample.

The advantage held by sons of business owners and executives has been further examined by separating them into two groups, men in the same firms as their fathers and men in firms different from those of their fathers. Table 31 shows achievement time and the different types of influential connections. Sons of large business owners in the same firms as their fathers constitute 53 cases or 6 percent of the total. They assumed top executive positions at a substantially younger age than the average of 53.1 years. Although sons of owners of large business concerns who are in the same firms as their fathers are few, they also attained positions of leadership earlier (7.4 years) than the average. Sons of owners or executives of large business firms who work for firms different from those of their fathers account for 145 cases or 16 percent of the total. These men achieved positions of leadership at about the average age. Evidently they attained their positions without having the direct advantage of inheriting their fathers' positions. It should be noted that the number of sons in firms different from those of their fathers is markedly greater than that of sons in the same firms as their fathers. In relation to inherited advantages, two additional points should be noted. First, sons of owners or executives who assume the same positions as their fathers are found mostly in the smaller firms of our sample. Second, among the business leaders studied, the positions of chairman and president are distinctly more often inherited than the positions of vice president and managing director. In general, our data suggest that inheritance of positions is presently not especially common.

The occupational status of the father is not the only influence affecting careers. Other relatives in one's company might also exert influence. Men in the same firms as their fathers assumed positions of leadership at an average age of 45.1 years. Twelve men, or 1.5 percent of the total, had wives' fathers in the same firm. These men attained their positions of leadership at an age (49.3 years) somewhat younger than the average. Those who had uncles or brothers in the same firm constitute 19 cases or 2 percent of the total. They assumed their present positions at 48.0 and 48.9 years, respectively, on the average. In general, it appears that the incidence of nepotism in large Japanese firms is rather low, and

Table 31.   Influential Connections and Achievement Time of 1960 Japanese Business Leaders

Type of Connection	Percent	Age Leader Assumed Present Position
Son of large business owner in same firm as father	6	44.6
Son of large business executive in same firm as father	2	45.7
Son of large business owner in firm different from father's	7	54.1
Son of large business executive in firm different from father's	9	52.3
Others	76	53.8
Total percent	100	53.1
Total number of individuals	985	

nepotism does not strongly affect achievement time. (We will refer again to nepotism in relation to size of business firm later in this chapter).

The educational backgrounds of the Japanese business elite and their subsequent careers will now be examined. Age data on the 1960 business leaders, classified according to education, are given in table 32. Average ages upon entering business employment, average ages at which the leaders assumed their present position, average years in business employment before attaining present position, and average present ages of respondents are given for each of five educational categories.

As we have already noted, men with superior family occupational backgrounds entered employment at later ages and achieved leadership in relatively less time than men with inferior occupational backgrounds. It is also clear that men with superior backgrounds tended to receive more formal education than the others. Education is then an important factor in causing men with superior backgrounds to begin employment later in life.

In table 32, the column on the extreme right lists the average present age of business leaders divided into groups based upon level of formal education. The average age decreases as the amount of formal education increases. The average age of men who are not high school graduates is 61.7 years. At the other extreme, the average age of men who have had some graduate work at universities is 53.8 years. This wide variation in age, when viewed from the standpoint of formal educational experience, indicates first that business careers are substantially lengthened when education is limited. It also reflects the fact that education of the nation as a whole has increased rapidly. In any kind of sample, the older group will have had less formal education than the more youthful.

The first two columns of table 32 show an expectable relationship between age at first employment and educational attainments. Men with little formal education started work at very early ages; the average for men who are not middle school graduates is 17.6 years. The group with the most education, graduate study at a university, entered business at an average age of 24.7 years. A noteworthy relationship is observed between Average Years to

Achieve Position and education. Men with little or no formal education required an average of 36.2 years to achieve their positions, whereas the time for university graduates was 28.3 years.

Table 32.   Education and Speed of Career Rise

Level of Education of Business Leaders*	Average Age Leader Entered Business	Average Years to Achieve Position	Average Age Leader Assumed Present Position	Average Present Age
Less than primary school	17.6	36.2	53.8	61.7
Middle school graduate	20.0	34.3	54.3	60.4
Specialist school graduate	22.7	31.8	54.5	60.2
University graduate	24.5	28.3	52.8	57.9
Graduate school	24.7	22.6	47.3	53.8
Average of total sample	23.6	29.5	53.1	58.6

*Levels of education of business leaders are defined in chapter 4.

When the effect of education is measured only by the number of years required to achieve business leadership, education appears to have a very large effect on the subsequent career. This single measure fails, however, to take account of the fact that men with less education begin their careers at an early age and in effect are educated on the job. Combining the two sets of figures to obtain a measure of the length of the total career before achieving business leadership substantially reduces the apparent impact of education, as is indicated in column three, table 32. For men with less than primary school education, the average age at which present positions were attained is 53.8 years. For men who graduated from universities, the average age is 52.8 years.

Our examination of the business careers of the 1960 business leaders in relation to their occupational background and education may be summarized as follows. Movement from one firm to another is not common. Most men either have been employed by only one firm or have changed employment only once. Only a few men have had experience in professions outside the commercial world. Achievement of positions of leadership requires a long period of service and seniority in the firm by which a man is employed. Above all the amount of formal education seems to be important in contributing toward a successful career. Differences of family occupational background appear to exert rather minor influences upon careers. Inheritance of positions of business leadership is not common in present-day Japan. In general, the Japanese business elite is recruited primarily on the basis of personal achievement. Yet the great emphasis that is laid upon education, seniority, and lifelong commitment to a single enterprise as qualifications for top executive positions suggests a closed rather than an open system in selecting business talent.

Occupational Mobility and Business Expansion

In the following analysis, Japanese commerce and industry are examined in further detail in terms of occupational mobility according to three variables: first, the expansion of the industries and of the firms in which business leaders hold their present positions; second, the types of business or industry in which leaders hold their positions; and third, the positions in the business hierarchy held by the leaders. These categories by no means exhaust the range of possible analytic variables by means of which the business community may be studied. They are, however, three of the most critical variables and constitute the points of reference from which occupational mobility is commonly discussed.

It is especially important to examine occupational mobility of the Japanese business leaders against the expansion of industry and of business firms. The Japanese national economy has experienced a high rate of growth in gross national product during the period of the careers of the 1960 business leaders. Industrial production in 1960 had increased 3.8 times over that of 1920.[7] Certain types of industry and some business firms have shown spectacular growth in recent years. Whether rapid expansion of business does in fact encourage increased occupational mobility is an unresolved question. It is our assumption that the rapidly expanding firm or industry offers increasing opportunities for filling executive po-

---

[7] *JSY*, 1961, p. 198.

sitions by personnel with occupational and educational backgrounds wider than those of executives of former years.

Table 33 offers data useful for an empirical examination of this assumption. The 1960 business leaders are classified by the rate of expansion of the industries and by the growth of the firms with which they are associated. Data presented here are limited to the mining and manufacturing industries. (For a discussion of the categories employed, see appendix 2). Distinctions made between an industry as a whole and individual firms are somewhat arbitrary, but they offer a basis for considering the role of business expansion in occupational mobility. This approach was formulated and successfully used by Warner and Abegglen in their study of American business and industry.[8]

Table 33 presents five categories of occupational background. If our assumption of accelerated mobility in expanding business is warranted, the table should provide an approximation of a nine-point scale, from the slowly expanding firm in a slowly expanding industry to the rapidly expanding firm in a rapidly expanding industry, and the degree of mobility should correlate directly with the scale of expansion. An examination of table 33 indicates that the expected relationship is not present in a clear form.

Let us first examine the incidence of occupational mobility of the business leaders against the rate of expansion of industry. Sons of small business owners who hold executive posts are more common in rapidly expanding and moderately expanding industries than in slowly expanding industries. Conversely, proportionately fewer sons of owners or executives of large business firms are in rapidly expanding industries. Sons of laborers and white collar workers appear more frequently in slowly or moderately expanding than in rapidly expanding industries. A larger proportion of sons of professional men is present in moderately or rapidly expanding types of industry than in slowly expanding industries. Sons of farmers are well diffused among all types of industry.

Secondly, we compare occupational mobility with the rate of expansion of firms. No consistent pattern is observed. Sons of farmers more frequently appeared in rapidly expanding firms in rapidly and moderately expanding industries, but not in rapidly

[8]Warner and Abegglen, p. 139 and pp. 284–8.

Table 33. Occupational Mobility and Industrial Expansion*

			Occupation of Father				
Rate of expansion of firm	Laborer and white collar worker	Owner, small business	Owner or executive, large business	Government official or professional	Farmer	Total	Number
Slowly Expanding Industries							
Slow	15%	17%	29%	15%	24%	100%	68
Moderate	9	14	28	15	34	100	44
Rapid	13	20	33	20	14	100	15
Moderately Expanding Industries							
Slow	9	24	19	26	22	100	46
Moderate	13	19	23	24	21	100	135
Rapid	16	21	16	19	28	100	43
Rapidly Expanding Industries							
Slow	5	26	22	33	14	100	42
Moderate	8	29	18	23	22	100	87
Rapid	7	24	20	13	36	100	45
All Industries	11	21	23	21	24	100	525

*Limited to mining and manufacturing industries.

expanding firms in slowly expanding industries. Again sons of owners or executives of large business firms are more commonly found in slowly expanding firms in slowly expanding industries, but this trend is not present in rapidly and moderately expanding firms in rapidly and moderately expanding industries. There is no clear evidence that occupational mobility is generally greater in rapidly expanding firms than in slowly expanding firms.

Table 33 summarizes data on occupational mobility in terms of the expansion of both industries and firms. When the two factors are considered together, accumulative and consistent trends toward accelerating occupational mobility are not evident. Relationship between business expansion and occupational mobility as indicated by father's occupation is vague. It is observed that stable firms and stable types of industries do recruit leaders from all occupational backgrounds in much the same proportions as do rapidly expanding firms and industries.

When the education of the Japanese business elite is examined, patterns of movement to business leadership in different types of expanding businesses become evident. Table 34 presents the results of an analysis of the education of business leaders in the several types of industry and business. When types of business are categorized by their rate of growth and individual firms by their rate of expansion during the career of their executives and these factors are related to the amount of formal education of executives, important and consistent differences appear. Among the elite in slowly expanding firms in slowly expanding types of business, 71 percent are university graduates. Only 6 percent have had education less than completion of middle school. On the other hand, only 38 percent of the business leaders in rapidly expanding firms in rapidly expanding types of business have had a university education, and 30 percent have not graduated from middle school.

The comparison given between the two extreme types of business firms (i.e., slowly and rapidly expanding) is, on the whole, consistent throughout the range of types analyzed. Within the two types, a much higher proportion of executives who are university graduates directs the most slowly expanding firms, and many more of the leaders of rapidly expanding firms have relatively little formal education. Thus, the rate of expansion of the firm appears to be a critical variable in the selection of the business elite, and a high level of formal education is much more common among leaders in the slowly expanding firms.

Expansion of industry as a whole bears relatively little relationship to the amount of formal education of its leaders. Moderately expanding industries do have a higher proportion of university graduates than do slowly expanding industries, and more men with relatively high formal education are in a position of leadership in concerns where expansion has been moderate or rapid. These circumstances are somewhat contradicted, however, by the fact that leaders in rapidly expanding firms have less formal education

Table 34. Education and Industrial Expansion*

Education of Leaders

Expansion of Firm	Less Than Middle School Diploma	Specialist School Degree	University Degree	Total Number	
	Slowly Expanding Industries				
Slow	6%	23%	71%	100%	69
Moderate	14	34	52	100	44
Rapid	31	38	31	100	16
	Moderately Expanding Industries				
Slow	8	30	62	100	47
Moderate	5	24	71	100	137
Rapid	7	23	70	100	44
	Rapidly Expanding Industries				
Slow	0	26	74	100	42
Moderate	3	23	74	100	87
Rapid	30	32	38	100	47
All Industries	9	26	65	100	533

*Limited to mining and manufacturing industries.

on the average than those in slowly expanding firms. It should also be noted that differences in formal education of leaders in different types of expanding industry are small in comparison with differences of formal education of leaders as related to different rates of expansion of firms.

In reviewing the effects of business expansion on the recruitment of the Japanese business elite, two general trends may be seen. First, there is no marked tendency for men of lower occupational backgrounds to be represented more frequently in rapidly expanding types of business than in moderately or slowly expanding types of business. However, when education is considered, rapidly expanding types of business do indeed offer more substantial opportunities to men with less formal education. These men make up a much larger proportion of the leadership of rapidly growing sectors of the Japanese industrial world.

At this point the question of the relationship of family occupational background and education arises. We have noted that a relatively high level of formal education is evident among leaders in the more stable business sectors, and that levels of education are generally lower among leaders in expanding firms and industries. It is important to note that the same relationship has been found in a study of American business leaders, where the researchers offered the following explanation: ". . . the son of a laborer or farmer would balance the disadvantage of birth by advanced education in order to achieve mobility in a stable industry."[9]

Careers in Various Industries

Expansion is only one dimension of observation of the total complex of Japanese business. The type of industry or business may also affect occupational mobility among the business leaders. In order to examine this question, twelve categories of business and industry have been set up. Table 35 presents information on occupational mobility of the business elite as related to occupations of fathers and to these twelve types of businesses in rank order with the largest category—sons of large business owners, government officials, or professional men—appearing first. Men from these backgrounds comprise 51 percent of the leadership in the textile and food industries. This compares with an average of 44 percent for all types of business. Some types of business and industry are low in this respect: 28 percent of the business leaders in service industries and 36 percent in the steel industry are sons of big business owners, government officials, or professional men.

Sons of owners of small business firms are overrepresented in service industries and public utilities. They are underrepresented in mining, food, and finance. Sons of white collar workers and laborers are found more frequently in trade and less frequently in service industries. Sons of farmers are overrepresented in mining, steel, transportation and communication, machinery, and service industries, and the proportions of leaders from big business and professional backgrounds are low in these industries.

---

[9]Warner and Abegglen, p. 142.

As we have noted, our data show that the higher the occupational status of the father, the higher the level of educational attainment of the son. It might be expected that the occupational status of fathers and the educational level of the business leaders in relation to the types of business and industry would be consistent, but they are not. Information on education and types of business (table 27, chapter 4) reveals that public utilities and financial sectors in the tertiary industries and heavy and chemical sectors in the manufacturing industry require higher education among their business leaders than do other industries and types of concerns.

Table 35. Occupational Mobility and Type of Business Firm

Type of Business of Leaders	Owner or Executive, Large Business, Professional and Gov't Official	Owner, Small Business	White Collar Worker, Laborer	Farmer	Total	Number
	Occupation of Fathers					
Textile	51%	20%	12%	17%	100%	128
Food	51	17	9	23	100	47
Finance	49	17	10	24	100	143
Construction	46	25	12	17	100	48
Power, gas	45	29	6	20	100	49
Chemicals	44	23	12	21	100	115
Transportation or communication	44	19	8	29	100	101
Mining	44	15	9	32	100	34
Trading	37	19	19	25	100	48
Machinery	37	25	10	28	100	163
Steel	36	25	10	29	100	59
Services	28	41	3	28	100	32
All types of business	44	22	10	24	100	967

The proportion of leadership in each type of business in accordance with region of birth has also been examined. The Kinki region, which includes the cities of Osaka, Kobe, and Kyoto, and is the traditional commercial center of Japan, produces somewhat more business leaders in trading and somewhat less in mining than any other area. The Kanto region, which includes Tokyo, produces the greatest number of leaders in the construction and food industries. Although representation in leadership is not truly uniform in all regions of the nation among the various businesses and industries, it nevertheless shows no great variation from region to region.

The proportion of leadership in each type of business in relation to size of place of birth was also examined.[10] Leaders in construction, finance, trading and services tend to have been born in cities. More leaders in public utilities and the steel industry were born in towns than was expected. The types of business whose leaders were most commonly born in rural villages are mining, transportation and communication. However, no clear pattern emerges that relates place of birth of business leaders to different types of business.

Our analysis of family occupational background, region of birth, and educational background of Japanese business leaders reveals no marked trends toward association with specific types of business or industry. Only the leaders in finance are typically upper class by birth and have university educations and urban backgrounds. Japanese business leaders share many characteristics of social origins and education regardless of the type of business and industry in which they are engaged.

Size of Business Enterprise and Positions Achieved

Occupational mobility of the 1960 Japanese business leaders will now be examined from the standpoint of the size of business enterprises. Table 36 presents the size of business firms of the 1960 business leaders in terms of capitalization and also gives the occupations of the fathers of the leaders. Sons of small business owners, professional men, or government officials are markedly overrepre-

---

[10]Definitions of city, town and village are given in the section on geographical mobility in this chapter.

sented in the firms with capitalization exceeding 10 billion yen and somewhat underrepresented in smaller firms. Background occupational groups that are underrepresented in the leadership of the larger business firms include sons of owners or executives of large business firms, laborers, white collar workers, landlords, and farmers. These latter groups are overrepresented in smaller firms. It appears that the opportunity for movement to leadership measured in terms of the amount of capitalization of firms is slightly greater for men with upper-middle class backgrounds than for others.

Table 36. Size of Business Enterprise and Occupation of Fathers of 1960 Business Leaders

Size of Firm in Capitalization	Owner, Small Business	Professional and Government Official	Land-lord, Farmer	Executive or Owner, Large Business	Laborer, White Collar Worker	Total	Number
More than 20 billion yen	34%	29%	17%	15%	5%	100%	41
More than 10 billion yen	25	27	27	14	7	100	71
More than 5 billion yen	22	20	20	24	14	100	119
More than 1 billion yen	21	20	25	23	11	100	699
All business leaders	22%	21%	24%	22%	11%	100%	930

It should be noted here that the incidence of leaders who assume the same positions as their fathers is greater in smaller firms than in larger firms.

Attention has also been given to the question of the effect of kinship ties between leaders and other persons in the firms of the leaders, and these data were related to the size of business firms. Nepotism in Japanese business and industry is most common in small firms. The smaller the firm, the greater the ties of kinship within it. Sons of owners or executives of large business firms are more common as leaders of smaller firms in our sample because they assume their executive positions by inheritance or through other direct familial influence.

The criterion of business achievement we shall next employ is that of executive position of the leaders. Table 37 classifies the respondents according to positions held into four categories: chairman, president, vice president, and senior managing director. It is evident that degree of business achievement as measured by these categories varies much more when related to occupational backgrounds than when related to size of business firms. We may note, for example, that the proportions of respondents holding the position of chairman or president who are sons of executives or owners of large business concerns are markedly larger than those holding the position of vice president or senior managing director. Sons of landlords or farmers also more commonly hold positions as chief executives rather than the lower positions. Occupational groups that are markedly underrepresented in chief executive positions are sons of professional men, government officials, laborers, and white collar workers. Sons of owners of small business firms are also underrepresented in chief executive positions.

Data relating positions in business firms and size of business firms to occupations of fathers of the 1960 Japanese business leaders reveal some important trends in occupational mobility. Sons of

Table 37.   Position in Business Firm and Occupation of Fathers of 1960 Business Leaders

Position	Executive, or Owner, Large Business	Land- lord, Farmer	Owner, Small Business	Profes- sional, Gov't. Official	Laborer, White Collar Worker	Total	Number
Chairman	36%	29%	20%	12%	3%	100%	56
President	29	27	18	17	9	100	256
Vice president	19	22	23	26	10	100	356
Senior managing director	19	23	24	21	13	100	299
All leaders	22%	24%	22%	21%	11%	100%	967

owners or executives of large businesses are more commonly leaders of small rather than large firms. However, a large proportion of them are chief executives of smaller firms. A similar pattern is observed for sons of landlords and farmers. The proportion of sons of small business owners, professional men, and government officials who are executives of big firms is large. However, the proportion who hold positions as chief executives in large firms is relatively small. Sons of laborers and white collar workers are least well represented in large firms and as chief executives of firms of any size.

Marriage and Movement to Business Leadership

Occupation of Wives' Fathers

In the foregoing pages, we have considered the question of occupational mobility of Japanese business leaders on the basis of characteristics of their fathers. In order to explore the social origins and mobility of our subjects more fully, it is useful to consider the family occupational background of their wives and maternal grandfathers. Data were gathered on the occupational status of the wife's father and leader's maternal grandfather for each of our respondents. Do men who become business leaders marry women of backgrounds different from their own? Do peculiar Japanese customs of adoption and primogeniture tend to maintain the occupational status of big business families, and what influence do they exert on movement upward to positions of business leadership?

At the time this research was conducted, 98 percent of the business leaders were married, 0.5 percent were widowers, and the balance of 1.5 percent did not indicate their marital status. It is safe to say that virtually all business leaders were married at some time during their careers, and it appears that marriage may be one of the means by which they advanced their status.

Our data on the relationship between marriage and mobility employ four occupational categories: the occupation of the leader's father, of his wife's father, of his father's father, and of his mother's father. The distribution of these four groups is shown in table 38.

Table 38.   Occupation and Marriage: Occupation of Father, Wife's Father, Father's Father and Mother's Father of 1960 Business Leaders

Occupation	Father	Occupation of Wife's Father	Father's Father	Mother's Father
Farmer or landlord	24%	13%	48%	47%
White collar worker	9	7	2	3
Owner, large business	12	11	6	5
Owner, small business	21	23	18	20
Executive, large business	11	16	2	2
Government official	11	14	4	6
Professional	10	14	6	7
Laborer	1	1	1	1
Samurai and others	1	1	13	9
Total, percent	100	100	100	100
Total number of individuals	974	926	857	818

Two trends stand out. First, there is little difference in the distribution of types of occupation of paternal and maternal grandfathers. Differences are of a magnitude that might be expected in a stable society emphasizing arranged marriages. It may be noted that considerable occupational movement took place between the grandpaternal and paternal generations. Marriage to women with backgrounds of higher status, or with different backgrounds, does not seem to have played an important part in this earlier mobility. This circumstance is consistent with the fact that such mobility as took place in the grandpaternal generation was largely horizontal, from one occupational sector to another of similar status.

Figures on the occupation of mother's father and wife's father show a massive drop in farmers and landlords and a great increase in white collar workers and businessmen. Forty-three percent of the mothers' fathers were businessmen, government officials, professional men, or white collar workers; and 85 percent of the wives' fathers were in these occupations. These trends are also observable in the occupations of the fathers' fathers and fathers of the business leaders. Marriages of women to the business leaders indicate a pronounced trend of movement, on the part of the women, toward urban life and identification through their husbands with the business world and away from various other socioeconomic identifications. In general, the distribution of occupations of wives' fathers represents the most highly urbanized occupational group in Japanese society.

A comparison of the distribution by occupation of father and wife's father presents a somewhat different picture from that of the grandparental generation. Only 13 percent of the wives' fathers are farmers or landlords whereas 24 percent of the business leaders originated from these backgrounds. White collar workers are somewhat less common among wives' fathers than among the business leader's fathers. The proportions of leaders' fathers and wives' fathers who are owners of large businesses and of small businesses are much the same. However, more wives than husbands had fathers who were executives of large business firms, government officials, or professionals. The over-all shift then is toward marriage in the direction of higher status and toward urban rather than rural marriage partners. It must be added that a pronounced shift from rural to urban life has been characteristic of the whole Japanese population for many decades.

A question arises as to how marriages between spouses of differing backgrounds came about. Did the sons of farmers characteristically marry the daughters of farmers? And did the daughters and sons of small business owners tend to marry at their own level or upwards? Marriages of paternal grandfathers and maternal grandfathers of the business leaders were largely confined to women of the same occupational backgrounds, extending only a little to contiguous classes and more distant classes. In contrast, marriage of leaders' fathers and wives' fathers occurred both within and without any given socioeconomic class and level. Table 39 indicates to what extent the business leaders married women of backgrounds different from their own.

Sons of farmers were more likely to marry women of the same occupational background (46 percent). Men whose fathers were laborers or white collar workers married less frequently within their own group (6 percent) than did men of other backgrounds. They were more likely to marry the daughters of farmers, owners of small businesses, government officials or professional men. Men whose fathers were government officials or professionals married women of backgrounds different from their own more frequently than did men of the other categories of occupational background. The sons of farmers, owners or executives of large businesses, and owners of small businesses married women of their own occupational backgrounds in 46 percent, 41 percent, and 40 percent of the cases, respectively. When the sons of owners or executives of large business firms married out of their own occupational background groups, they usually married the daughters of government officials or professional men. These data on marriage provide moderately accurate measurements of the social distance between the business elite and other occupational groups. Although the general tendency among the business leaders is to marry partners with backgrounds the same as their own or with other socially equal backgrounds, it is also clear that a considerable number of business leaders selected wives of higher status than themselves and of urban background.

When customary practices of marriage in Japan are considered, a certain amount of marrying upward seems doubtless the result rather than cause of mobility. That is, a young man with a rural or other background of low status who has managed to complete college would ordinarily marry a woman with a background of higher status than his own. Given higher education and the promise of a successful career, marriage upward would be entirely suitable, indeed requisite, and then might in turn accelerate social mobility.

The observed tendency to marry upward gains significance for the subjects of our study when they are compared with the urban population as a whole, among which choice of wives tends to be in the opposite direction. A comparison with data from a 1955 study of social class in Japan is given in table 40. The subjects of this 1955 study do not match our sample, of course, and thereby they suggest how much our subjects vary from the urban norm.

In reviewing the marriages of the fathers of business leaders and of the wives of business leaders, we can see that many men married upward and thereby enhanced their social status. Now we shall go back another generation and examine the occupation of paternal grandfathers of the leaders. Do the occupations of the

Table 39. Occupational Mobility and Marriage: Occupation of Wife's Father and Occupation of Father of 1960 Business Leaders

	Occupation of Business Leader's Father					
Occupation of Wife's Father	Laborer, White Collar Worker	Owner, Small Business	Owner or Executive, Large Business	Gov't Official, and Pro-fessional	Farmer and Land-lord	Total
Laborer or white collar worker	6%	10%	6%	10%	7%	9%
Owner, small business	29	40	13	20	12	22
Owner or executive, large business	2	10	41	20	20	23
Government official or professional	24	17	24	30	15	22
Farmer or landlord	39	23	16	20	46	24
Total percent	100	100	100	100	100	100
Total number of individuals	51	214	244	260	123	892

leaders' fathers and their wives' fathers differ in social prestige from those of the leaders' paternal grandfathers? In 60 percent of the cases grandfathers and fathers of business leaders and also the fathers of the leaders' wives were owners or executives of large business concerns. If we regard owners and executives of large firms, government officials, and professionals as holding positions of high prestige, we may say 78 percent of our cases have upper level occupational backgrounds through all three of these relatives. It appears that once high social status is achieved it tends to be maintained in subsequent generations. The number of men from socially inferior backgrounds who have moved upward neverthe-less shows that there is a fair degree of occupational mobility.

We shall now examine the relationship between educational attainment and marriage of the Japanese business leaders. It has

Table 40. Marriage and Occupational Background of Business
Leaders and of the General Tokyo Population

	Business Leaders		Tokyo Population (Sample)*	
Occupation	Occupation of Father	Occupation of Wife's Father	Occupation of Father	Occupation of Wife's Father
Professional or executive	44%	55%	21%	17%
White collar worker or small business owner	30	30	27	28
Laborer or farmer	25	14	49	49
Other or no answer	1	1	3	6
Total percent	100	100	100	100
Total number of individuals	974	926	1,138	782

*Nihon Shakai Gakkai Chōsa Iinkai, *Nihon Shakai no Kaisōteki Kōzō* (Hierarchical Structure of Japanese Society) (Tokyo: Yūhikaku, 1958), pp. 118, 126.

long been clear that higher education is the most important channel for occupational advancement in Japanese society.[11] Men born to high status usually attend universities or colleges. Men born to lower social levels among our business leaders are also likely to have attended institutions of higher education and to have used their education as an important means of advancing their careers. It is clear from our review of mate selection among the business leaders that higher education is associated with marriage upward for those with socially inferior occupational backgrounds and that for men of socially high backgrounds higher education increases the likelihood of marrying within one's own class. Men with university educations most frequently take in marriage the daughters of executives of large businesses and government officials. They are least likely to marry the daughters of laborers or farmers. Men with less education tend to marry the daughters of owners of small

---

[11]Education and social mobility in Japanese society are discussed in chapter 4.

businesses, white collar workers and laborers. In general, university-trained men (68 percent) are more likely than those with less education to marry women of high social status.

When they are university trained, do the sons of farmers or white collar workers marry women of higher status in the same manner as university-trained sons of professional men? Among our respondents who are university graduates, 14 percent of the sons of farmers and 18 percent of the sons of white collar workers married daughters of owners or executives of large business firms, whereas 36 percent of the sons of professional men married daughters of elite backgrounds.

Men lacking higher education who are sons of farmers or owners of small businesses generally married women of similar occupational backgrounds. Men lacking a middle school education whose fathers were executives of large firms also tended to marry women with backgrounds resembling their own. In one way or another, education may be said to play an important role in the selection of mates of the business leaders. In general, higher education serves to help them advance or maintain their occupational status, in part through marriage. Men with backgrounds of lower status and little formal education have found the road to business leadership difficult.

Adoption and Mobility

Sansom's comment on an earlier Japan has not lost its relevance as a description of present customs: "Great importance has always been attached in Japan to the inheritance of occupations, not only among traders and artisans, but also among painters, poets, historians, doctors, lawyers and even philosophers: and where there was no suitable successor in the family recourse was had to adoption."[12] Our data on occupational inheritance among business leaders include information on adoption. Our questionnaire asked for principal occupations of fathers, including foster fathers, and the statistics hitherto presented thus include some foster fathers. The questionnaire also included items inquiring whether or not

---

[12]Sansom, G. B., *Japan, A Short Cultural History* (New York: Appleton-Century-Crofts, Inc., 1943), p. 394.

the respondent had been adopted and asking for the principal occupation of the natural father in cases of adoption.

Eleven percent of our subjects stated that they had been adopted. This figure is not so unusual as it might appear, since a study of Tokyo families in 1934 also showed that 11 percent of the heads of families were adopted.[13] The adoption rate for our business leaders is thus probably about the same as that of the general population a generation ago.

Adoption in Japan is not confined primarily to infants. Matsumoto discusses the background and nature of Japanese practices of adoption:

> Patrilineal descent made the ranking of a son over a daughter largely an unquestioned value. . . . If no son was born, the ingenious system of *yōshi* (adopted husband) helped to cope with the resultant problems, and adoptions were frequent. A *yōshi* assumed the name of his adopted family group, married a daughter, and became legally the son and heir.[14]

In considering occupational mobility in Japan, then, some attention must be paid to the influence of adoption practices. From our data, it appears that adoption is indeed one channel by which some upward mobility is possible. A comparison of occupational distribution between occupation of real father and foster father among adopted cases indicates that only 20 percent of the sons of owners or executives of large business firms and of professional men were legally the sons of their natural fathers, and 40 percent had foster fathers. Fifty-eight percent of the leaders who are sons of farmers, government officials, white collar workers, or laborers were reared by natural fathers, and 37 percent had foster fathers. Among business leaders who are sons of owners of small businesses, 22 percent were adopted and 23 percent reared by natural fathers. Thus it may be concluded that adoption spurs movement from

---

[13]From *Tōkyō Shi Kazoku Tōkei* (Tokyo City Family Statistics) (Tōkyō Shiyakusho, 1935), pp. 38–39, 341. This report discusses a sample of 13,210 Tokyo families. The incidence of adoption appears to be declining, since a 1955 survey reports an adoption rate in Tokyo of only 5 percent (Nihon Shakai Gakkai Chōsa Iinkai, *op. cit.*, p. 110).
[14]Matsumoto, Yoshiharu Scott, "Contemporary Japan, the Individual and the Group," *Transactions of the American Philosophical Society*, New Series—Vol. 50, Part I, January 1960, p. 46.

lower-middle class urban backgrounds to higher status. A young man from a "good" but not affluent family who has displayed some unusual capacity or skill appears to be a favored candidate for adoption into a family of higher status and some mobility does occur through this social device.

In his discussion of adoptive marriage, Matsumoto concludes that "this custom has provided an avenue for higher mobility in both urban and rural Japan. Some of the most powerful men in Japan today have attained their position through this means of adoption into influential families."[15] Our data suggest, however, that adoption is less important as a factor in business mobility than Matsumoto's statement indicates. The incidence of adoption among our leaders, as we have noted, seems little different from that among the general population. Although there is a general trend toward upward movement through adoption and some tendency toward higher status among foster fathers, the distribution by occupation of real and foster father of our subjects are generally similar. There are two notable exceptions to the foregoing statement. The proportion of real fathers who were landlords is high, whereas the proportion of foster fathers who were landlords is low. Conversely, the proportion of real fathers who were owners or executives of large business firms is low, but one-third of the adoptions are into this category. There is then a special pattern of mobility through adoption of men from rural families of higher status.

Birth Order and Business Leadership

Closely related to the question of the role of adoption is that of the influence of rules of primogeniture. According to prewar Japanese law, the eldest son inherited family property and assumed responsibility on death (or retirement) of the father for the well-being and continuation of the family. The eldest son was subjected to special discipline and training and was favored in treatment and education. When a son was adopted, he normally played this role. Younger sons, especially, in rural families were less favored in attention given to their training but were given greater

---

[15]*Ibid.,* p. 46.

freedom to plan their own careers. Accordingly, an investigation of birth order seems highly relevant to our study of business leaders. It might be expected that birth order would exert influence upon careers in two rather different ways. First, consideration of occupational backgrounds suggests that eldest sons of rural landlords would appear infrequently in our sample because they might be expected to inherit substantial real property and secure social positions outside the business world, whereas eldest sons of men in larger business firms would be well represented. A second hypothesis regarding birth order would assume that, since younger sons are both socially free and psychologically prepared to seek careers in the cities and to adapt themselves to the demands of the changing economy and society, they should be well represented among our leaders.

Information on occupation of fathers and birth order of sons is given in table 41, which correlates adoption, birth order, and occupational background. This table may be compared with information from the 1934 Tokyo study referred to earlier,[16] in which 11 percent of the total number of heads of families were adopted sons, 37 percent eldest sons, and 52 percent younger sons. Our sample of business leaders shows more eldest sons (41 percent) and fewer younger sons (48 percent). The proportions of eldest sons in the urban middle or upper classes are overrepresented among the general population, but among the business leaders they are underrepresented for men with occupational backgrounds as farmers, laborers and landlords.

The proportion of adopted sons to natural sons is highest among owners and executives of large business concerns, indicating again the special role of adoption in social mobility. The high proportion of eldest sons for this occupational background reflects also the special importance of occupational inheritance. Among business families of high status, the expected tendency to give advantages to eldest sons is evident. With respect to our hypothesis that in a society emphasizing primogeniture, younger sons will be especially instrumental in social change and will be more mobile than eldest sons, we may note that the proportion of younger to eldest

---

[16]*Tōkyō Shi Kazoku Tōkei*, pp. 38–9.

Table 41. Birth Order of Business Leaders and Occupation of Father

Occupation of Father	Adopted Son (Occupation of Foster Father)	First Son	Younger Son	Total Percent	Number
Owner, large business	17	45	38	100	115
Executive, large business	15	43	42	100	103
Owner, small Business	12	39	49	100	212
White collar worker	12	55	33	100	87
Government official	10	45	45	100	111
Farmer	9	28	63	100	65
Professional	8	46	46	100	95
Laborer	8	31	61	100	13
Landlord	7	35	58	100	165
All business leaders	11	41	48	100	966
Tokyo, 1934*	11	37	52	100	13,210

*Tōkyō Shi Kazoku Tōkei (Tōkyō Shiyakusho, 1935), pp. 38–9.

sons is largest among men who are sons of laborers, farmers, and landlords. Among members of the urban white collar class, including professional men, government officials, sales people, and clerical workers, opportunities for occupational mobility appear to be nearly equally shared by all sons regardless of birth order. The research findings on the relationship between birth order and size of community are more striking, in that only a small proportion of business leaders who were eldest sons were born in a town (3 percent) or village (7 percent). Eldest sons of rural origin were especially confined to their inherited occupations. However, younger sons in rural communities were forced to move out. The differences between eldest sons and younger sons are most significant among the urban born.

Geographical Mobility

There has long been a stereotype of Tokugawa merchants as men born in Kinki who migrated to Osaka or Tokyo to achieve success. One might ask if the 1960 Japanese business leaders have any regional characteristics of this kind. What regions produce the most business leaders? To what regions do they move? Is there any disproportion in the urban-rural ratio within the business elite? There is considerable variation in region of birth and size of community of birth among the business leaders of our study. The variations describe patterns, and for this reason it appears that geographic origin also plays a considerable part in vertical mobility in the Japanese business world.

It has been noted that men with rural backgrounds are markedly underrepresented in Japan's business leadership. The very great predominance of the leaders who are graduates of a few universities in metropolitan centers has also been discussed. It then seems expectable that the business leaders were drawn predominantly from certain regions of the country and also that size of community of birth exerts a selective influence.

Table 42 gives the proportions of business leaders born in the several conventionally recognized regions of Japans and compares them in this respect with the total population of the nation in 1903 (the nearest census year), which approximates the average year of birth of the executives of our sample. The two largest urban centers of Japan, Kanto (Tokyo area) and Kinki (Osaka, Kobe, and Kyoto area), are the regions of birth of nearly half the leaders (47 percent), but only one-third of the population (34 percent) was born there. Eighteen percent were born in Chūbu (the central area). The rest of the leaders (35 percent) were born in the remaining regions—Kyushu, Chūgoku, Shikoku, Tōhoku and Hokkaido—in which 45 percent of the total population was born.

The regional productivity ratio of business leaders is given in table 42 in the column at the right. Where the proportion of business leaders and the proportion of Japanese population born in any region are the same, as in Chūgoku and Hokkaido, the ratio in the column on the right is 100. Kinki and Kanto rank highest with ratios of 144 and 133, respectively. Chūbu, Kyushu, and Shikoku produced somewhat smaller proportions of the business leaders than we had expected statistically. Relatively few business leaders were born in Tōhoku, which has been an isolated and

Table 42. Distribution of 1960 Business Leaders by Region of Birth and 1903 Population by Region of Residence

Region	Percent of Business Leaders Born in Region	Percent of Total Japanese Population in Region, 1903	Productivity Ratio of Region
Kanto	14%	18%	133
Kinki	23	16	144
Chūbu	18	21	86
Kyushu	13	15	87
Chūgoku	11	11	100
Shikoku	5	6	83
Tōhoku	4	11	36
Hokkaido	2	2	100
Total percent	100	100	
Total number	977	48,543,000*	

*Source: *JSY*, 1906, pp. 36–7.

backward area. In general, regional productivity of business leaders closely parallels industrial development, as is revealed by the marked overrepresentation of Kinki and Kanto, the two greatest industrial centers of Japan.

Geographical mobility of the 1960 business leaders can also be examined in relation to the region where they were born, attended school, and presently work, as shown in table 43. The three sets of data show wide regional variation. The greatest variation is between place of birth, on the one hand, and places of schooling and present employment, on the other.

Almost two-thirds of the business leaders with a specialist school education studied in Tokyo or other places in the Kanto region, as against only one-fourth in the region of their birth. Twenty-three percent of the leaders were born in the Kinki region, and 21 percent received their specialist school or university training there. Eighty-seven percent of the men who attended specialist schools or universities did so in Kanto or Kinki. The other regions are all underrepresented in terms of college or university training of the business leaders. Thus, geographical mobility of business leaders seems clearly to be linked with higher education. In prewar

Japan, even more than elsewhere in the world, specialist schools and universities were concentrated in or near a few urban centers and drew their students from all regions of the nation.

The headquarters of the large business firms of Japan are also concentrated in the Kanto and Kinki regions. These areas account for 88 percent of the business leaders studied, whereas the Japanese population in these regions in 1960 represented 42 percent of the total.

Table 43.   Region of Birth, Region of Schooling and Region of Present Employment of the 1960 Business Leaders

Region	Region of Birth	Region of Schooling	Region of Employment
Kanto	24%	66%	60%
Kinki	23	21	28
Chūbu	18	2	6
Kyushu	13	5	2
Chūgoku	11	2	1
Shikoku	5	0	1
Tōhoku	4	2	1
Hokkaido	2	2	1
Total percent	100	100	100
Total number of individuals	977	893	985

The extent to which each of the regions retains business leaders was also examined. The Kanto region retains 78 percent of the business leaders born there; there is little movement out of this region but much movement into it. The Kinki region retains 49 percent of the leaders who were born there, and nearly all of the others moved to the Kanto region. Chūbu retains only 17 percent of the leaders born there, and those who move go principally to Kanto (52 percent) or to Kinki (25 percent). The remaining regions retain few business leaders and serve to supply Kanto and Kinki.

Graduates of the major institutions of higher education in

Kanto tend strongly to be employed in that area and the same circumstances apply to the Kinki region. Graduates of any given specialist school or university within these regions tend to be diffused widely within the particular region.

Finally we examine the role of family occupational background in relation to region of birth. The data reveal considerable regional variation in the occupation of fathers of the business leaders. Sons of owners or executives of large business firms, government officials, and professional men represent 58 percent of the total number of business leaders born in Kanto, 44 percent of those born in Kinki, 38 percent of those born in Chūbu, and 32 percent of the leaders from Chūgoku and Shikoku. The proportion of sons of farmers is largest in Chūbu (33 percent) and smallest in Kanto (10 percent). As might well be expected, the two most heavily industrialized regions of Japan, Kanto and Kinki, produce most of the business leaders stemming from executive or professional backgrounds, and regions with the least industry most of the leaders coming from families of landlords and farmers.

Rural versus Urban Contributions to Business Leadership

The region of birth has been established as an important variable in the origins of business leaders. Places of birth appear also to be related to the extent of industrialization of the region. Since the size of a community is an index of its urbanization, it is worthwhile to examine the size of the community in which the individuals were born to determine what effect this factor might exert upon the selection of business leaders.

Table 44 gives the populations of the place of birth of the 1960 Japanese business leaders at about the time the leaders were born. Less than one-third of the leaders were born in villages, which accounted for nearly three-fourths of the total population in 1903.[17] Twenty-seven percent of the leaders were born in towns, which contained 14 percent of the national population in 1903. Cities of

---

[17]*Meiji Taishō Kokusei Sōran*, p. 632.

small or medium size, which produced 19 percent of the leaders, then held 6 percent of the total population. Almost one quarter of the leaders are from the six cities of Tokyo, Osaka, Kyoto, Nagoya, Yokohama and Kobe, which were then, as now, the largest cities of Japan, but accounted for less than one-tenth of the total population.

The third column of table 44 gives the ratio between business leaders and the general population as related to the size of community of birth. If the distribution of the population and that of the business leaders according to size of place of birth were approximately the same, the proportions given in this column would be 100. A lesser figure indicates smaller representation and a figure over 100 indicates greater representation than the proportion

Table 44.   Size of Place of Birth of 1960 Business Leaders

Size of Community of Birth	Business Leaders	Total Population (1903 census)	Ratio of Business Leaders to Population (1 = 100)
Village	30%	72%	42
Town	27	14	193
Small or medium city	19	6	317
Large city	12	4	300
Tokyo	12	4	300
Total percent	100	100	
Total number of individuals	977	48,543,000*	

*Source: *JSY*, 1906, pp. 36–7. In 1903 there were 12,139 villages of which 90 percent had less than 5,000 population and the rest mostly less than 10,000. Towns numbered 1,114 then and usually had less than 30,000 people. Most (92 percent) had a population between 2,000 and 10,000. Cities of small or medium size, which included a population range from 30,000 to less than 250,000, numbered 55 in 1903. Only 16 of these cities had a population exceeding 50,000. Large cities included Kobe (285,000), Nagoya (289,000), Yokohama (326,000), Kyoto (381,000), and Osaka (996,000). Tokyo had a population of 1,819,000.

expected on the basis of the distribution of the total population. The ratio for villages is less than one-half that expected, whereas the ratios for small or medium cities and large cities exceeds by three times the expected proportions. The ratio for towns is almost twice the expected proportion and is markedly higher than that for villages.

The importance of cities as the provenance of business leaders is sharply revealed. There is, however, little difference in the rate of productivity of business leaders between large and small cities. The national capital, the large commercial and industrial cities, and the smaller prefectural capitals and regional business centers produced leaders in about the same proportions. The marked underrepresentation of rural villages and provincial towns as a group is almost twice as high as expected. In summary we may say that the birth places of the Japanese business leaders are as follows: villages, 30 percent; towns or small cities, 46 percent; large cities, 24 percent. Men born in villages, towns, and small cities moved to the large cities for schooling and remained there to enter the business world. Changes in the national population between 1903 and now are of course great and show the rural-urban distinction we have implied. Nevertheless, our data make it clear that among the business leaders there has been very considerable social mobility among men from humble rural and provincial backgrounds.

We may now ask what size of community in each region of Japan has produced the greatest number of business leaders. Access to positions of business leadership among village men is observed to differ from region to region. Men from villages of western Japan (Chūbu, Kinki, Chūgoku, Shikoku and Kyushu) are invariably overrepresented among the business leaders, whereas those of northern Japan (Hokkaido, Tōhoku and Kanto) are underrepresented. It appears that villages in the more urbanized and advanced agricultural regions tend to produce more leaders than do villages in backward regions. As we have stated, cities produce proportionately more business leaders than villages and towns. It is interesting to note that cities of the north, which is economically the least favored region of Japan, produce a larger proportion of business leaders than do cities in other areas of

Japan. This circumstance seems to stem from the fact that rural-urban differences in ways of life have been much greater in the north than elsewhere. The young man of rural Tōhoku in 1903, for example, was ordinarily very poor, and few opportunities were available to him to secure in any of the cities of that region the education or employment that might raise his social position.

Table 45 presents data on the relationship between occupational status of fathers of business leaders and the size of the community in which the business leaders were born. As might be expected,

Table 45. Occupation of Father and Type of Community of 1960 Business Leaders

Occupation of Father	Type of Community			Total	
	City	Town	Village	Percent	Number
Owner or executive, large business	61%	23%	16%	100%	215
White collar worker, laborer	53	29	18	100	98
Government official, professional	52	24	24	100	205
Owner, small business	50	33	17	100	208
Landlord, farmer	7	26	67	100	233
All business leaders	43	27	30	100	959

a great majority of the sons of owners or executives of large business firms were born in cities, and a great majority of sons of landlords and farmers were born in villages. About one-half the men who are sons of white collar workers, laborers, government officials, professional men, and owners of small business concerns were born in cities and the other half in towns or villages. Town-born sons of small business owners, white collar workers, and laborers are overrepresented.

Since the time of birth of these business leaders, the movement of the Japanese population from country to city has proceeded very rapidly and represented a national change from a primarily agrarian to a primarily industrial economy. In 1960 the population in villages and towns represented only 37 percent of the total[18] as against 85 percent in 1903. In view of these circumstances, our findings on the backgrounds of business leaders are not surprising.

In our investigation of the background of business leaders, we thought it useful to learn the proportions that stemmed from different social backgrounds in pre-Meiji times, especially samurai and commoners. During the Tokugawa period (1603–1867) Japanese society had a status hierarchy dominated by the governing warrior class. From our data it becomes clear that the proportion of samurai descendants is greatest among the city born. Especially among the village-born leaders, commoner ancestry is more usual, and their fathers were principally farmers and landlords. Among town-born leaders, commoner ancestry is also usual, and the fathers are overrepresented as owners of small business. Among city-born leaders with samurai ancestry, men whose fathers were farmers or landlords are especially few.

A definite pattern is discernible in the social and geographical mobility of the Japanese business leaders. Men of samurai background were typically born in cities or towns in upper-middle class families, and their fathers had considerably more formal education than the average man. Although a substantial number of men of humble background are included among the modern business leaders, it is clear that the descendants of samurai have played an important part in the industrialization of Japan. Primarily city born and retaining in Meiji times some measure of their traditional prestige, they were perhaps in a favored position to acquire higher education and the other prerequisites of business leadership.

---

[18] *JSY*, 1961, pp. 16–7.

Chapter 6

SUMMARY AND CONCLUSIONS

The major concerns of this study may be stated in question form: (1) What is the social background of the business leaders of modern Japan? (2) Are the various categories of occupational background equally productive of business leaders? (3) What are the characteristics of recruitment of business leaders in other countries? (4) What are the personal qualifications of Japanese business leaders and what patterns do their careers follow?

We shall summarize our findings under these headings and discuss their significance with reference to the broader problems of social stratification and mobility.

(1) What is the social background of the business leaders of modern Japan?

An outstanding fact revealed by our data on family occupational background is that no single occupational group is dominant; that is, no one occupational background group may be said to be the principal source of modern business leaders. This circumstance, we may note, contradicts the Marxian idea that, under capitalism, the sons of capitalists monopolize directive positions.

The business leaders of Japan stem principally from occupational backgrounds that confer high social prestige, but these occupations are varied. Men of middle class background are less well represented among the modern business leaders, and men of lower class background are poorly represented. The following table, which combines various categories of comparable social status, gives the range of parental occupations:

Landlord and farmer   24%
Owner and executive of large business concern   22

Owner of small business concern	22
Governmental official and professional man	21
White collar worker	9
Laborer and others	2
	100%

It is clear that the present business leaders come from quite diverse occupational backgrounds. If, however, we combine the two categories "owner and executive of large business concern" and "owner of small business concern" into a single classification, it is possible to say that men from business backgrounds are most common among the modern business elite. Very few are sons of industrial laborers. Sons of farmers, most of whom were landlords, are very well represented, a circumstance that relates in considerable measure to the national shift from farming to industry. Proportionately fewer fathers than grandfathers of the business men were farmers, and proportionately more fathers than grandfathers were business executives. It is not wholly clear, however, whether the declining position of farming as a background for business leaders is due solely to the decrease in the relative number of farmers in the nation or whether other factors of motivation and opportunity are involved. An answer to this question must be left to the future.

The following statements may be made with respect to social background and social stratification:

A. The modern business leaders are recruited most frequently from upper social strata. In general, representation among the leaders diminishes as background familial status diminishes.

B. The modern business leaders do not constitute a castelike group. They stem from diverse occupational backgrounds and show no marked tendency toward inheritance of positions.

Let us now review the evidence in support of each of these statements.

The occupational categories we have used do not represent economic or social classes that may firmly be placed in a scale of prestige. Nevertheless, approximate judgments may be made. Our questionnaires were designed to bring out such distinctions as whether employment in government service was as a supervisory official or in a rank-and-file position, whether farmers were land-lords or small owner-operators, and the like. Of the eleven occupations we have used, the following five may safely be regarded as both economically and socially superior: owner of large business concern, executive of large business concern, government official, professional man, and landlord. Men in these occupations have generally been well-to-do and have held high social status. The greatest number of exceptions is doubtless among professional men and landlords, some of whom might more appropriately be assigned to middle class status, at least from the standpoint of income. Setting aside consideration of these exceptions, we may say that the 61 percent of our respondents whose fathers were in one or another of these five occupations constitute the proportion drawn from the upper levels of Japanese society.

From the standpoints of average income and social prestige, it is appropriate to label owners of small business concerns and white collar workers as members of the Japanese middle class. Thirty-one percent of the business leaders sprang from these occupational backgrounds. Farming (owner-operator) and common labor may be regarded as lower class occupations, and 8 percent of our respondents may then be said to have come from lower class backgrounds.

Evidence of the diversity of occupational background has already been presented in the foregoing paragraphs. Some additional remarks may be in order. Two of the eleven occupational categories—owner of large business concern and executive of large business concern—represent occupations on the parental level essentially the same as those of our respondents, and only 22 percent of our respondents had these occupational backgrounds. Thus, the majority of the business leaders did not follow the occupation of their fathers. Nevertheless, this occupational background is presently important, and will likely assume greater importance in the future, as Japan's short history as an industrial nation lengthens. There is no evidence, however, to justify describing the Japanese business leaders as a caste. Additional remarks on this subject will be presented later.

Closely related to occupational succession is the question of inheritance of positions of business leadership. Among our respondents who were sons of owners or executives of large business concerns, approximately one-third (including 45 percent of the sons of owners and 19 percent of the sons of executives) are associated with the same firms as were their fathers. Some tendency toward inheritance then exists, but this tendency is strongly weighted toward ownership rather than outright occupational succession; that is, a considerable number of men become owners of business enterprises through normal channels of legal inheritance of property. The proportion does not seem high as compared with circumstances in other nations, as we shall later see, and it does not indicate any significant trend toward direct inheritance of positions in a top-management caste. Although our data show that sons of the elite tend themselves to be among the elite, all evidence points to a fair degree of occupational and social mobility.

(2) Are the various categories of occupational background equally productive of business leaders?

Comparison of the occupational background of the business leaders with the occupational distribution of the total Japanese population shows a number of occupational classes as overrepresented in the backgrounds of the business leaders and others as underrepresented. Sons of government officials, owners and executives of large business concerns, and professional men are strongly overrepresented; sons of owners of small business concerns and white collar workers are somewhat overrepresented; and sons of farmers (owner-operators) and laborers are markedly underrepresented. As is obvious from our previous discussion of social class background, there are substantial differences in representation according to occupational background. It seems most probable, however, that these differences have significance with reference to the recruiting of the business elite, which go beyond social status and lead to questions of values and motivation outside the scope of this study.

(3) What are the characteristics of recruitment of leaders in Japanese business and industry as compared with circumstances in other countries?

Comparison was made with data on the United States and the

United Kingdom. The proportion of business leaders whose fathers were executives, professional men, or held other positions conferring high social status is greater in these countries than in Japan. The number of business leaders who are sons of business leaders is especially smaller in Japan, since Japan's industrialization is more recent and the number of men in big business a generation ago was relatively small. In the United States, few business leaders are the sons of government officials, but in Japan, sons of government officials are an important category of business executives.

Certain especially marked differences are evident among the three countries. The proportion of business leaders who are sons of farmers is, as expected, by far the largest in Japan. Inheritance of business leadership is more common in the United Kingdom. It occurs less commonly and at about the same rate in the United States and Japan. Sons of white collar workers and laborers are much more common among the business elite in the United States than in the United Kingdom or Japan. (Additional comparative data on the formal education of business executives is given below.)

Factors involved in the recruitment of the business elite in the three countries thus appear to differ, and these are doubtless multiple, relating to the extent and nature of industrialization as well as to cultural factors of other kinds.

(4) What are the personal qualifications of Japanese business leaders and what patterns do their careers follow?

Higher education plays an extremely important role in the selection of the Japanese business elite. The proportion of business leaders who hold undergraduate degrees is higher in Japan than in either the United States or the United Kingdom, and higher education seems to hold a unique position with reference to business success in Japan. A university degree in economics, law, government, or engineering is ordinarily a prerequisite. Most of the Japanese business leaders attended one of a small group of leading educational institutions in Tokyo, Osaka, Kyoto, and Kobe, and thus graduation from a prestigious university may be regarded as an important qualification if not prerequisite. Throughout the various types of business and industry in Japan, the executives may be said to constitute a fairly homogeneous and highly selected group from the standpoint of educational background.

Although high social status by ascription is obviously a very influential factor in the process of selection that produces business leaders in Japan, unlike higher education it is not a prerequisite. It is possible by means of higher education to move from a rural farming or an urban white collar background to positions as executives.

No emphasis is placed upon graduate training at universities as a requirement for business executives in Japan, and few have had such training. In the United States, university graduate training is regarded as important for business executives. In Japan, the bachelor's degree is regarded as vital to give the business executive professional competence, but training in industrial management is not regarded as being within the scope of the universities. Such training is nearly always given by the industrial firms themselves and constitutes an important element in the professional career of the business executives.

The careers of the Japanese business leaders may be described as following a bureaucratic course. They enter the business world immediately after graduating from college, and most men remain in the employ of the same firm during their entire careers. Climbing the occupational ladder takes them through a fairly well-defined series of steps, which, for the rank and file, form plateaus at some point or another. Appointment to positions of importance invariably depends in part upon seniority, and many years are required to climb the ladder. The average age of the Japanese business leaders is several years greater than that of their American and British counterparts. Slow progress through a bureaucratic maze is characteristic, but this does not deny importance to individual talent. Given the personal traits that allow successful adjustment to bureaucracy, the final governing factor in the selection of a few individuals to the topmost positions is unquestionably personal ability. To become or remain successful, the industrial concern must recognize talent.

Our findings may be still more briefly summarized in the following statements. No single occupational or social class monopolizes positions of executive leadership in Japanese business and industry. Although heterogeneous in occupational and social background and region of birth, the modern business leaders are homogeneous in educational background. Attainment of positions of leadership in the large commercial enterprises of Japan cannot be described as a matter of inheritance. In this respect, big business in Japan has freed itself for the most part from tradition. Considerations other than familial background dominate, and among these personal achievement, including higher education, is the prime requisite. Japanese business leaders are almost invariably recruited from among men who have devoted their whole occupational careers to the business world, and who, in the course of their careers, have had narrow training that clings closely to immediate problems of their firms and industries. Outsiders, such as professional men, presently do not and cannot enter their ranks. Despite the fact that there has been considerable movement to business leadership from other occupations on generational levels, business leadership in Japan is inflexible in the sense that attainment of positions of business leadership comes only through life-long employment. Further advancement in the industrialization of Japan would be greatly aided by, and ultimately will undoubtedly require, greater flexibility in this respect.

All in all, our data reveal that the rigid system of class stratification of Japanese society in preindustrial times has softened if not entirely dissolved, and that a considerable degree of social mobility now exists.

PART II

MOVEMENT OF JAPAN'S ELITE GROUPS, 1880-1960

Chapter 7

TRENDS OF MOBILITY INTO JAPAN'S ELITE GROUPS

Introduction

Part II presents some results of a study of changes in the backgrounds and careers of Japan's business, political, and intellectual leaders at three points in time representing distinct generations and spanning Japan's modern period: the 1880s, 1920, and 1960. This discussion is directed particularly to trends in social origin and education of business leaders over this period and to comparisons of Japan's business leaders with those of the United States and the United Kingdom.

The analysis of the origins and careers of the men who led Japan from agrarian isolation to industrial power is helpful not only for a better understanding of Japan itself but also in deriving implications for presently developing nations. Insofar as the data are unusual, their interest would lie in the effort made in this research to obtain comparability over time in the analysis of elite recruitment. Several studies of the leaders of the early period of Japan's modernization have recently been made available, including the work of Everett E. Hagen, Johannes Hirschmeier, and R.P. Dore.[1] The results of this study are somewhat different again. This is not the occasion to attempt a reconciliation or close analysis of these differences. It is perhaps sufficient to note that each of the studies has had a different objective and has used a somewhat different

---

[1]Hagen, Everett E., *On the Theory of Social Change* (Homewood, Illinois: The Doresay Press, Inc. 1962); Hirschmeier, Johannes, *The Origins of Entrepreneurship in Meiji Japan* (Cambridge, Massachusetts: Harvard University Press, 1964); and Dore, R. P., "Mobility, Equality and Individuation in Modern Japan", *Aspects of Social Change in Modern Japan*, edited by R. P. Dore (Princeton: Princeton University Press, 1967).

definition of sample and varying methods of obtaining data. Details of research methods and sampling in this historical study are discussed in appendix II. At present a brief description of the methodology of this study is in order, therefore, to place its results in better perspective.

This is, first of all, a study of men who occupy the top positions in business, political, and intellectual organizations and communities. It is assumed that the men who have occupied these positions have been leaders, that is, members of Japan's elite. It is not assumed that the sample includes all of Japan's leaders but rather that all of the men studied have been leaders, recognizing that outstanding men may well not have happened to occupy a position under scrutiny. It is quite possible to employ other definitions, as for example, "innovators" or "entrepreneurs," and undertake a sample selection in terms of individuals deemed to fit these definitions. Some differences in results would be expected from varying definitions of the sample.

The three elite groups—business, political, and intellectual—in this study are defined as follows. Business leaders include only those who occupied the position of chief executive in the largest firms in mining, construction, manufacturing, trading and other service industries in 1880, 1920, or 1960. It should be noted that business leaders of 1960 in part II are not identical to the sample of business leaders examined in part I, because the latter sample includes not only chief executives but also vice presidents and senior managing directors.

Political leaders include cabinet members, leaders in the Diet, officials of political parties, senior members of the civil service, and union leaders. While they are different in their activities, they collectively represent a major concentration of political power in Japanese society and have played important roles in modernizing the nation.

Intellectual leaders are men who have held leading positions in professional organizations. In Japan members of the university community, professional men in religion, law, and medicine, artists, critics and journalists provide social leadership and enjoy high prestige. While hardly homogeneous in major activities, they make up a group distinguishable from the political and business groups.

The fact that this is a study of time trends has influenced the selection of samples. In effect, each sample has been selected backward over time, beginning with those positions judged to be most important in 1960 and then selecting for the 1920 and 1880 periods a comparable number of what are judged to be comparable positions, identifying the men in those positions, and then including them in the study sample. The limited numbers of positions in the earliest period made sampling of a single year impracticable; therefore the sample drew from the 1880s.

A judgment as to the effectiveness of this approach can be made on the basis of appendix III. The number of positions studied was arbitrarily fixed. Four hundred positions were included for each of the three periods: two hundred from various branches of the business community; one hundred from the several categories of political leadership; and one hundred from the groups described as intellectual leaders. Special interest in the business elite resulted in enlarging that part of the total sample. There is therefore no thought that the results for business, political, and intellectual leaders might somehow be averaged or combined to provide a composite of Japan's leadership as a whole. In most instances, especially in view of the wide variance between sectors, separate examination of each group is necessary.

Recruitment of Leaders, 1880s

Japan's business, political, and intellectual leaders of the 1880s were remarkably young. The median age of the Meiji business elite was 39.8 years in 1885, slightly younger than the political and intellectual elites (40.4 years and 41.0 years). Sixteen percent of the total group were less than 30 years of age, while only 17 percent were 50 or more years of age. These men were born typically about 1845 and reached maturity at the time of the Meiji Restoration of 1868. They died at an average age of about 65 years, or around 1910. Slightly over 40 percent of the group lived to be more than 70 years of age, much longer than the average life span of the population at that time.

A first indication of the considerable and important differences in recruitment to leadership between the three types of leaders appears in terms of place of birth. In comparison with the population distribution by region at the time of the first national census in 1872, more than one-half of the business leaders were born in the two more urbanized regions, the Kanto (Tokyo area) and the Kinki (Osaka-Kyoto area), which contained less than one-third of the national population. In contrast, the western regions of Kyushu, Shikoku, and Chūgoku, again with about one-third of the national population, were the regions of birth for nearly three-quarters of the political leaders. Demonstrating still another pattern of recruitment, intellectual leaders came in large proportion (46 percent) from the Tōhoku and Kanto districts, which together comprised about one-quarter of the population.

A further aspect of place of birth may be noted: the size of the community in which the members of the Meiji elite were born. It will be noted from table 1 that villages and smaller towns are markedly underrepresented in each of the elite groups, while the eighty-four towns that in 1886 had a population of ten to twenty-five thousand supplied eight times the proportion of leaders that would be expected on the basis of population proportion. Most of these towns were castle sites of the daimyo, or feudal lords, and it

Table 1.   Size of Community of Birth: 1880s Leaders

Size of Community	Total, Japan 1886*	Total, Leaders	Business Leaders	Political Leaders	Intellectual Leaders
Village or town					
(less than 10,000)	88%	43%	55%	33%	28%
Town (10–25,000)	2	17	14	20	21
Small city (25–50,000)	3	11	6	27	8
Large city (50,000)	4	13	14	13	12
Tokyo	3	16	11	7	31
Total	100%	100%	100%	100%	100%
Number	38,507,000	384	200	84	100

*Adapted from Bureau of Statistics, Imperial Cabinet, *Dai 7 Nihon Teikoku Tōkei Nenkan* (Japan Imperial Statistical Yearbook, No. 7), Tokyo, 1888, pp. 42–6.

is appropriate therefore in this description of the origins of the postfeudal leadership of Japan to turn immediately to the question of feudal affiliation. The feudal affiliation of the families of these young men from the castle towns and cities of Japan who led the early modernization is shown in table 2. Feudal ties were defined by family allegiance to a daimyo, not by place of birth, since, for example, a man affiliated with the Satsuma fief might have been born at Edo in Bakufu (shogunal) territory. Table 2 also provides an estimate of the proportionate size of each of the groups of feudal domains shown. These estimates are based on *koku* of rice held by each grouping, and thus only loosely approximate whatever the population proportions may have been. They do provide a rough

Table 2. Type of Feudal Affiliation: 1880s Leaders

Feudal Group	Total, 1861	Total, Leaders	Business Leaders	Political Leaders	Intellectual Leaders
Shogunate & bannermen	27%	32%	32%	19%	44%
"Inner" daimyo & retainers	26	23	31	8	18
Tokugawa collaterals & retainers	10	8	9	2	10
"Outer" daimyo & retainers (total)	37	37	28	71	28
Choshu	2	7	4	17	4
Tosa	1	6	2	19	4
Satsuma	3	5	3	12	3
Hizen	2	2	1	6	0
Total	100%	100%	100%	100%	100%
Number	25,190*	381	199	84	98

*Thousands of *koku*.
Source: Department of Japanese History, Kyoto University (ed.), *Kindaishi Jiten* (Handbook of Modern History) (Tokyo: Tōyō Keizai Shimpō Sha, 1958), pp. 647–654, and Kodama, Kota, "Bakuhantaisei", *Sekai Daihyakka Jiten* (Encyclopedia of the World), Vol. 23, pp. 157–9 (Tokyo: Heibonsha, 1958).

measure, however, against which to compare leadership proportions.[2]

The central role of men from the *tozama* or "outer" domains in
the overthrow of Tokugawa hegemony, and especially of the 4
shown in detail in table 2, has received much attention. A good
deal has been made in historical studies of the leadership contribution of men from these 111 domains headed by "outer" daimyo
(tozama). The critical importance of separate examination of
leadership in each sector of national life is therefore underlined
when it is noted that these domains did indeed provide an overwhelming proportion of the political leadership during the early
Meiji period, but that business and intellectual leaders were drawn
from these groups in substantially smaller proportions than would
have been expected on the basis of their size. Indeed, it was precisely those groups that held feudal power—the officials of the
shogunal government *(bakufu)*, the shogunal retainers or banner-
men *(hatamoto)*, and the shogun's "inner" or hereditary vassals,
the *fudai* daimyo—that supplied the larger proportion of business
and intellectual leaders following the Meiji Restoration.[3]

The central issue in this study of elite recruitment in Japan's
modern century is that of patterns of mobility into elite positions
from families of varying occupational status. In terms of the 1880
elite groups, occupational status of father and feudal status of family correlate closely, of course, and must therefore be considered
jointly. Table 3 presents the feudal status of the fathers of members
of the elite groups of the1880s. (The detailed occupational and
feudal positions on which these categories are based are listed in
appendix IV.)

In evaluating these data, it is useful to bear in mind the general
status composition of the pre-Meiji population. About 6 percent of

---

[2]The taxable rice yield of feudal domains was measured in *koku*. One *koku* (about five
bushels) was the quantity of rice theoretically needed to feed one person for one year.
Thus the *koku* figures bear at least a rough relationship to population and are so used
here, in the absence of reliable census statistics for this period.
[3]Direct vassals of the shogun with holdings below 10,000 *koku* were called *hatamoto*;
those with 10,000 *koku* or more were daimyo. *Fudai* or "inner" daimyo were heirs of
those who had been vassals of Tokugawa Ieyasu prior to the battle of Sekigahara
(1600). Heirs of those who were Ieyasu's equals (allies) or his enemies at Sekigahara
and of those who were neutral in that battle, were all classified as *tozama* or "outer"
daimyo.

the households of Japan at the time of the Meiji Restoration enjoyed higher status as court nobles *(kuge)* or as samurai. The nobility numbered some 470 families, or 0.007 percent of all households. The number of upper class samurai families has been variously estimated but probably numbered about 9,000 or 0.13 percent of the national total, these including hatamoto of the shogunate, and ministerial and managerial positions under the daimyo. Middle status samurai and samurai in professional positions may be estimated to have headed about 250,000 households, or 3.6 percent of the population. Lower status samurai comprised about 2.4 percent of all households. (This group is made up of the 168,000 households classified as *sotsuzoku* in the census of 1872.)[4] Out of a total then

Table 3. Feudal Status of Father: 1880s Leaders

Feudal Status of Father	Total, Leaders		Business Leaders	Political Leaders	Intellectual Leaders
Kuge or daimyo	3%		0%	12%	3%
Samurai	47		23	79	67
Upper class		5	1	7	10
Middle class		14	10	23	14
Professional		12	4	11	30
Lower class		16	8	38	13
Farmer	15		22	6	10
Country samurai		3	3	4	3
Village head		9	14	1	7
Peasant		3	5	1	0
Townsman	35		55	3	20
Merchant		10	19	0	1
Owner, small business		17	31	0	1
Profession		7	3	3	17
Clerk, artisan		1	2	0	1
Total	100%		100%	100%	100%
Number	381		198	84	99
Unknown	3		2	0	1

[4]These estimates are based on a review of several sources including Dajōkan Kosekiryō (Census), 1872; *Dai Bukan* (The Great Directory of Samurai) (Tokyo: Daigō Sha, 1936, Vol. 10); Fukuchi, Shigetaka, *Shizoku to Samurai Ishiki* (Samurai and Samurai Consciousness) (Tokyo: Shunjū Sha, 1956).

of more than 7,000,000 households, some 10,000 held highest status under the feudal system, with another 420,000 households in lesser but advantaged position.

Two general remarks may be made about the patterns of Meiji leadership recruitment as shown in table 3. First, it is evidently quite impossible to generalize about Meiji leadership as a whole in terms of social origins. There is a great diversity in background of different sectors of leadership. Second, it would hardly appear that the change from the formal feudal system of status caused a revolution in leadership. While the men under study occupied the highest positions in Japan some twenty years after the Meiji Restoration, it is evident that occupational continuity and status continuity are more characteristic than dramatic or even substantial changes in leadership recruitment patterns.

The business leaders studied are drawn for the most part not from the disaffected samurai groups so frequently described as the source of change in modernizing Japan, but rather from the townsmen and farmer groups who had for centuries been assigned the chief roles in commerce and preindustrial manufacture. Only a small percentage of business leaders came from any one of the several higher status feudal groupings traditionally aloof from commercial activities. Further, as indicated in table 4, those men of samurai origins who entered business tended to hold top positions in business organizations, including the chamber of commerce, in public utilities—transport and communication—and in finance, which had the most intimate connections with the government, and indeed may be seen as direct extensions of government activity. Similarly, the leadership of businesses in the new manufacturing sectors of chemicals and pharmaceuticals, metals, machinery and textiles was not disproportionately drawn from samurai ranks. These data do not then support the frequently expressed view that a frustrated and dispossessed higher status group provided a special entrepreneurial impulse in the early industrialization of Japan. Rather, they indicate that while there was increased mobility into top level business positions in Meiji Japan from nonbusiness backgrounds, a majority of business leaders came from those groups that had traditionally been engaged in commerce and industry.

Similarly, Meiji political leadership shows strong continuity from the feudal period. The very small number of families of highest feudal rank supplied about one-fifth of the top political leaders. Less than 10 percent of the political elite were recruited from the lower status background of farmer or townsman, and the largest group of these were country samurai, or *gōshi*, whose feudal status was marginal to and not clearly differentiated from that of samurai proper. Lower status samurai did indeed supply a large proportion of political leaders, again suggesting some increased mobility but within a general pattern of status continuity. In any event, the contrast between the social background of business leaders and political leaders is very great, demonstrating the difficulties of generalizing about "the leaders of Meiji Japan."

Table 4. Family Feudal Status and Type of Business: 1880s Leaders

Type of Business	Samurai	Farmer	Townsman	Total
Business organization	45%	22%	33%	100%
Transport and communication	36	28	36	100
Finance	35	30	35	100
Chemicals & pharmaceuticals	28	11	61	100
Steel & machinery	21	21	58	100
Textile	21	27	52	100
Mining	20	0	80	100
Food	11	6	83	100
Trade	3	34	63	100
Construction	0	0	100	100
All business leaders	23%	22%	55%	100%
Number	46	44	108	198

Recruitment of Leaders, 1920

Since the sample for this study was selected on the basis of the position occupied, rather than on the basis of personal characteristics of individuals, it was quite possible that a single individual might be included in the leadership groups for two points in time. Owing to the youth of the leaders of the 1880s, some might be expected to continue in an elite position through the 1920 period, and this was in fact the case. Of the total 1920 sample of 400 men, 29 or 7 percent were also included in the Meiji group.

This direct continuity in leadership suggests and is a partial cause of a first contrast of the 1920 leaders studied with the men of the earlier generation. Over the generation the median age of the business leaders advanced some 12 years, to 52.1 years of age, with a median age for political leaders in 1920 of 49.8 years and of intellectual leaders of 50.7 years. Some part of this shift in the age of the leadership group may also be laid to the changes that occurred in educational background, away from the apprentice training of the previous generation and toward formal, longer, advanced education, delaying the beginning of the career.

Men of this 1920 group were born around 1868 at the very beginning of the Meiji Restoration and matured at a time when the slogans and policies of the Meiji government were well developed. Typically too these men belonged to the first generation to receive their formal training under the new educational system installed by the Meiji government. Their careers went forward during a period of extraordinary social change, and therefore corresponding differences in background and experience might be anticipated.

In 1920 as in the preceding generation, somewhat over one-half of the business leaders were born in the Kanto and Kinki regions. Regional recruitment of political leaders changed sharply in the interval, however. Kanto and Tōhoku, source of only 11 percent of Meiji political leaders, supplied 45 percent of the political leaders of 1920, with the proportion from Chūgoku, Shikoku and Kyushu declining from 71 percent in the 1880s to 27 percent in 1920. This change does not reflect a shift in families to other regions. Table 5 indicates the extent to which men of the four leading *tozama* domains lost their hold on channels of elite recruitment over this generation. As for intellectual leaders, by 1920 they were drawn from the various regions in proportions similar to the distribution of population by residence, no doubt because of nationwide recruitment of able students for the new imperial universities.

Table 5. Leadership Representation of the Four Major "Outer" Domains in the 1880s and 1920 Leaders

Families From Satsuma, Chōshū, Tosa, or Hizen	Total, Japan 1861*	Total, Leaders	Business Leaders	Political Leaders	Intellectual Leaders
1880s	8	20	10	54	11
1920	8	11	11	13	4

*Department of Japanese History, Kyoto University, *Kindaishi Jiten* (Handbook of Modern History) (Tokyo: Tōyōkeizai Shimpō Sha, 1958), pp. 647–54.

As with region of birth, the recruitment of business leaders in terms of size of birthplace changed little in the 1920 period from the earlier generation, as shown in table 6. The larger towns and cities remained the source of a great disproportion of business leaders. The pattern for political leaders, however, shows here too a major change in one generation. The proportion of the political elite coming from the villages and small towns increased from one-third to more than one-half. Similarly the proportions of intellectual leaders from rural backgrounds increased markedly.

There is therefore an indication that while the pattern of recruitment of business leaders changed little in the generation 1880 to 1920, some major shifts in elite recruitment took place in other sectors of the society. There is here another reminder of the care necessary in generalizing on these matters from one hierarchical structure to another in the society, and it is necessary to turn again to materials on family status to examine further the nature of the changes that took place.

The family social status of the men who made up Japan's 1920 leadership can be examined in terms of two variables, related but separable. There is first the feudal status of the family of origin, which can be compared with the 1880s sample. A meaningful examination of family origins for this group is also possible, since the majority of the fathers of the 1920 elite held jobs that can be classified under present-day categories. (The detailed feudal

Table 6. Size of Community of Birth: 1920 Leaders

Size or Community	Total, Japan 1886	Total, Leaders	Business Leaders	Political Leaders	Intellectual Leaders
Village or town					
(less than 10,000)	88%	49%	48%	54%	47%
Town (10–25,000)	2	11	13	11	9
Small city (25–50,000)	3	8	6	14	6
Large city (50,000)	4	17	20	14	12
Tokyo	3	15	13	7	26
Total	100%	100%	100%	100%	100%
Number	38,507,000	400	200	100	100

Sources: *JSΥ*, 1888, p. 25 and pp. 45–7.

and occupational positions on which the categories are based are listed in appendix IV.)

The predominance of men from that 6 percent of the population having noble or samurai backgrounds continues through the 1920 generation, with 43 percent of the total sample. Within this broad pattern however, as shown in table 7, some substantial shifts took place over the generation. Men from a samurai background appear in larger proportions in business leadership in 1920 than in the 1880s, 37 percent as compared with 23 percent earlier. No doubt the prestige of business positions had increased, as also the capability of men from samurai families to hold business positions.

A sharper shift from 1880 to 1920 occurred in the political hierarchy. Almost exclusively the domain of the sons of nobles or samurai in the 1880 period (91 percent), by 1920 just under one-half of the political elite were from such families. Men from farm backgrounds, in particular, made great gains in the political field, as did also men from the feudal townsman status. A similar but less dramatic change occurred in recruitment of intellectual leaders. As indicated earlier, this reflects in part a break from the hold of the "outer" domain families on national leadership, but more important it also signals the move to national leadership of men

Table 7. Feudal Status of Father: 1920 Leaders

Feudal Status of Father	Total, Leaders	Business Leaders	Political Leaders	Intellectual Leaders	
Kuge or daimyo	2%	0%	4%	4%	
Samurai	41	37	46	46	
Upper class	7	8	3	6	
Middle class	5	2	11	6	
Professional	5	2	5	12	
Lower class	12	8	19	15	
Status unknown	12	17	8	7	
Farmer	25	21	38	17	
Country samurai	4	2	7	4	
Village head, landlord, rural trader	18	17	26	10	
Peasant	3	2	5	3	
Townsman	32	42	12	33	
Professional	7	3	2	20	
Businessman	22	35	9	10	
Artisan	3	4	1	3	
Total	100%	100%	100%	100%	
Number	390	200	96	94	
Unknown (number)	10	0	4	6	

from rural backgrounds. As will be shown below, the driving force in these changes in political and intellectual elite recruitment appears to have been the changes in the educational system. It must be noted again, however, that the patterns of recruitment to leadership of business and industry appear not to have shifted substantially.

The occupations of the fathers of Japan's 1920 leaders provide a more sensitive measure of the nature of recruitment than does feudal status. As shown in table 8, the great mass of farmers (tenant or operating), along with the industrial labor force, were virtually excluded from elite positions. One-half of the business leaders of 1920 were sons of owners or executives of businesses. Sons of landowners or samurai made up another third of the business elite, with sons of professional men and government officials comprising most of the balance.

The source of change in political leadership may also be identified in table 8. Nearly one-third of the group are sons of landowners, and it would appear that it was the movement of this group to top governmental positions that provided most of the contrast noted earlier between the Meiji and Taishō periods.

Special attention should be paid to the considerable proportion of men in all three leadership categories whose fathers were government officials. As will be noted in more detail later, this pattern of elite recruitment, in the business sector in particular, sets Japan off sharply from the historical pattern of business leadership recruitment in the United States. The very small proportion of men occupying government positions at the time of Japan's first occupational census in 1883 supplied, to all three hierarchies,

Table 8.   Occupation of Father: 1920 Leaders

Occupation of Father	Total, Japan 1883	Total Leaders	Business Leaders	Political Leaders	Intellectual Leaders
Laborer	3.4%	0%	0%	0%	1%
Farmer	} 77.9	3	1	5	3
Landowner		18	15	30	12
White collar	0.8	4	2	6	7
Owner, small business	} 7.1	13	17	9	9
Owner or executive, large business		19	32	7	4
Government official	0.02	9	7	14	9
Professional	0.9	15	7	9	36
Unclassified	9.9	0	0	0	0
Samurai	—	19	19	20	19
Total	100%	100%	100%	100%	100%
Number	21,689,000	399	200	100	99

Note: The sources of the occupation distribution of 1883 into the above categories are stated in table 2 in chapter 2 of this book.

numbers of leaders vastly out of proportion to their number in the population.

Recruitment of Leaders, 1960

The median ages of the 1960 leaders reveal a curious fact when compared to the ages of the two earlier generations of leaders. Each succeeding generation is about ten years older on the average than the earlier one, with the median age of the total group of leaders studied in 1960 about 60 years, compared with slightly over 50 years in 1920 and about 40 years in 1880. The advance in median age for 1960 over 1920 cannot be attributed to direct continuity of individuals in the same or similar positions, since only ten of the 1960 sample were also in the 1920 sample selected for study. (Another study by the author suggests that in the business community at least the postwar period has seen a temporary extension of tenure by men in the topmost positions owing to wartime interruptions in the careers of potential successors.) In any event, the political leaders of 1960 were somewhat younger (median 55.7 years) than the intellectual and business leaders (61.7 and 61.0 years, respectively). A good proportion of the total, 13 percent, were over 70 years of age. The typical member of this 1960 leadership group then was born at the turn of the century, educated in the "liberal" '20s, and has seen the full working out of Japan's industrialization.

Patterns of recruitment by region of birth more nearly approximate the population distribution in Japan in 1900, the average birth year, than was the case for the earlier leadership generations. The urban areas supply a disproportionate share of intellectual leaders, and business leaders to a lesser degree, with rural and less-developed areas, notably Tōhoku, underrepresented. Political leaders are drawn in proportions very like the population distribution, no doubt reflecting the nature of the distribution of political power under postwar electoral conditions.

Size of birthplace remains, however, closely associated with leadership recruitment, at least insofar as the villages of Japan are markedly underrepresented, while the great cities and Tokyo especially supply a vastly greater proportion of leaders in comparison with population, as shown in table 9. Nearly one-third of the business leaders are drawn from the six largest cities, and more than 40 percent of the intellectual leaders. The explanation of course is not difficult to find. Both in occupational (social) background and in educational opportunities the villagers are disadvantaged in Japan (as elsewhere) when compared with urban residents.

Table 9. Birthplace of 1960 Leaders

Size of Community of Birth	Total, Japan 1903*	Total, Business Leaders	Business Leaders	Political Leaders	Intellectual Leaders
Village	72%	31%	29%	41%	26%
Town	14	25	27	30	15
City, small or medium	6	15	15	11	18
Five large cities	4	13	16	9	13
Tokyo	4	16	13	9	28
Total	100%	100%	100%	100%	100%
Number	48,543,000	409	210	99	100
Outside Japan		3	2	1	

*Adapted from *JSY*, 1906, pp. 36–7.

The occupational origins of the leaders of Japan in 1960 are summarized in table 10. Nearly one-half are from executive or professional families. One-quarter are sons of landlords. Only one-tenth are from laboring or farm-operating backgrounds.

As in the preceding two generations of Japanese leadership, the differences in origins of leaders in the three sectors studied are considerable. Patterns of social mobility are once again seen to be different in business careers from political and intellectual careers. As would be expected, most businessmen are sons of businessmen, and 57 percent of the business leaders studied are sons of owners or executives of large or small businesses. Perhaps less expected however is the fact that it is in the business sector that sons of laborers and of farm operators appear in smallest proportions. While the notion of the poor boy working his way to the top of a large company may have some currency in Japan, the odds on such an Alger-style hero emerging appear slight indeed.

The young man of humble origins might do better to look to the political arena, where a small but perceptible group of the 1960 leaders are from laboring or farming backgrounds. In fact, landowning or farm-operating backgrounds would seem a positive advantage since these backgrounds comprise the largest single grouping, with more than one-third of the political leaders sons of landlords or tenants. The next largest grouping of political leaders is that of sons of government officials, another evidence of the considerable continuity in at least the bureaucratic leadership of Japan over several generations. The quite small proportion of political leaders who are sons of small businessmen is more puzzling; perhaps they lack the constituency for electoral efforts that a rural background might provide and yet also lack easy access to a bureaucratic career.

The recruitment of intellectual leaders shows no striking pattern. One-third are sons of professional men, just as precisely one-third of the business leaders are sons of executives or owners of large businesses; perhaps this proportion can be taken as a general rule for continuity of position. A small proportion of intellectual leaders are from farm backgrounds, and this fact might fairly be attributed to the disadvantage rural origins impose in obtaining a higher education.

The examination of occupational origins thus far has been in such terms as may be useful in characterizing these groups generally. A question of no less importance has to do with social mobility and the extent to which one or another sector of the society is over- or underrepresented in national leadership. An adequate measure can be obtained only by adjusting for population proportions from the several occupational backgrounds, and the distribution of 1920 adult males shown in table 10 provides a basis for such an adjustment.

Since the men studied were sixty years of age, it may be assumed that in the early 1920s their fathers were well along in their careers. Thus their report of their father's occupation may be taken to

Table 10. Occupation of Father: 1960 Leaders

Occupation	Japan: 1920 Adult Employed Males*	Total, Leaders	Business Leaders	Political Leaders	Intellectual Leaders
Government official (civil or military)	0.4%	11%	9%	17%	10%
Executive or owner, large business	1.7	23	33	13	14
Professional	1.3	14	5	11	33
White collar	7.9	9	8	12	9
Owner, small business	13.2	15	19	7	15
Laborer	26.3	1	0	3	1
Farm owner or tenant	48.3	26	24	37	18
Landlord	7.3	17	18	24	9
Operator or tenant	41.0	9	6	13	9
Other occupations	0.9	1	2	0	0
Total	100%	100%	100%	100%	100%
Number	17,081,000	406	207	99	100

*Bureau of Statistics, Imperial Cabinet, *Shokugyō: Kokusei Chōsa Hōkoku*, Vol. II (Occupation, The Census Report of 1920), and *JSY*, 1929.

be approximately comparable to the distribution of adult males by occupation as reported in the 1920 census. While that census does not provide a breakdown of occupations entirely comparable to the occupational categories used in this study, the author has drawn on the sources indicated, as well as others, to arrive at the distribution shown in table 10. Special mention should be made of the estimated division of the total landowning and land-working group into landowners and operators or tenants. The assumption is made here that landlords constituted some 15 percent of this total group, although there is some indication that the proportion may have been less. To the extent that this proportion is less than the 15 percent shown, the calculations following would tend to overstate the amount of occupational mobility out of farm operator and tenant backgrounds.

To derive a single measure of the degree to which an occupational group has advantages or disadvantages as a source of national leadership in the succeeding generation, the proportion of leaders from a given background is compared with the presumed proportion of persons in the total population from that occupational background as given by the 1920 census. Unity then is 1.00 or, as shown in table 11 for simpler reading, 100. In this event, the leadership representation of a given group reflects something like "equal opportunity," or entirely equitable sharing of national leadership on the basis of population proportions. To the extent that the ratio is greater than 100, a given group is overrepresented in national leadership.

The measure of mobility rates is shown in table 11. They bring into sharp relief the features of leadership recruitment in 1960 already remarked on. There is an extraordinarily high rate of recruitment from government executive backgrounds into all sectors of leadership, a disproportion in elite recruitment unusual not only within Japanese leadership patterns but so far as is known for mobility rates of any similar group in any other industrial society. These rates of recruitment surely indicate more than some special prestige attaching to official families in Japan, or special favors in access to education or career openings. While these data provide

Table 11. Occupational Origin of Japan's 1960 Leaders
(Proportional representation = 100)

Occupation of Father	Total, Leaders	Business Leaders	Political Leaders	Intellectual Leaders
Government official	2,750	2,250	4,250	2,500
Executive or owner, large business	1,353	1,941	765	824
Professional	1,077	385	846	2,538
White collar	114	101	152	114
Owner, small business	113	144	53	113
Laborer	4	0	11	4
Farm owner or tenant	54	50	77	37
Landlord	233	247	329	123
Tenant	22	15	32	22

no direct evidence, the proportions might suggest a close social interaction among the several elite groups in Japan with the government group at or near the center of the pattern. They might also suggest that in the transition to a modern and industrial society the kind of family patterns and familial training resulting from governmental occupational roles are especially favorable to success in the next generation in a variety of careers.

It is sufficient to note further, from the data of table 11, that the mobility advantages conferred in Japan by birth into the higher occupational statuses appear to be very great indeed. What may be taken to represent middle class status, occupational backgrounds of white collar and small business levels, are fairly represented in all leadership groups, as are also men from landowning origins. The enormous disadvantage then is suffered by men whose fathers were industrial or farm laborers.

Trends in the Recruitment of Business Leaders, 1880–1960

The backgrounds of the men occupying Japan's topmost business positions over three generations may now be compared for trends in mobility to business leadership. The period covers the entire span of Japan's industrial development. Some reply can therefore be provided to the question of whether in the course of this economic development Japanese society has become more open.

Some special interest attaches to the question of the feudal status of Japan's business leaders in the earlier period of industrialization. There has been debate over the role of men of the samurai class in supplying the initiative for modernization in the business and industrial sectors. As indicated in table 12, and perhaps not surprisingly, these data suggest a mixed answer; samurai did indeed play a considerable part in business leadership, but it does not appear that men from this background dominated the business scene.

It should first be noted from table 12 that men from a samurai background appeared in business leadership in the 1880s in a proportion about four times greater than their proportion in the population. It may be noted too that within the group of business leaders from a samurai background, there is no striking imbalance in favor of one or another of the several samurai statuses. There is, in short, no marked tendency for "underprivileged" samurai to exercise business leadership, in contrast to men from the topmost samurai status.

From the fact that about one-quarter of the business leaders held samurai status in the preceding feudal order, it might be considered remarkable that so large a proportion as three-quarters of the business elite of the 1880s had been villagers or townsmen without feudal rank. Townsmen, less than one-tenth of the total population at the end of the Tokugawa period, produced more than one-half (55 percent) of the Meiji business leaders. Despite their lower formal status under the feudal regime, a majority of the Meiji business elite were men from families that had earlier been engaged in trade and industry; and when it is kept in mind that a number of the men from a village background were undoubtedly from families engaged in such rural businesses as *sake* and *shōyu* processing, the proportion of Meiji business leaders from business backgrounds appears to have been very substantial.

Comparing this first generation of leadership with succeeding ones, a conclusion of remarkable stability must be drawn. The proportion of men whose families had claimed higher feudal status increased to just over one-third by 1920, chiefly at the expense of men from families that had been in merchant status during the feudal period. The change in proportions from the 1880s to 1920, making some skeptical allowance for those cases where specific samurai status is not known, is hardly substantial. Oddly, from the 1920 to 1960 groups, there is no change in proportions of business leaders by feudal status claimed for family.

In summary, then, there is little support in these data for the assertion that men from samurai background supplied the leadership of the early industrial revolution in Japan. True, they are proportionately more numerous in leadership positions than in the total population, but this is an outcome entirely to be expected simply on the basis of superior familial financial resources, social status, and educational opportunity. Further, there is a striking

Table 12.   Family Feudal Status and Business Leadership: 1880s, 1920, 1960

Family Feudal Status	Total Japan 1872		Business Leaders		
			1880s	1920	1960
Kuge or daimyo	0.007%		0%	0%	2%
Samurai	6		23	37	35
Upper class		0.1	2	8	–
Middle class		3.6	9	2	–
Professional		–	4	2	–
Lower class		2.4	8	8	–
Status unknown		–	0	17	–
Commoner	94		77	63	63
Villager		85*	22	21	–
Country samurai (gōshi)			3	2	–
Village head			14	17	–
Peasant			5	2	–
Townsmen		9*	55	42	–
Merchant, businessman			50	35	–
Professional			3	3	
Clerk, artisan			2	4	
Total	100%		100%	100%	100%
Number	31(million)		198	200	200

*These two figures are based on calculations by economic historian Sekiyama Naotarō, who estimated the distribution of population by feudal status at the very end of the Tokugawa period as follows: samurai 6–7 percent; priest 1.5 percent; farmers 80–85 percent; townsmen 5–6 percent; outcast 1.6 percent. He also estimated the distribution of population by occupation as follows: farmers 80 percent or more; artisans 3 percent; traders 6 percent. See Sekiyama, Naotarō, *Kinsei Nihon no Jinkō Kōzō (Structure of Population in Modern Period in Japan)* (Tokyo: Yoshikawa Kōbunkan, 1957), pp. 307–14.

similarity over the entire eighty-year period in the proportions of business leaders by family feudal status. There is little evidence that any single status group was the driving force in Japan's economic modernization.

Some indications of the pattern of occupational movement from a given feudal status to business leadership can be derived from an examination of the occupations of the fathers of 1920 business leaders and their family feudal status as shown in table 13. Where the father was in a white collar, governmental, or professional occupation, samurai background is by far the most frequent. In those cases among 1920 business leaders where the father had been in business, much the largest proportion is from families whose feudal status was that of townsmen. It would appear from these data therefore that rather commonly the sequence of occupational mobility was from samurai status to a white collar or professional position, culminating in the next generation in business leadership.

Trends in recruitment of business leaders by occupation of father are indicated in table 14. The overall impression is one of singular stability in the proportions of leadership from these several backgrounds, despite great changes in the occupational structure of society and in the national economy and polity. Through all three generations of business leaders, an almost unvarying 50 percent are sons of businessmen. Within this, there were more men in the early period whose fathers had been owners of small businesses, and fewer whose fathers had owned large businesses, consistent of course with the relatively small scale of enter-

Table 13. Occupation of Father by Family Feudal Status: 1920 Business Leaders

| | Family Feudal Status | | | |
Occupation of Father	Samurai	Villager	Townsman	Total
Samurai	100%	0%	0%	100%
White collar	75	25	0	100
Government official	70	22	8	100
Professional	68	7	25	100
Executive, large business	27	13	60	100
Owner, large business	10	12	78	100
Owner, small business	9	6	85	100
Landlord or farmer	6	74	20	100
All fathers	37	21	42	100
Number	74	42	84	200

prises at that time and the presumably greater opportunities to build a small firm to a predominant size. Over the past two generations, however, even in this respect there has been little change in proportions. The business elite from business backgrounds are drawn about equally from families where the father managed a large business and the son continues in this firm's management, where the father managed a large business and the son directs a similarly large firm, and where the father had owned a small business.

Slightly less than one-quarter of the business leaders of both the 1880s and 1960 were from farm backgrounds, with a ratio of landlord to operator backgrounds of about three to one in both periods. Again, the emphasis must be on a singular stability in proportions, although in the case of men from farm backgrounds there was a curious decrease in proportions in the 1920 business leader group, a decrease most marked in the thinly represented operator-tenant class. There is no direct evidence as to the cause of this temporary falling-off in the supply of business leaders of rural origin. It is possible however that, relative to the urban occupational groups, the men of the villages were not able to take advantage of the new educational system as rapidly, or perhaps schools were not available to them as rapidly. Whatever the cause of the 1920 decrease, by 1960 the proportion of business leaders from a farm background had returned to the 1880 level.

The remaining occupations, including both clerical and industrial workers, government personnel, professional men, and samurai, form a miscellaneous group. It does not seem unreasonable, however, to include the samurai in this largely clerical and professional group, since in feudal society the samurai did provide much of the clerical and professional services. If they are so included, then the proportion of men in business leadership from this composite group has not changed greatly over this eighty-year period.

The conclusion from these data, however one might combine specific occupations into categories, seems inescapable: the topmost level of Japan's business world has been recruited in very similar proportions since the very beginning of the modern period in terms of the occupation (and thus, in good part, social class) of the father. This is the more singular when it is remembered that the

Table 14. Occupational Origin of Business Leaders: 1880s, 1920 and 1960

Occupation of Father	1880s	1920	1960
Owner or executive, large business, same firm as son	10	20	18
Owner or executive, large business, different firm from son	9	12	15
Owner, small business	31	17	19
Total, Business	50%	49%	52%
Landlord	17	15	18
Farm operator or tenant	5	1	6
Total, Farm	22	16	24
White collar or other	2	2	9
Government official	—	7	9
Professional	3	7	5
Samurai	23	19	1
Total, government, clerical and professional	28	35	24
Total, all occupations	100%	100%	100%
Number	200	200	207

occupational composition of Japan has undergone very great changes. For example, slightly over three-quarters of the Japanese labor force in 1883 was employed in agriculture. The proportion for 1960 was one-third. Despite so great a decline, recruitment of business leaders from this group has remained almost constant at just under one-quarter. On the other hand, the proportion of owners and executives of large and small businesses in the population has increased from about 7 to about 11 percent, while the proportion of the business elite from these backgrounds has held steady at about one-half of the total. More dramatically, while the proportion of laborers in the population has increased from less than 4 percent of the 1883 work force to one-third of the 1960 work force, there were no sons of laborers in the business leader groups studied for either 1880 or 1960.

This report on research results is not the proper platform for an extended effort to explain these data, if indeed an explanation could readily be arrived at. It seems fairly clear that sons of the lowest stratum of the farm population and the entire laboring population of Japan have almost no access to the top levels of the business hierarchy. It may then prove to be the case (and the review of the education of these men in the following section provides a basis for this argument) that for the balance of the society—sons of clerks, landlords, professional men and the like—the steady improvement in access to higher education has fairly neatly canceled out changes in the class and occupational structure.

For each of the three generations studied, some two-thirds of the business elite are from higher status backgrounds: government (and samurai), business, professional, and landowning status. There is the question of career patterns, however, and possible changes in the career patterns that have led to elite business positions. Table 15 summarizes these trends, in three groupings. The

Table 15. Business Leaders' Career Patterns, 1880–1960

Career Pattern	1880s	1920	1960
Founded own business as partner, owner, or director	57%	32%	10%
Inherited family business (owner or director, same firm as father)	23	24	18
a. Large business	10	20	18
b. Small business	13	4	—
Neither founded nor inherited firm	20	44	72
Total	100%	100%	100%
Number	200	200	207

proportion of business leaders in the 1880s who founded their own businesses comprised more than one-half (57 percent) of the total. This indicates that for the first generation of Japanese business leaders there were ample opportunities to establish enterprises through their own talents and ambitions. Those who inherited small business firms and expanded them to large business firms in the 1880s account for 13 percent. If we add them to the groups of founders, then a total of 70 percent achieved their top positions in large business firms by so-called entrepreneurship. However, these opportunities were largely reduced by 1920. About one-third of the 1920 business leaders are in this category. By 1960, only one-tenth of business leaders had reached the top by this route.

The proportion of business leaders who inherited their positions, in the sense of directing the same firm as that managed by their father, has not changed greatly in the total, declining from 23 percent to 18 percent over the three generations. However, separating the inheritance of top executive positions in large business firms from small ones, it appears that about one-fifth of inheriting business leadership occurred in 1920 and 1960, as against one-tenth in the 1880s.

The substantial change is that expected in an economy reaching industrial maturity with very large business units; the proportion of business leaders who in the Weberian sense pursued bureaucratic careers,[5] neither inheriting nor founding their firm but achieving leadership positions through some kind of merit, had increased from only one-fifth in the 1880s to nearly three-quarters in 1960. Again, education and formal training are implicit in these changes.

From the beginning of industrialization to the present period, some marked trends in mobility to business leadership in comparison with political and intellectual elite can be found, as follows.

Initially, business leaders had largely different family feudal status backgrounds from the members of the political and intellectual elites. A majority of business leaders were sons of merchants rather than of samurai or villagers. While the great majority of men in the political and intellectual elite were from various ranks of samurai and while Meiji political leaders undoubtedly played the most important role in Japan's early modernization, early business enterprises were established and run by the men who had previously engaged in manufacturing and trading in the feudal society. This may suggest that early development in Japanese modern business and industry is in significant part an outgrowth

---

[5]Weber, Max, *Essays in Sociology* (Translated by H. H. Gerth and C. Wright Mills) (London: Routledge & Kegan Paul, Ltd., 1948) pp. 196–244.

of management methods developed in traditional manufacturing and trading.

The second generation of Japanese business leaders (1920) reflects the transition from a traditional society to a modern industrial society. Substantial numbers of sons of samurai entered the business world with modern higher education and achieved top executive positions on merit. Direct family inheritance of chief executive positions from their founders increased their numbers. In terms of family occupational backgrounds, business leaders in 1920 are not similar to political and intellectual leaders, mainly due to occupational continuities of professional men among intellectual leaders and overrepresentation of government officials and landlords among political leaders. There were no revolutionary changes in succession of elite groups, but elite positions were gradually opened to sons of small business owners and landowners for business leadership, to sons of land owners for political leadership, and to sons of professional and landowners for intellectual leadership.

In 1960 Japanese society became more open in recruiting men into elite groups. The research results do not deny that inequality in family occupational status was a factor in success in national leadership. However, the present elite groups are more similar in social composition and are in general less determined by family occupational status than in the earlier periods. Almost all occupational groups are better represented in positions of leadership as a whole. Present notable trends in recruitment for leadership positions are that sons of government officials and executives or owners of large business firms have the most favorable prospects for getting into all three areas of national leadership. This reflects not only a special pattern of elite recruitment in Japan but also maturity of economic development.

Chapter 8

TRENDS OF EDUCATION OF JAPAN'S ELITE GROUPS

Development of Japan's Educational System

A brief review of the development of Japan's educational system in the modern period will help us understand the role of education in the recruitment of political, business and intellectual elites. Of the many forces that have played a part in Japan's industrialization, the central role must surely be assigned to the carefully planned and massive investment undertaken early in the Meiji era in support of formal education. The facts mentioned below clearly indicate that, in pursuing a national policy of industrializing Japan after the Western model, the leaders of the new government of the Meiji Restoration drew up very ambitious educational plans and made real efforts to carry them out.

Japan's traditional educational system was rather well developed by the end of the Tokugawa period. Domain schools owned by the daimyo were responsible for the literacy training of sons of their retainers. These schools numbered 285 in 1872 and were located in castle sites in all parts of Japan. Countless voluntary schools known as *terakoya*, or writing schools, and private schools in towns and villages were responsible for teaching commoners. Indeed, Japan had already attained a high literacy rate by the end of the feudal period. It is estimated that somewhat more than 40 percent of all Japanese males and 10 percent of all Japanese females were getting some formal education outside their home by the time of the Restoration.[1] However, these schools were all administered by separate daimyo and individual schoolmasters.

---

[1]Dore, R. P., *Education in Tokugawa Japan* (Berkeley and Los Angeles: University of California Press, 1965) p. 254.

The task of the Meiji government was to establish a few principles in public education, to tie the numerous separate schools into a unified education system, and to develop a new curriculum. In spite of the existence of a well-developed traditional system teaching Confucian doctrine and Japanese classics, the introduction of Western science and technology convinced the political leaders of the Meiji government as well as the common people of the superiority of Western over traditional learning. As a result there was almost no organized resistance from traditional scholars and teachers.

The Meiji government published a "School Ordinance" in 1872 and initiated general education. By 1877 about 26,000 schools—a university, colleges, high schools and primary schools—had been established. The distribution by school, teacher, and enrollment is shown in table 16.

Table 16. Distribution of Japan's Schools, Teachers, and Student Enrollment by Level of Education: 1877

(Number)

Level of Education	Schools	Teachers	Students
University	1	91	1,760
Specialist school	53	252	4,112
Middle school	389	910	20,522
Primary school	25,459	59,825	2,162,962*
Total	25,902	61,078	2,189,356

*The proportion of enrollment in primary school among school agers in 1878 was 40 percent (male 56 percent, female 23 percent).
Source: Ministry of Education, *Gakusei 80 Nenshi* (Eighty Years' History of Educational System) (Tokyo: Finance Ministry Printing Bureau, 1954), pp. 1043–63.

Tokyo University was the first and until 1897 the only university. It inherited the shogunal higher educational and research institutions and transformed inself into a modern university in a short period. In 1877 it expanded to four faculties: law, sciences, letters, and medicine; the faculties of law, sciences, and letters then had 710 students, 32 Japanese faculty members, and 24 foreign faculty members; the faculty of medicine had 1,040 students, 24 Japanese and 11 foreign faculty members.[2] The Meiji government hired many foreign professors, drawn about equally from the United States, the United Kingdom, Germany, and France. The number of foreign scholars working in Tokyo University and Japanese specialist schools gradually decreased in the 1880s and their positions were taken by Japanese scholars trained in Western universities under government support.[3] They numbered about 20 persons each year from 1876 to 1885.

The Meiji government also established specialist schools in Western languages, education, engineering, law, business and medicine. These schools accounted for 53 schools, 161 teachers and 3,361 students in 1877.[4] In addition to these government supported specialist schools it should be noted that private higher institutions played an important role in introducing Western sciences and languages in the initial period of industrialization in Japan. These schools were directed mostly by individual scholars. They used Western textbooks and taught Western sciences, arts and thought. Private specialist schools accounted for 38 schools, 79 teachers and 1,874 students in 1877.[5] Many of these schools did not last long, but most of the present private universities in Japan are outgrowths of one of these early institutions.

Middle schools in the 1877 period required a curriculum very similar to that of the present high schools. They not only trained pupils for specialist school and university work, but also provided polytechnic training in engineering, commerce, agriculture, and foreign languages. Many of the earliest middle schools were transformed from domain schools in the Tokugawa period, but there were also new establishments to meet new needs. Primary schools spread most rapidly over every part of Japan. They numbered 25,000 in 1878 in contrast to 26,000 at present. This implies that from the very beginning Japan provided the number of primary schools needed for national compulsory education. This rapid

---

[2]Ministry of Education, *Gakusei 80 Nenshi* (Eighty Years' History of Educational System) (Tokyo: Finance Ministry, Printing Bureau, 1954), p. 73.
[3]*Ibid.*, p. 68.
[4]*Ibid.*, p. 77.
[5]*Ibid.*

development of the primary school is due mostly to the existence of a voluntary school system in the Tokugawa period. The traditional *terakoya,* or writing schools, and teachers provided the basis for school faculties and teaching personnel in the new public schools. The proportion of school enrollment of pupils among children of school age was 28 percent in 1874, 40 percent in 1883, 51 percent in 1887, and 80 percent in 1900.[6]

These data show that Japan started her industrialization with well-developed traditional educational institutions but with only a few modern scientific higher institutions. We shall compare the education of Japan's leaders of the 1880 period with data on the educational system in the Tokugawa and Meiji periods.

Education of Leaders of 1880

Formal Education

Scientific education and training, which are essential to industrialization, were foreign to Japan till the mid-nineteenth century, the period when the Meiji leaders were growing up. Most of the education provided by the feudal regime was the teaching of centuries-old Confucian ethics. Only a few institutions were beginning to teach science and technology. Apprenticeship was the predominant characteristic of training. An attempt is made in this section to determine the kinds of educational experiences that the Meiji leaders received, i.e., level of formal education, field of study, institution of higher education attended, and education abroad. These data reveal the actual role of Japan's earlier educational system in industrialization.

The leaders of the 1880s, men about forty years of age in 1885, received their education under the systems in effect under the feudal regime. The education of villagers and townsmen was confined largely to temple schools and apprentice programs, and this educational background accounts for about one-third of the total, as shown in table 17. A *terakoya,* or writing school, was a voluntary private institution for literacy training of commoners in towns and villages during the Tokugawa period. Literacy training

---

[6]*Ibid.,* p. 38.

Table 17.   Level of Formal Education: 1880s Leaders
(Percent)

Level of Education	Total, Leaders	Business Leaders	Political Leaders	Intellectual Leaders Artists	Others
None or *terakoya*,	5	8	1	0	1
Apprentice	28	45	1	76	6
Private school or domain school	39	30	70	12	34
Higher education	28	17	28	12	59
Total	100	100	100	100	100
Number	371	189	82	17	83

in Japan was maintained in Buddhist temples throughout the medieval period. However, it was not necessary to hold these classes in the Tokugawa period. Toward the end of the feudal period and with the necessity of reading and writing ability for commercial and administrative activities, sons and daughters were enrolled in these voluntary schools at an earlier age. These schools numbered 4,293 in the 1860s, contrasted with 58 in 1800.[7] These schools were managed and taught by educated samurai, townsmen, villagers, and priests. Their curriculum included reading and writing of Japanese and sometimes mathematics. Until the compulsory education system was installed by the Meiji government in 1872, the *terakoya*, or writing school, provided literacy training for commoners. Only 5 percent of the Meiji leaders received less than a *terakoya*, or writing school, education.

Besides *terakoya*, most commoners acquired their business and professional skills and knowledge under an apprenticeship program. The apprenticeship was divided into two parts: training in family work and apprenticeship outside the family. Thirty

[7]Details of historical development, general characteristics, distribution, curriculum, teachers and pupils of the *terakoya* are found in Ishikawa, Ken, *Terakoya* (Tokyo: Shibundō, 1960).

percent of the business leaders were apprentices in their family business, and 15 percent were apprenticed to an outside business. There was almost no apprenticeship among political leaders. Among intellectual leaders only artists (actors, painters, musicians and the like) had been apprentices. Most of these had training in their family profession. The proportion of apprenticeships among the three types of leaders reflects the different practices in training and recruitment in each sector.

Domain schools *(hankō)* were established by individual daimyo and provided training primarily for sons of their retainers. There were 285 such schools in 1872.[8] Their curriculum covered Confucian doctrine and Japanese classics. However, by the end of the Tokugawa period, they had come to include more and more sciences and Western languages. It should be noted that 43 percent of the domain schools explicitly prohibited entrance of commoners.[9] The others did not restrict the entrance of commoners. The category of private school included private tutoring, community schools, and various other private schools. The community school *(kyōgaku)*[10] was run mostly by the daimyo or village and town headmen and provided more systematic education than the temple school for sons of commoners. Private schools *(shijiku)* were owned by individual scholars and specialized in specific subjects; they were not limited to samurai. According to Ishikawa, *shijiku* numbered 1400 to 1500 throughout the Tokugawa period.[11] They were mostly owned by Confucian scholars or, to a lesser extent, Japanese classic scholars. Since no school had a fixed term, students frequently journeyed from one teacher to another in different places.

The higher education category includes the specific institutions provided by the shogunal government[12] and later the Meiji government, as well as colleges and universities in Western countries. Intellectual leaders and political leaders received more higher educa-

---

[8]Ishikawa, Ken, *Nihon Shomin Kyōikushi* (Educational History of Japanese Commoners) (Tokyo: Tokō Shoin, 1934), p. 121.

[9]*Ibid.*, p. 175.

[10]*Ibid.*, pp. 216–20.

[11]*Ibid.*, p. 174.

[12]Details of organization, curriculum of shogun-owned educational institutions are found in Ishikawa, Ken, *Tokugawa Jidai ni okeru Gakkō no Hattatsu* (Development of Schools in the Tokugawa Period) (Tokyo: Iwanami Shoten, 1951).

tion than business leaders, because they were mostly of samurai origin and had to study at their domain schools as well as at shogunal schools. However, it is notable that even among the business leaders the level of formal education seems high; 47 percent of them had received a higher education. This is to be contrasted with a very low level of education in the general population in those days.

Education and Feudal Status

Before getting into a review of the content of higher education among the leaders of the 1880s, let us determine to what extent the level of education of the leaders is related to family feudal status. It is important to know whether men of different feudal backgrounds received different amounts of education. Table 18 presents the education of the Meiji elites in relation to family feudal status. The amount of education was widely different in each status group. It is clear that the samurai entered political, business or intellectual careers in the Meiji era with distinctly higher education than men of other origins. Whatever careers samurai followed after the Meiji Restoration, their success depended on educational qualification.

Townsmen, in contrast to former samurai, assumed leadership positions with markedly less formal education. They depended on apprentice training. More than two-thirds of leaders of townsman

Table 18. Family Feudal Status and Education of Meiji Leaders

(Percent)

Level of Education	Samurai	Villager	Townsman	Total
None or *terakoya*	1	11	7	5
Apprenticeship	6	27	61	28
Private school or domain school	53	36	23	39
Higher education	40	26	9	28
Total	100	100	100	100
Number	176	55	124	355

status received apprenticeship or less than a temple school education. Townsmen without higher education appeared more often in business leadership and distinctly less so in political and intellectual leadership. The culture of the merchants and artisans, who attached less importance to higher education for their sons, no doubt affected, in part, the educational level of townsmen. If modernization is conceived as a concomitant to the advancement of the educational level of the population, then townsmen in Japan were the slowest to adapt to the concurrent social change. We shall trace the differences of educational levels among different occupational groups in successive generations and try to illuminate to what extent formal education is related to movement to a position of leadership in Japanese society. We shall add here an indication to what extent university education was made available to nonsamurai families in the early Meiji period. The Japanese government's 1962 report on education[13] shows that 78 percent of the students enrolled in Tokyo University in 1879 were sons of samurai. By 1882, within only three years, this proportion had dropped to 50 percent of the total. It is rather surprising to discover that sons of commoners accounted for one-half of the students of Tokyo University, which was the outgrowth of the shogunal higher institutions and was organized for the purpose of recruiting higher civil servants and research personnel of the Meiji government.

Higher Education

Location of School. The locations of schools where leaders studied show some marked trends. The well-known predominance of Tokyo's schools, and particularly Tokyo University itself, began to appear in the 1880s. Of the three groups of leaders, intellectual leaders studied in the largest proportion in the nation's capital (61 percent). So did many business and political leaders (39 percent and 25 percent, respectively). Schools in Kyoto and Osaka, then the largest cities, are not as productive as might be expected; however, Nagasaki, which was the only trading port open to

---

[13]Ministry of Education, *Nihon no Seichō to Kyōiku* (Japan's Growth and Education) (Tokyo: Teikoku Chihō Gyōsei Gakkai, 1962), p. 35.

foreign countries during the Tokugawa period, was an important learning center for later intellectual and political leaders. *Higher Institutions Attended.* Higher institutions that the Meiji leaders attended are shown in table 19. Toward the end of the Tokugawa period, shogunal institutions consisted of the schools of Confucian studies *(shōheiko)* and Western studies *(kaiseisho)* and the Medical Institute *(igakusho).* These institutions were combined to form Tokyo University in 1877 under the Meiji government. The graduates of the three institutions are well represented in the intellectual leader category. It appears that intellectuals under the Tokugawa regime remained in the Meiji government despite the revolutionary political changes. While Tokyo University later became the predominant source of Japan's leadership groups, it was not the dominant institution for political and business leaders in the 1880s. Keiō Gijuku, a private institution founded in 1858 by a great enlightenment leader, Fukuzawa Yukichi, was the single largest source for the Meiji business leaders. Hitotsubashi, which was founded in 1875 and has lately become another large training institution for business leaders, had not begun to play that role during this period. In general, Japanese leaders in the 1880s were drawn from rather varied educational institutions

Table 19. Higher Institutions Attended: Meiji Leaders
(Percent)

Institution	Total, Leaders	Business Leaders	Political Leaders	Intellectual Leaders
Shogunal institution	9	3	8	16
Tokyo Imperial University	12	6	3	26
Keiō Gijuku	9	18	3	5
Hitotsubashi	1	2	0	0
Others (including domain schools)	69	71	86	53
Total	100	100	100	100
Number	250	88	81	81
No higher education	134	112	3	19

of higher learning. This is because the country experienced a great political and educational transformation during the period when these leaders were brought up. It was a time when traditional institutions were destroyed or reorganized, and new institutions began to grow.

Table 20 presents the figures for foreign education among the 1880s elites. Eighteen percent of the total group of Meiji leaders studied abroad. Thirty-three percent of intellectual leaders and 28 percent of political leaders had studied abroad, but only a few business leaders. It is notable that the men who studied in the United Kingdom and in the United States account for three-fifths of those who studied abroad. This implies that the Anglo-American countries were the major source of Western influence in Japan in the early Meiji period, but a substantial number also studied in Germany and France.

Table 20.   Foreign Education: 1880s Leaders
(Number)

Country	Total, Leaders	Business Leaders	Political Leaders	Intellectual Leaders
United Kingdom	23	5	11	7
United States	19	3	5	11
Germany, Austria	12	2	2	8
France	10	1	5	4
Other European countries	4	0	1	3
Other countries	1	1	0	0
Total	69	12	24	33
Percent of foreign education	18	6	28	33

According to the earlier record of foreign education in Japan, there were 250 students studying abroad under government support and 123 privately financed students in 1872. However, because of government policy to limit foreign study only to very promising candidates, the number engaged in foreign study decreased to 11 in 1875 and 26 in 1885.[14] It is clear that Western education was not only an important way of adopting modern sciences and arts but also a most important factor in the achievement of leadership positions.

A final aspect of the higher education of Japan's leaders in the 1880s is the major subject of study. As shown in table 21, more than one-third of the leaders had majored in Confucian or traditional Japanese studies. Business and political leaders did so more often than intellectual leaders. Presumably the intellectual leaders learned mostly Western sciences and arts and played a major role in transmitting Western civilization into Japanese society. Study of Western languages was a step toward learning Western sciences and technology in the Tokugawa period. Study of Dutch, English, and French did not separate learning science from learning the language. Fifteen percent of the total number with higher education were included in this category. Political and intellectual leaders more often studied law and government, medicine, military sciences, and navigation. Business leaders were more likely to study engineering and economic subjects.

A discussion of the education of Japan's earlier elite would be incomplete without some examination of the foreign travel of these men. It has been noted already that 18 percent studied abroad, but these were only part of a larger group (41 percent) who had traveled abroad. Among these more than one-third had traveled abroad more than twice. For the most part these were not casual visits, since over two-thirds of the men who traveled abroad had more than one year of foreign residence. Fifty-four percent were in residence in foreign countries for over four years each. These foreign residences were virtually all in European countries and the United States, rarely in Asia. Foreign trips were longer and more frequent among intellectual and political leaders than among business leaders.

The education of the Meiji elite can be briefly summarized in the following manner. They received their education under the feudal regime or in some new higher institution after the Meiji Restoration. The education of commoners who became leaders was confined largely to apprenticeship. However, samurai received markedly higher education either in traditional Confucian

[14]Ministry of Education, *Gakusei 80 Nenshi*, pp. 64–7.

Table 21.   Major Field of Study: 1880s Leaders
(Percent)

Major Field of Study	Total, Leaders	Business Leaders	Political Leaders	Intellectual Leaders
Confucian or Japanese studies	35	43	42	19
Western languages and sciences	15	14	15	17
Law & government	14	2	12	27
Medicine	9	5	7	16
Military science and navigation	8	5	18	1
Engineering	6	13	2	5
Economics and commerce	6	16	1	1
Science and mathematics	3	1	2	5
Agriculture	1	0	1	1
Art	1	0	0	2
Other	2	1	0	6
Total	100	100	100	100
Number	250	88	81	81
No higher education	134	112	3	19

doctrine or in Western sciences and arts. The predominant characteristics of the education of the Meiji business leaders were apprenticeship training and learning in traditional doctrine. They were far more predisposed to conserving traditional values in contrast to political and intellectual leaders. Among political leaders almost all received some higher education. About one-third studied traditional subjects, and the rest studied Western languages and sciences. Intellectual leaders progressively adopted Western sciences. They studied more often in Tokyo in shogunal institutions, Tokyo University and Western universities. In general, the Meiji elites in political, business and intellectual sectors represent rather varied experience in education in terms of level and types among different feudal backgrounds.

Education of Leaders of 1920

Formal Education

The Taishō leaders, the second generation of Japan's industrializing elite, received substantially different education from the Meiji leaders in terms of level of formal education, major subjects, and foreign education. Table 22 shows the level of education among these leaders to be very high. Slightly over one-half graduated from a university. Including three to four year specialist school graduates, a total of 71 percent of the Taishō elite received higher education. Before examining table 22 in further detail and the role of education in national leadership, some explanation of the categories used is necessary. These men are the first product of the educational system that the Meiji government had designed for its modernization policy. This stystem was expanded during the Taishō and Shōwa periods and lasted until the reorganization of the educational system after the Second World War by the occupation forces. The several levels of formal education are not quite comparable to the American stages, and thus the translations employed can be misleading in making comparisons. Broadly stated, the term "middle school graduates" refers to graduates of the former *chūto gakkō*, extending five years after the six years of primary school. By "specialist school graduates" is meant graduates of the three- to four-year schools that extended beyond this "middle school" level.

There are no directly comparable data on the level of education of the 1920 elite in Japan's total population. However, it is possible to identify the number and proportion of graduates in several levels of education in Japan from 1890 to 1910.[15] From 1890 to 1900, when the 1920 leaders received their higher education, Japan had 1.6 to 1.7 million graduates from all levels of school, including the nonenrolled school-age population. University graduates during the period were 431 to 679 men each year or 0.03 to 0.04 percent of the total. Specialist school graduates were 3,930 to 4,830 men or 0.2 to 0.3 percent of the total. Middle school gra-

---

[15]The data are adapted from *Monbushō Nempō* (The Annual Report of the Ministry of Education) 1890–1910.

Table 22.   Level of Education: 1920 Leaders
(Percent)

Level of Education	Total, Leaders	Business Leaders	Political Leaders	Intellectual Leaders Artist	Others
Less than primary school	21	30	10	58	7
(Apprentice)	(9)	(9)	(5)	(46)	(5)
Middle school	3	7	7	12	7
Specialist school	20	17	27	24	19
University	51	46	56	6	67
Total	100	100	100	100	100
Number	397	198	99	17	83

duates are still less than 1 percent of the total in 1900. The majority of the school-age population (83 percent) was not enrolled in primary schools in 1890, but 91 percent of the school-age population in 1910 completed the term of compulsory education. It is clear that men attending universities and specialist schools in the Meiji period were only a small minority of the total population. Let us compare the level of the 1920 elite with the educational level of the general population.

Presumably more than 90 percent of Japan's male adult population had a formal education of less than primary school in 1890, when the average 1920 elite received his education. However, only 31 percent of the leaders had less than primary school education or apprentice training. Middle school education before 1910 is rare among the general population and is counted as higher education. Middle school graduates comprised 8 percent of the 1920 elite. The Taishō leaders who graduated from specialist schools and universities amount to 71 percent, while the accumulated population of graduates of higher institutes by 1900 was sizable among the general population. It is clear that university and specialist school training was a most important means of attaining leadership positions in the Taishō period.

What are the reasons why Japan found educational attainment prerequisite to leadership positions in political and business careers during this period? At present we can only assume: first, that Japan had a tradition of placing importance on learning in pre-modern society; second, that new technological demands of political and industrial organization required scientific training regardless of family background. Having emerged from a feudal patrimonial social system that placed great emphasis on inheritance of socially important positions, Japan promptly adopted a rational, achievement-oriented social system that was functionally related to industrialization. It should be noted that the distribution of education among the three groups of leaders is rather even. However, two exceptions deserve special mention. First, the leading artist in the study sample (actors, painters, musicians and the like) are shown separately from other intellectuals in table 22 since their distribution by formal education is unique. The relatively low level of formal education of this group is due, of course, to the continuation of apprentice training methods for these occupations. Second, the level of education is lower for the business leaders than for the other two groups of leadership. This is due to the fact that business training in the Taishō period was in some aspects still dependent on traditional practices in business succession. However, a more important trend is that the recruitment for executive positions in business had become more dependent upon educational attainment than on the apprenticeship characteristics of the 1880s.

Higher Education

The most significant aspect of the recruitment in the Taishō elite is that graduates of specialist schools and universities founded under the Meiji government had achieved the topmost leadership positions. We will examine the role and content of higher education in the recruitment of the three leadership groups. We define institutions of higher education as specialist schools and universities. Let us examine the location of school attended, the name of college and university studied at, field of specialization and foreign education of the 1920 elite.

Education for the 1920 elite is concentrated in specialist schools and universities in Tokyo. Three-fourths of the leaders completed their higher studies in Tokyo. Schools in large cities other than Tokyo hardly share in training national leaders. Of the three groups, most political leaders (85 percent) were educated in the nation's political capital. Even the business leaders are predominantly graduates of Tokyo (71 percent) with only 4 percent graduates of universities in the Osaka-Kyoto area, the traditional center of business activities.

A single university, Tokyo, is the source of higher education of 40 percent of all the men studied, while this proportion is 21 percent in the 1880s. Tokyo University supplied 34 percent of the business leaders in 1920, and 9 percent in the Meiji period. Similarly, it supplied 43 percent of the political leaders in 1920, compared to 11 percent in the 1880s. It is notable that Keiō University produced a distinctively larger proportion (15 percent) of the business leaders in 1920, as was the case in the sample of Meiji business leaders examined. Except for Tokyo and Keiō universities, there were no dominant institutions in recruiting the Taishō leaders.

The major subject of study among the Taishō elite at higher institutions is shown in table 23. Most of the leaders are graduates of the curricula of law and government, economics and commerce, and engineering. Concentration in a few curricula is most marked among the political leaders: two-thirds of them studied law and government. Major subjects for the business leaders are mostly the three fields of economics, law, and engineering, with a marked increase from 1880. Specialized fields for the intellectual leaders include many subjects in the sciences and arts. Important trends from 1880 to 1920 are a marked decrease in traditional learning (Confucian and Japanese studies) and a marked increase in law and government.

Foreign higher institutions in Western countries account for 23 percent among the 1920 leaders in contrast to 18 percent among the 1880 leaders. Of the three leadership groups, intellectual leaders had studied abroad most frequently. The distribution of those with a foreign education is shown in table 24. Twenty-three percent (92 men) of a total of 460 Taishō elite studied abroad. Of this total, 41 of the men studied in the United States, 22 in the United Kingdom, 22 in Germany and Austria, 4 in France and 3

Table 23. Major Subject Studied: 1920 Leaders
(Percent)

Major Subject	Total	Business Leaders	Political Leaders	Intellectual Leaders
Law & government	33	23	60	21
Economics & commerce	17	31	10	2
Engineering	10	20	2	2
Western language	6	6	6	7
Sciences & mathematics	4	2	2	9
Confucian & Japanese studies	4	3	6	4
Navigation & military science	3	2	6	1
Medical science	5	2	0	16
Art	2	0	0	6
Agriculture	1	0	0	5
Other curricula	15	11	8	27
Total	100	100	100	100
Number	310	133	90	87

in various other countries. A significant trend in foreign education is that almost one-quarter of the business leaders in 1920 studied in Western countries as against 6 percent in the Meiji period. They were trained mostly in the United States and the United Kingdom. Most of the political leaders who studied in foreign countries also went to the United States and the United Kingdom. In terms of foreign education the 1920 leaders were influenced by the United States first, then the United Kingdom and Germany.

Sixty-one percent had traveled abroad. Of these about one-half made one trip while the rest traveled twice or more. As in the earlier period, these were not for the most part casual visits since over three-fourths of the men who traveled abroad had more than one year of foreign residence, with about one-half of the men in residence in foreign countries for over four years. Both the frequency

Table 24.   Foreign Education: 1920 Leaders
(Number)

Country	Total	Business Leaders	Political Leaders	Intellectual Leaders
United States	41	25	7	9
United Kingdom	22	12	5	5
Germany & Austria	22	3	1	18
France	4	2	1	1
Other European countries	2	1	1	0
Others	1	0	1	0
Total	92	43	16	33
Percent with foreign education	23	22	16	33

and duration of foreign travel among the Taishō leaders had substantially increased in comparison with the Meiji elite. Japanese
leaders in the 1920 period are not only well educated in Japan's
domestic specialist schools and universities, but also a substantial
portion of these leaders extended their university work in Western
countries. Their frequent travels gave them extensive foreign contacts and experiences.

In traditional Japan, formal learning had largely been the
monopoly of the samurai. The Meiji government established an
educational system and provided an opportunity for higher learning to commoners as well as samurai. We have indicated already
that among the 1880 leaders, samurai with higher formal education achieved leadership positions in political, intellectual and business careers while townsmen achieved these positions through apprenticeship and less formal education.

Regarding the relationship between feudal status of family and
level of education of the 1920 elite, it is clear that the three status
groups provided for their sons in different degrees. Not all sons of
samurai received a higher education after the Meiji Restoration,
but the percentage that did was much higher than among sons of
villagers and townsmen. Proportionately more sons of villagers in

the 1920 elite received university training than sons of townsmen. It appears that in the process of Japan's modernization, the value of higher education among the three status groups was shared differently. The samurai, the ruling class in the feudal society, saw the importance of Western learning in higher institutions and were anxious to provide this education for their sons. Presumably this was because (as Thomas C. Smith pointed out recently)[16] the samurai, professional, military and civil officials in feudal Japan had been moved from the countryside to towns and cities, taken out of farm production, and lived on stipends provided by their feudal lords. As a result, their social norms were bound to be bureaucratic, and they placed great importance on education for administrative and professional work. Well-to-do farmers also adopted these values and gave higher education to their sons. However, townsmen, generally wealthier than the others, shared the values less during the transition period from the feudal to the industrial society.

Table 25 shows the occupational status of their fathers and the education of the 1920 leaders. It indicates that the 1920 leaders from different occupational origins received different levels of education. Who achieved national leadership positions with more university education? Who assumed these positions with less formal education? Sons of government officials among the 1920 leaders received the highest formal education. Sons of samurai, white collar workers, executives of large businesses, and professional men received higher formal education. It should be noted that these occupations tended to include a large number of former samurai. Leaders from farm backgrounds received less formal education, but it is surprising to find that sons of business owners, including large businesses, received the lowest formal education among the various occupational groups.

The discrepancies in recruiting the 1920 leaders among the various occupational statuses of their fathers should account for the different amount of education given to their sons. It appears

---

[16]Smith, Thomas C., "Japan's Aristocratic Revolution," *The Yale Review*(Vol. 50, No. 3, March 1961), pp. 372–3, and "Merit as Ideology in the Tokugawa Period," *Aspects of Social Change in Modern Japan*, edited by R. P. Dore (Princeton: Princeton University Press, 1967), pp. 71–90.

Table 25.   Occupational Status of Father and Education of 1920 Leaders
(Percent)

Occupation of Father	Less than Primary School	Middle School & Specialist School	University	Total
Government official	3	19	78	100 (36)
Samurai	12	26	62	100 (74)
White collar worker	13	27	60	100 (15)
Executive of large business	16	28	56	100 (18)
Professional	5	41	54	100 (46)
Farmer	23	30	47	100 (91)
Owner, large business	27	28	45	100 (58)
Owner, small business	39	22	39	100 (51)
Total	19%	28%	53%	100 (389)

that more samurai and government officials sought higher formal education for their sons. Consequently, their sons achieved leadership positions most frequently.

The characteristics of education among the 1920 leaders can be briefly summarized as follows. These men were the first products of the educational investment under the Meiji government. In comparison to the Meiji leaders they had much higher formal education in specialist schools and universities in Japan as well as Western countries. They majored primarily in modern sciences and arts, in law, economics, and engineering. They had extensive foreign travel. It appears that sons of samurai received the highest education and were most active in the political, intellectual and business leadership of Japan.

Education of Leaders of 1960

Formal Education

The level of formal education among the 1960 elite groups is shown in table 26. It is clear that the educational level of these intellectual, political and business leaders is significantly higher than that of the previous generations. The column at the left of table 26 lists the education of a sample of the fifty- to sixty-nine-year-old Japanese population in 1955. It is used here as the best measure of the total population group comparable to the leaders studied. It will be noted that only 7 percent of this population were graduates of a specialist school or university, while nearly 90 percent of the leaders are specialist school or university graduates. Almost 85 percent of the population ended formal education at the primary school level, while only 5 percent of the leaders studied did so.

Table 26. Level of Education: 1960 Leaders
(Percent)

Level of Education	Total* Japan	Total, Leaders	Business Leaders	Political Leaders	Intellectual Leaders Artist	Others
Primary school graduate	83	4	2	6	28	4
Middle school graduate	10	7	7	7	30	5
Specialist school graduate	7	15	20	12	30	2
University graduate	—	74	71	75	12	89
Total	100	100	100	100	100	100
Number	277	412	212	100	17	83

*Source: Adapted from Nihon Shakai Gakkai Chōsa Iinkai, *Nihon Shakai no Kaisōteki Kōzō* (Hierarchical Structure of Japanese Society) (Tokyo: Yūhikaku, 1958), p. 187.

It will be noted that the distribution of education among the three groups of leaders is rather even. Two exceptions deserve special mention. First, the leading artists studied (actors, painters, musicians and the like) are shown separately from other intellectuals in table 26, since their distribution by formal education is unique. The relatively low level of formal education of this group is due, of course, to the continuation of apprentice training methods for these occupations. Second, while the businessmen, as a whole, have more specialist school training than the other groups, somewhat fewer are university graduates. This is due to the technical nature of these specialist schools. The absorption of what are here termed "specialist schools" into the university system during the Allied occupation has meant that virtually all future business leaders will be university educated.

The 1960 leaders received their education in institutions established under the Meiji government and expanded by the successive generations of the Japanese government. They completed their schooling around 1920. By this time the proportion of graduates of specialist schools and universities was still small. University graduates totalled less than three thousand every year and various specialist school graduates numbered 16.7 thousand every year. A drastic increase in university graduates occurred after the Second World War. The current report of the Ministry of Education in Japan indicates that 12 percent of the population of college age were admitted to colleges and universities in 1961.[17]

Before looking further at the nature of higher education for the study's sample, the data presented in table 27 may be considered in the light of the analysis of occupational backgrounds. The table shows the education of the fathers of the present-day leaders along with the education of the fathers of a sample of the present Japanese population. As would be expected, the level of formal education of the fathers is much less than that of the men studied and is in turn much greater than that of the fathers of the total population.

About one-fifth of the fathers of the 1960 leaders were educated either in the special schools for children of the samurai established under the shogunate and daimyo or in the *terakoya*, or writing schools, for offspring of commoners. These distributions are indicated within parentheses in the table. It is interesting to note that those who received education under feudal institutions were mostly in domain schools, which later developed into middle schools. It will be noted that two-thirds of the fathers of the men studied received

---

[17]Ministry of Education, *Nihon no Seichō to Kyōiku* (Japan's Growth and Education) (Tokyo: Teikoku Chihō Gyōsei Gakkai, 1962), p. 49.

Table 27.   Education of Fathers of 1960 Leaders
(Percent)

Education	Total Japan*	All Leaders	Business Leaders	Political Leaders	Intellectual Leaders
Less than primary school	89	33	28	35	41
(*Terakoya*)		(4)	(2)	(5)	(6)
Middle school	7	25	33	18	14
(Domain school)		(19)	(26)	(13)	(9)
Specialist school		21	19	25	22
University	4	21	20	22	23
Total	100	100	100	100	100
Number	1,896	307	149	82	76
Unknown		105	63	18	24

*Source: Adapted from *Nihon Shakai no Kaisōteki Kōzō*, p. 196.

an education that might be taken to reflect relatively high social status. One-third of the fathers of the leaders received no more than primary school education.

The level of education for 1960 leaders is high, and almost all leaders had a university or specialist school education, as shown in table 28. There is a tendency for sons of urban upper class white collar men to receive a higher level of education than those with rural and middle or lower class backgrounds. However, in contrast to the 1880 and 1920 leaders, they show only slight differences among different occupations of their fathers. It is clear that elite positions invariably required higher formal education. Among the leaders the differences of formal education are minimal. However, this does not mean that there is no difference in education among sons of non-leaders. A sample survey of social mobility and stratification of Japan indicated that the amount of education of sons was largely determined by the occupational status of the father.[18]

From the two sets of data, it is safe to say that overrepresenta-

---

[18]*Nihon Shakai no Kaisōteki Kōzō*, p. 198.

Table 28. Occupational Status of Father and Education of 1960 Leaders

(Percent)

Occupation of Father	Primary School	Middle School	Specialist School	University	Total
Executive, large business	0	0	10	90	100 (33)
Government official	0	4	7	89	100 (45)
Owner, large business	3	0	10	87	100 (63)
Professional	6	4	11	79	100 (53)
Landlord	3	3	17	77	100 (70)
Owner, small business	2	11	22	65	100 (60)
Farmer	7	19	10	64	100 (42)
White collar worker	2	21	16	61	100 (38)
Laborer	67	33	0	0	100 (3)
Total	4%	7%	15%	74%	100 (407)

tion of sons of government officials, professionals, owners or executives of large businesses, and landlords among the 1960 leaders is due to the fact that they received university or specialist school education at a rate far exceeding that of sons of men in other occupations. The almost equal representation of sons of clerical and sales workers is due to the fact that their educational level in the general population ranges from university education to primary school education. Underrepresentation of elite positions for sons of farmers and laborers is due to their low opportunity for obtaining higher education.

Higher learning is the royal road to achievement of national leadership in Japan, as elsewhere. However, chances for higher learning a generation ago were limited to the upper or upper-middle class of Japanese society. Sons of laborers and farmers had almost no opportunity for receiving higher education a generation ago. Even government university scholarships were few, outside the military and teacher schools. University education began to become available for ambitious middle class boys only after 1940 and even more after the Second World War. When the 1960 leaders were being educated around 1920, the occupational status of their father was still an important determinant in whether they applied for university admission or not. Opportunity for higher education was far from equal in Japan. The real competition for the best education and the best careers in that period occurred among sons of government officials, professionals, owners or executives of large businesses, and landlords, which account for two-thirds of the total leaders in present-day Japan.

Finally it is worthwhile noting that there is considerable corre-- lation among family feudal status, education of father, and urban-rural difference of birthplace of the 1960 leaders. The general pattern of social mobility of the present elite from samurai origin appears to be that their fathers were in urban white collar occupations (e.g., government officials, professions, and managers of businesses) having distinctly higher education than the rest of the population. Most of the present leaders of samurai origin also received a university education. Commoners who became leaders were usually farmers or small business owners in towns and cities. Their fathers were less educated. Even though the present elite from commoner origins received specialist school and university education themselves, their upward generational mobility was more difficult.

Higher Education: 1960 Elite

The well-known predominance of Tokyo's universities, and particularly of Tokyo University itself, is entirely borne out by the data, as was found in the Taishō elite. Seventy-five percent of the 1960 elite studied in specialist schools and universities in Tokyo, where only 4 percent of the total population had lived in 1920. Of the three groups, the political leaders studied in greatest proportion (85 percent) in the nation's political capital. Kyoto, an older capital, produced one-tenth of all leaders. Eighty-five percent of the 1960 elite graduated in the Tokyo and Kyoto areas. Only 8 percent are graduates of universities in the Osaka-Kobe area, a traditional business center. The 1960 leaders, though born in cities, towns, and villages throughout Japan, were educated predominantly in Tokyo. The city is not only the political capital but also the chief training center of all the leadership groups of Japan.

A single university, Tokyo, is the source of higher education for nearly one-half of all the men studied. Indeed, five great universities—Tokyo, Kyoto, Hitotsubashi (the former commercial college), Keiō and Waseda—together account for the higher education of three-quarters of Japan's present-day leaders. Four of these five great universities are in Tokyo; three of the five are government-endowed institutions. The distribution by university attended is shown in Table 29.

It is clear that Tokyo University and other government-endowed universities (especially Kyoto, Hitotsubashi, Kyushu, Tōhoku, and Kobe) were the chief sources of Japan's top leadership. These higher institutions were established by the Japanese government for the purpose of supplying administrative and professional personnel for the civil, educational and industrial organizations. Among private universities, Keiō and Waseda, both in Tokyo, are important universities in producing national leaders. After 1897 the Japanese government started to establish new universities in addition to Tokyo University. Yet in 1922 the enrollment of Tokyo University was far greater than that of other government universities. This is one reason why the graduates of Tokyo

Table 29.   Higher Institution Attended by 1960 Leaders
(Percent)

Name of Institution	Total, Leaders	Business Leaders	Political Leaders	Intellectual Leaders
Tokyo	48	46	55	45
Kyoto	9	9	6	13
Hitotsubashi	8	13	2	2
Keiō	5	6	2	6
Waseda	4	4	5	3
Kyushu, Tōhoku, Kobe	6	8	2	4
All others in Japan	20	14	28	27
Total	100	100	100	100
Number	368	195	87	86

University among the present Japanese leaders outnumber those of the other universities. It appears also that Tokyo, Kyoto and other imperial universities supplied more leaders than the other government-endowed institutions and private universities. This explains differences of prestige existing among various universities and specialist schools.

A final aspect of the higher education of Japan's leaders to be considered is the major subject of study at the universities. As shown in table 30 the majority of the leaders are graduates of curricula of law or government, of economics, and of physical sciences or engineering. These three curricula account for 83 percent of the total. Ninety-four percent of the business leaders majored in one of these three curricula: 38 percent in economics, 32 percent in law or government, and 26 percent in physical sciences or engineering. Concentration on law or government is most marked among the political leaders. Major subjects of the intellectual leaders are scattered throughout all branches of sciences, arts and engineering. Other curricula include military sciences, medical sciences and others. The trends of major subjects of leaders between 1920 and 1960 are more or less similar for the three leadership groups with more concentration on law, economics and engineering.

In nearly all cases the men in the study sample received their higher education in Japanese institutions. Only 8 percent studied abroad, mostly at the graduate level. Intellectual leaders studied abroad most frequently among the three leadership groups (17 percent). Thirty-two men or 8 percent, out of a total of 412, studied abroad. Of this total, 10 studied in the United States, 9 in the United Kingdom, 4 in Germany, 3 in France, and 6 in other countries. If we contrast the foreign education of the 1960 elite with those of the two earlier elite groups, the numbers are surprisingly small in 1960—less than one-half of the Meiji elite and one-third of the Taishō elite. Presumably, in 1960 the educational prerequisite for leadership positions was the completion of undergraduate work in certain Japanese universities or colleges. Also the decrease of foreign education in the 1960 elite is due to the Second World War, which made it impossible to study in the allied countries. However, the advantage of foreign education in career success is less in the recent period.

Table 30.   Major Subject of Study: 1960 Leaders
(Percent)

Subject	Total, Leaders	Business Leaders	Political Leaders	Intellectual Leaders
Law or government	37	32	63	20
Economics	26	38	13	13
Physical science or engineering	20	26	7	23
Philosophy or social science	6	0	0	26
Literature or art	3	0	5	15
Other curricula	8	4	12	3
Total	100	100	100	100
Number	368	195	87	86

Less education in foreign institutions among the 1960 Japanese elite does not mean that they have had less experience abroad. Ninety-five percent have traveled abroad, and the average number of trips is slightly more than four per person. These are not for the most part casual visits since about one-half of the men who have traveled abroad have a total of more than one year of foreign residence, with 20 percent of them in residence in foreign countries for four or more years.

The education of the typical Japanese leader in 1960 can be quickly summarized as follows. He is a university graduate and a product of either a law, economics or engineering curriculum at a large Tokyo university. Although he has probably not studied abroad, he has made several lengthy foreign trips. He is then, by all odds, a highly literate person. Higher educational institutions were few a generation ago, and these were open only to the sons of the upper classes of Japanese society. An increasing proportion of university graduates among the total population in the post-Second World War period has had no effect on the recruitment pattern of the very top leaders of present Japanese society.

Trends in Education and Social Mobility in Japan's Elite Groups

The education and social mobility of Japan's elite groups in the modern era have been examined. In summarizing the data presented above, we consider four questions: (1) To what extent has the education of Japan's population at large changed in the course of modernization? Even before Meiji, Japan had a rather well-developed school system and had attained a relatively high literacy rate even among commoners. However, learning was dominated by Confucian doctrine and Japanese classics. Thus, the task was to integrate the separate schools owned by daimyo and individual school masters into a national educational system and also to introduce modern scientific learning. Above all the Meiji government early made the critical and far-sighted decision to invest heavily in public education, to make education compulsory, and to provide low-cost higher education. No more profitable investment in Japan's future could have been undertaken, and yet it must have seemed to many at the time an extravagant and risky undertaking.

The School Ordinance of 1872 provided elaborate educational plans for the country and the subsequent legal change supplemented them. These included the establishment of elementary schools, secondary schools, vocational schools, professional colleges and universities. The patterns of development are summarized in the recent publication, *Japan's Growth and Education*, as follows:

> The growth of Japanese educational facilities has been characterized by a very rapid growth of primary education in the early stages, followed by a rapid spurt in secondary education as the spread of primary education becomes complete, this being followed by an accelerating growth in higher education as the spread of secondary education in its turn reaches the saturation point. In speed and pattern of development, Japan resembles the United States and Russia more closely than either of the older European countries, Britain and France (where the growth in secondary education only starts

well after primary education has become universal) or new developing countries like India, where secondary and higher education expand more rapidly before the universal spread of primary education is completed.[19]

With regard to similar efforts on the part of other nations to industrialize, the conclusion is inescapable that education is the very center of an accurate explanation of Japan's industrial success. Very rapid enrollment into elementary schools of the entire school-age population attests to the range of the effort. Even though attendance at higher institutions was small in the early years, the extraordinary sacrifices made by families even today to gain for their sons not only admission to a university but admission to the finest universities shows the critical importance of higher education to modern career success.

(2) What were the levels of education in the political, business and intellectual elites in 1880, 1920 and 1960? The education of the 1880 elite can be characterized as follows: They all received education in the feudal school system, though a few also attended the new higher institutions after the Meiji Restoration. The education of commoners was confined largely to apprenticeship and temple schools. However, samurai received markedly higher education in traditional Confucian doctrine or in Western sciences and arts. Meiji business leaders were trained predominantly as apprentices or studied traditional Confucian doctrine. They were far more predisposed to conserving traditional values in contrast to the political and intellectual leaders. Almost all political leaders received higher education; about one-third had only traditional learning, but the rest went further by learning Western languages and sciences. The intellectual leaders were even more interested in Western languages and sciences and studied more often in Tokyo at the shogunal institutions, and later Tokyo Unitersity, or at Western universities. In general, the Meiji elite in the political, business and intellectual sectors represent rather varied education in terms of level and types among different feudal status backgrounds.

The 1920 leaders were the first products of the educational in-

---

[19]Ministry of Education, *Nihon no Seichō to Kyōiku*, pp. 18–23 (English translation by R. P. Dore).

vestment under the Meiji government. In comparison to the Meiji leaders they had much higher formal education in specialist schools and universities in Japan as well as Western countries. Most of them majored in law, economics, or engineering and travelled abroad extensively.

By 1960, the level of formal education of all elite groups was even higher. University graduation is now for all practical purposes an absolute prerequisite to advancement to a top level position in Japan. The education of the typical Japanese leader in 1960 can be characterized as follows: He is a university graduate, a product of either the law and government or the economics curriculum at a large Tokyo university, and although he has probably not studied abroad, he has made several lengthy foreign trips. He is, by all odds, a highly literate person.

(3) What are the contents of higher education among the political, business and intellectual elite in the modern era? Initial training in the earliest period of the modern era was in shogunal schools or in domain schools. These elites received further education in science in domestic or Western institutions. Political leaders in the 1880 period were far more disposed to Western influences than were the elite at that time. The early pattern was quickly changed and higher education in domestic universities very rapidly became customary for political leaders. By 1920 a specialist school or university education had already become a prerequisite to a political career. Almost all higher civil servants were educated at Tokyo University. Their schooling and subsequent careers constituted a closed system of bureaucracy in government as well as in larger political circles.

The group of business leaders experienced the greatest changes in the role of education in the recruitment of top executives over the period. Apprenticeship programs were soon superseded by a university education. The unusual receptivity of the Japanese business community to higher education and the early high demand for university-trained employees are characteristic interactions between business institutions and educational institutions in Japan. Since industrialization requires advanced sciences and technology, the rapid economic growth of modern Japan owes much to the special attention to and investment in education.

Trends of education for the intellectual elite over the period are no exception to the general patterns found in education for political and business leaders. It is evident that there are close relations between the academic and political and business communities in Japan. Since the positions of national leadership in the political, business and intellectual communities come largely from Tokyo University, the alumni of Tokyo University tend to form a school clique *(gakubatsu)* in important political, business, and professional organizations.

(4) Is educational opportunity open to all classes or limited to a certain privileged class? In traditional Japan, formal learning was largely the monopoly of the samurai, and the only form of technical training was the apprentice system. In the course of industrialization, Japan established an educational system functionally related to development of skill and technology and adopted Western learning. Though early classes in Tokyo University were dominated by samurai, the university and specialist schools established by the Meiji government were open to all classes. Sons of landlords, professional men, businessmen, and white collar people came to enroll in the leading university through a competitive examination. The low cost of the government-supported specialist school and universities provided a new channel for the recruitment of Japan's leadership positions. By expanding the chances for vertical social mobility, education no doubt accelerated the change from the traditional Japanese social structure to an industrialized society. Our research results on education of national leadership groups and population at large indicate that through educational facilities of various levels social mobility in Japanese society has steadily increased over the last eighty-year period.

Chapter 9

COMPARISONS AND CONCLUSIONS

Comparisons in Social Origins

A comparison of the business leaders of Japan, the United States, and the United Kingdom provides one kind of summary of the foregoing discussions. Historical data on the social origins and education of business and industrial leaders in these countries are available. It should be noted, however, that exact comparison is impossible because of differences in samples of business leadership and in classifications of social background of the business elite.[1] Despite the methodological difficulties we can observe some trends in family occupational backgrounds of business leaders in the three countries.

Table 31 includes the results of this examination of the occupations of fathers of business leaders over the past three generations with results obtained in the West in studies covering a comparable time range. Business leaders from economically privileged classes are dominant in all three countries. However, variations in the extent of industrialization and of social structure in each country

[1]The comparative data for the United States business elite are a total of 174 cases of industrialists of the 1870s in textile, railroads and steel by Gregory, Frances W. and Neu, Irene D., "The American Industrial Elite in the 1870's", in William Miller (ed.), *Men in Business* (Cambridge, Massachusetts: Harvard University Press, 1952), pp. 193–211, and a total of 1080 cases of big business executives in 1900, 1925 and 1950 in railroad, public utilities and industries of various kinds by Newcomer, Mabel, *The Big Business Executive: The Factor That Made Him, 1900–1950* (New York: Columbia University Press, 1955), pp. 52–64.

The business leaders in the United Kingdom, which we will use here for comparison, include 641 owners and directors in the steel industry from 1850 to 1953; see Erickson, Charlotte, *British Industrialists: Steel and Hosiery 1850–1950* (London: Cambridge University Press, 1959). See also *Management Succession* (London: The Acton Society Trust, 1956) and Copeman, G.H., *Leaders of British Industry* (London: Gee & Co., 1955).

Table 31. Occupational Origins of Business Leaders: Japan, United States, United Kingdom (Percent)

	Sons of Businessmen in Business Leadership			Sons of Farmers in Business Leadership			Sons of Professionals, and Samurai, Public Officials, in Business Leadership (Samurai Japan only, in parentheses)			Sons of Clerical Workers and Laborers in Business Leadership		
	Japan	United States	United Kingdom	Japan	United States	United Kingdom	Japan	United States	United Kingdom	Japan	United States	United Kingdom
1870–1889	50	51	57	22	25	13	7 (19)	16	19	2	8	11
1890–1909		49			21			23			7	
1910–1929	50	48	57	16	15	7	14 (18)	24	25	2	13	11
1930–1949			45			10			28			17
1950–1960	52	53	36	24	13	7	14 (1)	19	21	9	15	36

Sources: United States data from Gregory, Frances W. and Neu, Irene D., "The American Industrial Elite in the 1870s—Their Social Origins," in William Miller (ed.), *Men in Business* (Cambridge, Massachusetts: Harvard University Press, 1952), pp. 193–211; and Newcomer, Mabel, *The Big Business Executive* (New York: Columbia University Press, 1955), pp. 52–64.
United Kingdom data from Erickson, Charlotte, *British Industrialists: Steel and Hosiery 1850–1950* (London: Cambridge University Press, 1959). See also *Management Succession* (London: The Acton Society Trust, 1956) and Copeman, G. H., *Leaders of British Industry* (London: Gee & Co., 1955).

cause differences in the historical development of recruitment from occupational groups.

In the earliest period, sons of businessmen made up half or more of the business leaders in all three countries, in spite of the considerable disparity in the stage of industrial development achieved. In the industrially most advanced country, the United Kingdom, the proportion of business leaders from business backgrounds (industrialists, merchants, or bankers) was greatest. In succeeding generations that proportion remains similar in most industrial countries except in the United Kingdom, where the most recent group studied shows a marked drop in proportions of sons of businessmen. (It must be noted, though, that of the three national studies, that for the United Kingdom is by far the most limited in scope.)

The relative importance of family status in achieving business leadership is different in the three countries. The proportion of the business leaders who became the head of the same corporation as their fathers is surprisingly similar in the United States and Japan (10 to 20 percent).[2] Such inheritance was less common in the early period, increased in the next period, and decreased in the most recent period. Although the data for the United Kingdom show a pattern similar to that of the other countries, the amount of hereditary leadership is distinctly higher (21 to 36 percent).[3]

In the United Kingdom, a significant reduction in the proportion of business leaders who came from business families occurred after the First World War, and the downward trend was even more pronounced after the Second World War. It seems probable that since the First World War, business in the United Kingdom has given more opportunities for sons of white collar and manual workers to achieve leadership positions.

The unusual pattern in Japan of mobility of farmers' sons into business leadership is the more striking when compared with the other two countries. The proportions of sons of farmers were similar for the United States and Japan in the 1880s. Thereafter, consistent with the decline in size of the farm population, the representation of sons of farmers in American business leadership has declined sharply. In the United Kingdom, the proportion was low in

---

[2]Newcomer, p. 53.
[3]Erickson, p. 16.

the beginning, dropped even further, and has remained at a very low level, as would be expected given the minor role of British agriculture in the economy. In Japan, however, despite later but parallel declines in farm population, the proportion of sons of farmers has remained stable despite a temporary decline in 1920. It would seem then that a simple demographic explanation—e.g., that farmers' sons were forced to the cities in Japan by the shrinking of the farm population and thus turned to business—will not suffice since a similar phenomenon in the West shows different results.

There is a difference between Japan and the two Western countries that has an indeterminate influence on these proportions. Throughout this discussion, the landlord group and farm operators and tenants in Japan have been grouped together as "farmers." There is a real inaccuracy, of unknown degree, in this treatment since some part of the landlord group, by a considerable margin a greater source of business leaders than farm operators or tenants, were not "rural" or farmers, but were a renter group with urban interests. It appears that during the Meiji period, landlords were associated with their holdings more directly than was the case later when urban-located landlords lived off farm-based incomes. Thus grouping these as "farmers" is only partly accurate, and may to an unknown degree cause differences in trends between Japan and the West in mobility to business leadership.

In comparing the figures for sons of professional men and public officials we must remember the high proportion of sons of public officials in the Japanese case. For the United States only 10 to 15 percent of the combined group are sons of public officials (civil or military), while in Japan two-thirds are sons of public officials. Without definite information for separate comparison of the two occupational groups for the United Kingdom, it seems safe to state that mobility from professional backgrounds in Japan is much less than in the other two countries. This is due in part to a strong tendency to continue in the professions from father to son in Japan, and also no doubt to the much lower status in Japan of such professions as law, accountancy, and even medicine. However, it should be noted that if we count samurai (the Tokugawa civil and military administrative class) in this combined category, then the proportion with such background in the 1880s and in 1920 becomes distinctly higher in Japan than in the other two countries. The lower status occupational groups of white collar worker and laborer supply a much smaller share of business leadership in Japan than in the United States and the United Kingdom. This was initially due no doubt to the small size of these groups in the population. It is now due to inequality of social status of sons of laborers in Japanese society. It is of special interest to note the high proportion from these backgrounds in business leadership in the United Kingdom, suggesting that as the other economies move to similar maturity in development, a parallel decline in sons of businessmen in business leadership will occur to the advantage of men from white collar and laboring backgrounds who have received a university education.

With the close relationship to changes in family occupational status, career patterns in the business world in the three countries show a high degree of uniform change. The principal avenues to executive positions in business firms are founding a company, inheriting an executive position from one's father, and rising from the ranks within a firm or other firms.

On careers of United Kingdom industrialists of 1865, Erickson indicates that 56 percent of those studied had founded their own firms.[4] This percentage declined drastically in the following periods, to 15 percent in 1905–25 and only 3 percent in 1957. Hereditary leadership, with a strong association of family control of an industrial firm and apprentice training of sons for succession to executive position, was next in frequency. The peak of control by family or investor types occurred between 1905 and 1925 (51 percent). Even in 1953, family appointees who held leading positions in British industry in the most recent period still constituted 40 percent of the total. Although the percentage of salaried administrators or professional managers has gradually increased (from 14 percent in 1865 to 57 percent in 1953), the dominant characteristic of industrial leadership recruitment in the United Kingdom is the strong influence of aristocratic families. Inheritance in large firms in the United Kingdom involves not only ownership but also managerial positions. Erickson indicates that "the establishment of a family dynasty in British industry is not always the result of founding or investing in the firm. Two generations of the same family, whose role was primarily managerial rather than proprietary, have controlled some companies."[5]

The general trends of change in career patterns for United States business leaders are in much the same direction as in the United Kingdom, with some important differences. First, inheritance of executive office is far less common in the United States. Newcomer found that fewer than one in four (23 percent) executives in large American industrial corporations in 1950 had achieved their positions chiefly by inheritance or investment.[6] Second, success in another company is a more important means of achieving executive positions in the United States than in the United Kingdom. Newcomer indicates that these men constitute almost one-fifth (18 percent) of the business and industrial leaders studied in 1950. The most striking trend is the increase in the proportion of executives who have worked their way up within the company. They account for 18 percent in 1900 and 51 percent in 1950.

In comparison with these two countries, Japan has seen more drastic change in business career patterns. After two generations of industrialization, including periods of founding enterprises and some change by inheritance, a true managerial revolution took place in Japan. At present Japan's executive positions seem less related to direct family inheritance or investment than those in the other two countries. Achieving an executive position in a large business firm in Japan is for the most part determined by a bureaucratic career in the lower managerial echelons. Such careers require a higher formal education and long service. This special career pattern in Japanese business leaders suggests a need to examine the function of formal education for a business career.

Comparisons in Education

The question of what constitutes the best education for business leadership has not yet been agreed upon in either the United

[4]Erickson, p. 51.
[5]Erickson, p. 52.
[6]Newcomer, p. 102.
[7]Erickson, pp. 30–44; Newcomer, pp. 63–82.

Kingdom or the United States.[7] The relationship between the industrial community and education is different in the two. Acceptance of college or university graduates in the business and industrial community is higher in the United States than in the United Kingdom.

In Japan, a late industrializer, higher education has recently gained importance in recruiting executives for business and industry. A comparison of the proportion of university-educated business leaders in Japan, the United States, and the United Kingdom, as shown in chart 1, indicates striking differences. The business leaders of Japan are by a good margin the best educated. The very rapid rise in the proportion of univeristy graduates has already been remarked on.

The proportion of university or college graduates in business leadership in the United Kingdom is strikingly low. In the United Kingdom, 15 percent of the 1875–95 sample were men who are known to have had university or college degrees. The proportion has probably little more than doubled since. Of the 1940 sample, 31 percent of the men are known to have had a university education.[8] The United Kingdom lags very far behind both the United States and Japan in this respect. Other studies confirm the general proportion shown in chart 1. The Acton Society[9] found that 30 percent of the top managers in the large firms it studied were college graduates, and Copeman[10] gave a figure of 36 percent from his questioning of directors of public corporations.

Cultural conditions are related to this phenomenon. Erickson comments: "It is commonly believed that the university graduate was almost unknown in nineteenth century British industry, and that the practical man reigned supreme."[11] Furthermore, it is well known that business careers are viewed less favorably by graduates of British universities than are professional and civil service careers.[12] There is an increased number of university graduates in British industry in the more recent period; however, it is indicated that employment of university trainees "was not part of a conscious recruitment policy on the part of firms in the industry, but a

---

[8]Erickson, p. 37.
[9]*Management Succession,* p. 9.
[10]Copeman, p. 102.
[11]Erickson, p. 35.

reflection of the high degree of family control and the attitudes of those families that education for social status was to be preferred

Chart 1.   Proportion of University Graduates Among Business Leaders:
Japan, United States, United Kingdom
(Percent)

Sources: United States data from Newcomer, Mabel, *The Big Business Execu-*
tive (New York: Columbia University Press, 1955), pp. 65–82.
United Kingdom data from Erickson, Charlotte, *British Industrialists:*
Steel and Hosiery 1850–1950 (London: Cambridge University Press,
1959), p. 37 and Copeman, G. H., *Leaders of British Industry* (London:
Gee & Co., 1955), p. 100.

Note to Chart I

Japan	1880	17%
	1920	46%
	1960	71%
United States	1900	28%
	1925	40%
	1950	62%
United Kingdom	1885	15%
	1915	19%
	1940	31%
	1952	36%

to specific education for an industrial career."[13] In general the slow development of relationships between industry and scientific and technical institutions is characteristic of the United Kingdom.

The education of American business leaders is quite different from the common notion of the self-made man with little formal education. From the earlier period their recruitment was not based on a rigorous apprenticeship, but in large part on academic education. The percentage that had attended college was more than one-third (37 percent) even among the industrial elite of the 1870s although it is not known how many had completed college or university.[14] The figures in chart 1 for 1900–1950 indicate only those who graduated from a college or university.[15] They show the changes in formal education of the top executives over the period covered. The proportion of university graduates among large business leaders is distinctly higher in the United States than in the United Kingdom. Furthermore, there is as expected a marked increase in the level of formal education among younger executives in the United States. Also it should be noted that cooperation between industry and university for industrial activities is most extensive and intensive in the United States at present.

The proportion of business leaders with a university or college education shows a dramatic change in Japan. Beginning with a very low proportion of leaders with university education, Japanese business institutions soon found great value in university training and began to recruit top executives on the basis of educational qualifications. Conscious efforts to hire university graduates for training as future executives were made by the first generation of Japanese business leaders. The effect became evident in the higher educational level of the 1920 business leaders. The proportion of university graduates among the 1960 business leaders suggests that university education is now almost prerequisite for business leadership. It is quite clear that within another decade virtually every major business position in Japan will be filled by a university graduate.

There are different patterns of academic-industrial cooperation in the three countries. The close connection between formal edu-

---

[12]Lipset and Bendix, p. 41.
[13]Erickson, p. 38.
[14]Gregory and Neu, p. 203.

cation and a business career in Japan's early modern era may help to explain why organizational and technical innovations find so ready an audience in the Japanese business community. According to Thomas C. Smith, the reason for emphasis on educational qualification in Japanese industry is that "the later and more rapid industrial development is, the sharper must be the break between the axiomatic, technical knowledge handed down from father to son and from master to apprentice on the one hand, and the knowledge required by modern industry and finance on the other."[16] In order to adopt advanced technology and industrial arts in industrial operations it was necessary for Japan's business leaders to acquire basic knowledge and skills through the aid of scientific and technological institutions.

Conclusions

In concluding this empirical report on some aspects of Japan's business leadership in the modern era, it is worthwhile to note some implications of our data for economic development and changes in social structure.

First, some of the reasons why Japan succeeded in the take-off from a traditional agrarian society and in driving to industrial maturity are implicit in the dynamics of social mobility. The Tokugawa feudal regime rigidly defined the ascriptive status of people and prohibited mobility in status, residence, and occupation. However, this traditional social system gave way to industrialization. The process of recruiting an industrializing elite was not dominated by a single social status or class. From the beginning, there was no homogeneous business class monopolizing the direction of business and industry. Rather the elite came from the heterogeneous social origins of traditional merchants, samurai, and well-to-do farmers, from all parts of the country. No revolutionary change in leadership groups occurred, but there was a

---

[15]Newcomer, p. 68.
[16]Smith, Thomas C., "Landlords' Sons in the Business Elite," *Economic Development and Cultural Change*, IX, I, Part II, (October 1960), p. 100.

strong tendency toward stability in recruitment of leaders from various backgrounds. This stability was sustained by a principle of achievement and new channels for social mobility.

Secondly, the development of an education system provided a new channel for recruitment of leaders. The ready access of most levels of the society to universities and specialist schools has been essential to stability in leadership recruitment. Educational experiences for business leaders have changed from apprentice training in business firms to scientific and technological training in universities. Consequently, the prevalent pattern of mobility to business leadership has changed from a traditional inheritance or entrepreneur type to a bureaucratic or professional type. The role of education in opening up chances for vertical social mobility no doubt accelerated the changing of the Japanese traditional social structure to that of an industrialized society.

Education made it possible for all classes of people to move from an ascriptive status in a system of traditional social stratification to new positions in an industrialized society. Vertical mobility in Japanese society depended to a large extent upon how much education a man received. The availability of higher education for different people of feudal status in all three leadership groups in Japan has been discussed. The pattern of relationships between formal education and social classes is basically the same for business leaders as for other leadership groups.

The ways in which the business leaders of different status backgrounds received higher education were as follows: Samurai entered business in the early period of industrialization almost exclusively with higher education. Sons of merchants, however, had rarely received higher education other than apprenticeship. Although differences in amount of education among different feudal status groups persisted, as time passed the percentage of sons of government officials, professional men, executives or owners of large businesses, landowners, and finally owners of small businesses receiving university education increased. Sons of industrial workers and farmers lagged behind, but those who did receive a university education found that their social origin had little effect on the course of their bureaucratic career in government or private business.

Thirdly, in the career pattern of the Japanese business elite, some special practices of executive development are noteworthy. Methods of training executives have changed from rigorous apprenticeship in management for heirs and future entrepreneurs to modern development systems designed to produce professional and bureaucratic managers. Present-day Japanese business enterprises have institutionalized ways of selecting executives largely on the basis of education, length of service in the company, and career achievement. A typical career begins with entrance examinations on academic subjects right after graduation from a university. For those who are accepted, a lifetime commitment to the company is strongly implied. Men move up step by step in an intricate hierarchy. Promotion is shaped by a special merit system that has been based largely on seniority. However, it is now common for larger corporations to make promotion dependent on systematic performance appraisals often associated with examinations on specialized work and management problems.

Thus, Japanese executive development depends primarily upon training and experience within a company. Much less importance is attached to success in management or to professional skills demonstrated in another company. The qualification of a top executive is assessed not by his ability to deal with management matters but by his loyalty to the organization. Present-day Japanese business leaders must accept the goals, values, and patterns of authority and feel a lifetime commitment to the company. Management effectiveness or ineffectiveness in Japanese industrial organizations may depend on these special patterns of executive development.

APPENDICES

Appendix I

JAPANESE BUSINESS LEADERS IN 1970[1]

This appendix provides a more up-to-date profile of the Japanese business leaders. A questionnaire survey of the social backgrounds of the Japanese business leaders was given again in 1970.* The questionnaire were designed to be comparable to the one in 1960. Comparing the social backgrounds of 1970 Japanese business leaders to those of 1960 yields an accurate picture of the men who have led Japanese business and industry during the past decade.

The definitions of 1970 business leaders are the same as those of 1960 and include the five top executive positions in the largest firms in the Japanese business and industrial world: the chairman of the board of directors, the president, the vice president, and the two most highly placed or senior managing directors (*senmu torishimariyaku* and *jōmu torishimariyaku*). [The details of the research methods for the 1960 business leaders are described in Appendix II.]

The largest firms were identified in terms of amount of capitalization in 1960 and the four hundred largest firms were selected. Our research subjects in 1970 were the top executives of about five hundred of the largest firms. It seems legitimate to include more firms in 1970 than in 1960 since more large firms emerged during the period.

[1]This is a revised version of the paper by Mannari, Hiroshi and Abegglen, James C., "The Japanese Business Leaders in 1960 and 1970: Their Social Origins, Education and Career Patterns," *Social and Cultural Background of Labor-Management Relations in Asian Countries*, (Proceedings of the 1971 Asian Regional Conference on Industrial Relations, Tokyo, Japan) (The Japan Institute of Labour, 1972), pp. 43–67.

*The 1970 questionnaire research has been done by James C. Abegglen, president, The Boston Consulting Group, Inc., Tokyo and Hiroshi Mannari, professor, Kwansei Gakuin University, Nishinomiya. The questionnaire was mailed from the Tokyo office of the Boston Consulting Group in November, 1970.

Executive in the defined positions of the largest firms in 1960 totalled 1525 and in 1970, 3310. A questionnaire on family occupational background, education, and career (total of sixteen questions) was sent to each person. Replies received from 985 or 65 percent in the 1960 sample and 1080 or 33 percent in the 1970 sample. The distribution of respondents among Japanese business leaders both in 1960 and 1970 positions is shown in the following table:

Table 1.   Distribution of Respondents by Positions among Japanese Business Leaders in 1960 and 1970.

	1960	1970
Chairman	6%	6%
President	27	13
Vice president	15	15
Senior managing director (senmu)	22	26
Senior managing director (jōmu)	30	40
Percent total	100	100
Total number	985	1080
Total sample	1525	3310

The lower response rate in the 1970 sample than in the 1960 sample is largely due to the fact that we had the supporting letter from the Secretary of the Japan Federation of Employers' Association in our questionnaires to all the Japanese business leaders in 1960, but not in 1970.

The two following facts should be noted about the comparability of the responses to the questionnaire researches of 1960 and 1970. First, we had a higher proportion of responses from the 1960 presidents group but markedly less from the 1970 group. This is due to the fact that for the group of chief executives in 1960 we administered the questionnaires twice: the first time as a pilot study sample for 360 leading businessmen, mostly chief executives of the largest firms in 1959; the second time we included the chief executives as part of the five top executive positions in the 400 largest firms in 1960. Thus, the presidents group in 1960 received more requests to fill questionnaires than the rest. This is the major reason for the higher proportion on the part of the 1960 presidents.

Second, the proportion of senior-managing directors, especially jōmu, is higher in the 1970 sample. As we stated in the research methods section this is due to the fact that in 1960 we controlled this sample by including only one out of three men in this position in order to avoid overrepresentation of this group. However, there was no such control for the 1970 sample.

Therefore, there is the possibility of some distortion between the 1960 and the 1970 sample. This distortion may in turn produce a deviation in the research results. In order to examine this question we tried to review whether trend-patterns in the distribution of occupation of fathers, education and size of community of birth place of the business leaders in each of the five top executive groups in 1960 and 1970 are different or not. This examination indicated that the major trend-patterns of distribution for these variables over the period follow exactly the same patterns which are revealed in the total sample as well as in each of the five different top executive groups.

We acknowledge that this test will not make entirely clear the issue of sample dissimilarities. However, this allows us to conclude that our major findings in trend are sound. We also note that the respondents among the 1970 business leaders represent the top executives in Japan and still provide the best available comparative sample for the 1960 sample.

These data help us to determine the more recent changes in recruitment patterns for business leaders with regard to their backgrounds and qualifications. Since Japan has experienced very rapid economic growth and technological change in the decade, it is of special interest to explore whether any comparable changes in the social structure of the nation's elite have also occurred. During this period the Japanese gross national product has grown almost four times,[2] one of the highest increases among industrialized nations. Business activities have developed into multinational operations. The social structure in terms of division of labor has been drastically changed from primary industry to secondary and serv-

---

[2]Bureau of Statistics, Office of the Prime Minister, *Japan Statistical Yearbook, 1970*, p. 489.

ice industries. Recent studies[3] in occupational structure and economic development indicate that from 1960 to 1965 Japan transformed itself from an industry-dominated society to the service
industry type.

In accordance with these economic and social changes, social
mobility measured in terms of father's occupational position in
relation to the son's has increased both in terms of gross and net
mobility. We should analyze the occupational mobility of Japanese business leaders in 1970 with reference to the analysis of
social mobility in Japanese society from more recent studies.[4]

Also we have some new researches on the social characteristics
of American and European chief executives. These data will permit a comparison of Japanese business leaders with their American
and European counterparts.[5]

Age and Executive Hierarchy

The age factor in the Japanese business hierarchy is unique
among industrial countries. In spite of the rapid growth of their
economy from 1960 through 1970 the Japanese maintain a strong
seniority principle among other factors in selecting the various
ranks of top executives. Drastic expansion of business usually provides opportunities for new and young talent to run businesses. It
is thus strange that only a few younger businessmen are included
in the topmost positions.

In 1970 their median age is 58.9 years. Only 1 percent are under

[3]Tominaga, Ken'ichi, "Shakaiidō no Sūseibunseki, 1955–1965" (Trend Analysis of
Social Mobility 1955–1965), *Japanese Sociological Review*, Vol. 21, No. 1, June 1970, pp.
2–24. Naoi, Atsushi, "Keizai Hatten to Shokugyō Kōzō no Hendō, (Occupational
Structure of Japan and Economic Development), *Nihon Rōdō Kyōkai Zasshi*, Vol. 12,
No. 12, Dec. 1970, pp. 14–27.
[4]Yasuda, Saburō, *Shakaiidō no Kenkyū* (Studies in Social Mobility) (Tokyo: Tokyo
Daigaku Shuppan-kai, 1971); Tominaga, Ken'ichi, "Studies on Social Stratification
and Social Mobility in Japan: 1955–1967," edited by Norbeck, Edward and Parman,
Susan, *The Study of Japan in the Behavioral Sciences*, Rice University Studies, Vol. 56,
No. 4, Fall 1970, pp. 130–49; Tominaga, Ken'ichi, "Shakaiidō no Katei Bunseki,"
edited by Tominaga, Ken'ichi and Kurosawa, Susumu, *Kaikyū to Chiikishakai* (Class
and Community) (Tokyo: Chuō Kōronsha, 1971), pp. 133–89.
[5]Bettignies, H. C. de, "Leaders Across the Ocean: Comparing American and
European Chief Executives," *European Business*, No. 26, Summer 1970.

40 years of age and only 7 percent are under 50 years. A total of 23 percent of the business leaders is under 55 years, and a great majority of top executives (77 percent) are over 56 years old. Thirty-eight percent are over 61 years old.

In reviewing the age composition of the present Japanese business leaders, certain characteristics stand out. First, the age structure of the Japanese management hierarchy is very stable during the period betwen 1960 and 1970, as shown in the following table:

Table 2. Median Age of Japanese Business Leaders in 1960 and 1970 by Position

Type of Position	1960	1970
Chairman	66.6 years	67.4 years
President	62.4	61.8
Vice president	58.7	59.8
Senior managing director (I), (senmu)	57.7	58.5
Senior managing director (II), (jōmu)	55.9	56.6
	58.6	58.9

The age distribution by position for Japanese top management is almost identical in 1960 and 1970. Presidents are slightly younger in 1970, but the rest of the executives are slightly older. An important feature of the data is that as a whole Japanese top executives are not getting younger but older.

Second, the top management hierarchy has a definite order in accordance with seniority. Japanese top management personnel have been recruited on the basis of a long career within the organization. Most of the Japanese business leaders studied here (71 percent) have worked for their present firms more than twenty years and have assumed their present executive positions almost invaribly after 1960. The years of tenure relative to present age is shown in the following:

The median number of tenure years in 1970 is a little shorter (4.8 years) than that of 1960 (5.5 years). It is clear that recently the length of time required to assume each top position has been longer. The duration in each position varies and some notes are

Table 3.   Median Years of Tenure and Present Age of Japanese Business Leaders in 1960 and 1970 by Position

	1960		1970	
	Median Tenure Years	Present Age	Median Tenure Years	Present Age
Chairman	6.0	66.6	4.9	67.4
President	9.8	62.4	8.3	61.8
Vice president	4.8	58.7	3.9	59.8
Senior managing director I	3.7	57.7	3.9	58.5
Senior managing director II	4.7	55.9	4.3	56.6
Average	5.5	58.6	4.8	58.9

necessary. The average years of tenure for president are much greater than that of the others. It is almost 10 years in 1960 and 8 years in 1970. Also the president is nominated from among the vice presidents and senior managing directors. Moreover, in Japanese management, the position of chairman of the board of directors is not determined by ownership; rather it is the position that the successful president assumes after being chief executive. This is one of the reasons that Japanese chairmen are older than the others. Finally, the man nominated for president has usually assumed the topmost position for about 15 years in 1960, i.e., 9.8 years plus 6.0 years, and 13 years in 1970, i.e., 8.3 years plus 4.9 years. The other executives, besides the chairman and the president, stay in their positions a shorter time. They are either promoted to higher executive positions or retired.

The age factor in Japanese management seems to indicate that age and length of tenure for chairman and president are the bases for selecting major executives. These traits are somewhat different from those of other countries to be considered, but they provide a strong tendency for consistency and stability in Japanese management.

The age of Japanese top executives should be evaluated in comparative terms. Survey data for the U.S. and European business elites are available. Table 4 shows the age distribution of chief executives in several countries. The Japanese data are based on

141 presidents in our research. There are significant differences in the general pattern of age distribution among these industrial countries. Japanese presidents are by far the oldest, averaging 62 years in comparison with the U.S. presidents' 55 years and the average of 57 years for all European chief executives. The average within Europe varies.

Thus, Japanese presidents are about 7 years older than the U.S. presidents and 5 years older than the European presidents. These great differences in age mean that Japanese presidents become chief executives at an age when their U.S. and European counterparts are retiring from their positions.

While we concluded that for the 1960 business leaders age and the seniority principle tend to prevent innovative actions in modern management and technology in further advancement of industrialization, this is not the case. Considering the age distribution in several industrial countries in the world, it seems that the age factor is not directly related to the rate of economic development.

Table 4.   Age Distribution of President in Industrial Countries

Age	Japan 1970	U.S. 1966	All Europe 1968	France 1968	U. K. 1968	Germany 1968
Under 50 years	6	23	26	15	25	30
50–9	30	51	34	36	46	25
Over 60 years	64	26	40	49	29	45
Percent	100	100	100	100	100	100
Number	140	492	576			

Source: Hall, D. J., Bettignies, H. C. de and Amado-Fischgrund, G., "The European Business Elite," *European Business,* No. 23, October 1969 for European executives and Bettignies, H. C. de, "Leaders Across the Ocean: Comparing American and European Chief Executives," *European Business,* No. 26, Summer 1970, p. 57 for U.S. executives.

Social Origins and Mobility

What are the occupational backgrounds of the 1970 Japanese business leaders? Are there any changes in their social origins as measured by the occupation of their fathers and grandfathers? We will try to determine the occupation of their fathers and note changes from the 1960 sample.

The first two vertical columns of table 5 show the occupation of fathers for the Japanese business leaders of 1970 in comparison to that in 1960. It is clear that not all occupational backgrounds are equally represented in top level business positions. In 1970 sons of owners and executives of large or medium business concerns are represented in considerably greater proportion than men with other occupational backgrounds. More than one-fourth of the present leaders are sons of large business executives. Sons of laborers, operating farmers and white collar workers in private business are few.

In comparing business leaders of 1970 to those of 1960, a considerable change in patterns of recruitment is observable. Sons of laborers, owners of small businesses and professions are almost equally represented in 1960 and 1970. However, there are two marked trends. First, the proportion of sons of executives of large businesses, government officials and military officers, and professions, who constitute an upper white collar group, has increased remarkably from 43 percent to 53 percent. The lower white collar group, consisting of employees in public services and private businesses, has declined. Sons of owners of large or medium firms have decreased. In general these trends indicate that administrators or professionals rather than owners have been gaining as a recruitment source of business leaders. Second, the proportion of landlords and farmers, who were the single largest source of business leaders in 1960, has been decreasing in accordance with the decrease of those groups in the population at large.

The fourth vertical column provides the percent distribution of adult employed males in 1930. This distribution is drawn from the census[6] assumed to be comparable to the occupational distribution of the fathers of 1970 business leaders. A comparison of the second and fourth columns shows that less than 1 percent (.54 percent) of the 1930 adult male population were government officials, but 14.4 percent of the 1970 business leaders are the sons of government officials. Only 2.7 percent (estimated) of the 1930 adult

---

[6]Bureau of Statistics, Imperial Cabinet, *Shokugyō to Sangyō : 1930 Kokusei Chōsa Hōkoku*, (Occupation and Industry: Census Report of 1930), Vol. II, 1935.

Table 5. Occupation of Fathers of Japanese Business Leaders in 1960 and 1970 and Mobility Relative to the General Population

Occupation	Father of Leaders		Japan's Population, Adult Employed Males		Ratio of Leaders' Father to Population (1 = 100)	
	1960	1970	1920	1930	1960	1970
Government official	11.5%	14.4%	.36%	.54%	3194	2667
Government official	9.8	10.8	.27	.41	3629	2634
Military officer	1.7	3.6	.09	.13	1889	2769
Owner or manager, large or medium business	22.0	27.9	1.75	2.73	1257	1021
Owner	11.5	8.7				
Executive	10.5	19.2				
Profession	9.7	10.6	1.32	2.26	735	469
Professor	2.5	2.1	.04	.06	6250	3500
Lawyer	.7	.9	.03	.04	2333	2250
Engineer and others	3.3	3.7	.43	.76	767	487
Doctor	2.5	3.3	.45	.66	556	500
Priest	.7	.6	.37	.74	189	82
Small business owner	21.6	21.8	13.17	8.98	164	242
White collar worker	9.0	6.9	7.89	9.30	114	74
Teacher or clerk in public office	6.5	5.5	2.72	3.18	238	173
Clerk or sales, private business	2.5	1.4	5.17	6.12	48	23
Laborer	1.3	1.5	26.29	30.30	5	5
Farmer	24.0	16.9	48.31	43.32	49	39
Landlord	17.3	12.1	7.25	6.48	238	187
Operating farmer	6.7	4.8	41.06	36.84	16	13
Other occupations	.9	0.0	.91	2.57	0	0
Percent total	100.0	100.0	100.00	100.00		
Number total	974	1062	17 million	19 million		

males were business owners or executives of large or medium business firms, whereas 27.9 percent of the 1970 business leaders are sons of business owners or executives of large business firms. Although 30.3 percent of the adult males were laborers, only 1.5 percent of the 1970 Japanese business leaders are sons of laborers.

The third and fourth columns of table 5 show the distribution of population of adult employed males in 1920 and 1930. There has been an expected shift in occupations in response to industrialization. Along with gradual decreases of farmers and small business owners (traditional industries), all the new industrial occupations have substantially increased. Although Japan still had a larger proportion of farmers (43.3 percent) in 1930, the occupational structure had changed to that of industrial countries. The 1970 Japanese business leaders started their business careers in the 1930s, after Japan became fully industrialized.

The sixth column shows the ratio between the occupational distribution in the whole population and that of the fathers of 1970 business leaders. It is designed to be compared with the ratio for 1960 business leaders in the fifth column.

Government officials are by far the most overrepresented. Ownership or top executive positions may have played a certain role in determining the careers of their sons. Sons of professional men stand third in rank. Sons of college and university professors and lawyers are extremely well represented among the business leaders. Sons of doctors, engineers and other professions are moderately well represented. Sons of priests are underrepresented relative to their proportion.

Owners of small business firms stand fourth in rank. Nine percent of the 1930 population and 22 percent of the fathers of the business leaders of 1970 were in this occupation. The ratio is 242. This is the only group that had increased its productive ratio over 1960. Sons of white collar workers stand fifth in rank. The ratio (74) is below the average expectation. A sharp difference in frequency is observable among white collar workers according to specific occupations. Sons of teachers and clerks in public offices are much better represented than sons of clerks and sales people in private business. The latter group had sharply reduced its productive ratio over 1960.

It is clear that movement to business leadership is limited for sons of farmers and manual workers of all kinds. The chances for sons of laborers are also small. It is striking that sons of laborers comprise only 1.5 percent of the 1970 business leaders, whereas almost one-third (30.3 percent) of the population in 1930 were laborers. The ratio is 30.3:1.5 or 5 per 100. This occupational group is the least likely to produce business leaders.

Seventeen percent of the 1970 business leaders are sons of farmers, who constituted 43 percent of the 1930 population. They decreased as a source of business leaders from 24 percent in 1960 to 17 percent in 1970. Farmers also decreased in total population, from 48 percent in 1920 to 43 percent in 1930. The ratio also decreased, from 49 for 1960 business leaders to 39 in 1970. Thus it is safe to predict that in the future farmers, both landlords and operating farmers, will play an even smaller role in the recruitment of business leaders. However, if we look at landlords and operating farmers separately, we see that the former almost doubled the expected rate, but the latter's ratio is only 13.

The following points are noted in considering the class differentiation of productive ratios for the 1970 business leaders.

First, the order of the productive ratios for each occupation is generally consistent with the prestige hierarchy in occupational ranking given by Japanese society.[7] Those occupational groups that show the highest ratio (professor, government official, lawyer and executive of large firms) received the highest scores in studies of social ranking. These reveal that the order of productive ratios for business leaders in our research is closely paralleled by the score for occupational ranking in present-day Japan.

Second, the statistics leave no doubt that the 1970 business elite was composed chiefly of the sons of men who had relatively high occupational status: government officials, businessmen, and professional men. For sons of men of upper status chances of assuming leadership are markedly high. In spite of the great increase in top executive positions that has accompanied rapid industrialization, big business firms in Japan have tended to recruit their top executive force principally from the urban upper class.

Third, is Japanese society becoming more open or less open in

---

[7]Odaka, Kunio, *Shokugyō to Kaiso* (Occupation and Stratification) (Tokyo: Mainichi Shimbun), 1958. Nishihira, Shigeki, *Shokugyō no Shakaiteki Hyōka* (Social Evaluation of Occupations) (Tokyo: Tōkeisūri Kenkyūjo, 1965).

recruiting business leaders? On the basis of 1960 data, we initially assumed there were increased opportunities for business leadership for men of the middle and lower classes. However, this is not the case in 1970. The productive ratio of leaders in the urban upper class, consisting of government officials, business executives and professions in 1970, has dropped from 1960. This may indicate that access to business leadership is becoming more open. However, this is mainly due to the increase in the proportion of the urban upper class among Japan's total work force. Small business owners, a traditional middle class group, produced more in terms of productive ratio in 1970 than 1960. But this is also due to the reduction of their proportion in the total population. In the case of white collar workers, laborers and farmers, chances to achieve business leadership have remained the same or declined. For lower occupational groups movement into the business hierarchy was rare in 1970.

Fourth, these data tell us that for men of the upper classes chances for becoming business leaders have increased over 1960, but for the middle and lower classes, they have decreased.

In general the recruitment patterns of 1970 business leaders reveal a tendency to restrictiveness. They are more concentrated in sons of the urban upper class. The reasons behind these changes are beyond our present task, but it seems that the sources of leaders in 1970 has shifted from traditional occupational groups to urban industrial ones: 1970 business executives are recruited from the urban business class rather than from non-industrial occupation groups as was the case in 1960.

In the future, Japanese business leadership may continue to be drawn from urban business groups. Our research data suggest that the recruitment pattern has been tending to change in this direction.

Occupational Mobility Pattern from Paternal Grandfathers to Fathers of the 1970 Business Leaders

In examining occupational mobility across three generations we have indicated that there was a great deal of mobility into higher occupational groups from the grandfathers to the fathers of the 1960 business leaders. There was a major movement from farm into urban occupations. Almost one-half of the grandfathers of 1960 business leaders were farmers. One-half of them turned to urban occupations as a transitional step. Finally their sons reached the topmost positions. There was a pronounced tendency toward maintenance of high social status. It seems that a new pattern has been emerging with the 1970 business leaders.

The occupational distribution of paternal grandfathers and fathers of the 1970 Japanese business leaders in comparison to that of 1960 is given in table 6. General patterns in the occupational distribution of grandfathers and fathers in 1970 are similar to those of 1960. However, the patterns of occupational mobility are more pronounced in the reduction of landlords, farmers and samurai. There are great increases for all the rest of the occupations from grandfather to father in 1970.

A farm background for fathers of 1970 business leaders is substantially less than in 1960. But if we check the occupation of

Table 6. Distribution of Occupation of Paternal Grandfathers and Fathers of the 1960 and 1970 Business Leaders

	1960		1970	
Occupation	Grandfather	Father	Grandfather	Father
Laborer	1%	1%	1%	1.5%
Landlord and farmer	48	24	47	17
White collar worker	2	9	4	7
Owner of small business	18	21.5	20	22
Owner of large or medium business	6	11.5	5	9
Executive of large or medium business	2	10.5	3	19
Government official	4	11.5	6	14
Professions	6	10	8	10.5
Others including samurai	13	1	6	0
Percent total	100	100.0	100	100.0
Number total	857	974	956	1062

grandfathers of 1960 and 1970 business leaders, the two are at about the same level. Thus, in 1970 more movement off the farm into urban occupations had taken place in the generation from grandfather and father. About one-half of the grandfathers were farmers both in 1960 and 1970. While one-half of the sons of grandfathers remained farmers and the other half moved out in 1960, one-third remained farmers and two-thirds moved out in 1970. Most of them became executives of large businesses, government officials and professionals. These groups constitute the major sources of 1970 business leaders.

A category that shows an interesting pattern is that of samurai. The warrior class was abolished at the beginning of the Meiji period (1872). Six percent of grandfathers were identified as being samurai, but no fathers as samurai. However, 32.2 percent of the business leaders identified themselves as being of "samurai background." This proportion is almost the same as the 1960 level (31.5 percent). Thus, the warrior class of the late Tokugawa period assumes great importance as a source of modern business leaders. A recent analysis of social stratification and mobility in Japanese society[8] indicated that samurai descendants consistently tended to be more strongly oriented than other people toward upward social movement and were in fact were more upwardly mobile than others.

A separate analysis of samurai decendants in our 1970 data also shows that they appear significantly more frequently as government officials, large business executives and professional men in the fathers' generation of the 1970 business leaders. They appear less frequently as farmers, small business and large business owners. These occupational mobility patterns for the samurai are similar to the 1960 sample described in detail in chapter 2.

Nearly all the remaining occupational categories show percentage increases from the grandfather's generation to that of the father. The following occupations show substantial increases in the proportions of fathers over those of grandfathers: executives of large or medium business firms, white collar workers, government officials and military officers, professional men and owners of large or medium businesses.

---

[8]Yasuda, Saburō, *op. cit.* pp. 292–316.

For these occupational groups, generational upward mobility and maintenance of once achieved higher status are marked. It should be noted, however, that the laboring class, which greatly increased in the total population during the last three generations, failed to participate in the general upward mobility across the three generations both for 1960 and 1970 business leaders.

Three generations of occupational succession and mobility for business leaders during the period from 1960 to 1970 show that larger mobility in favor of urban executive, official and professional classes has taken place.

Comparison of the Origins of Chief Executives

For 1960 Japanese business leaders, we have made detailed comparisons with the fathers' occupation of business leaders in the U.S. and the U.K. in the 1950s. These comparisons suggest somewhat different rates of recruitment of business leaders from the several occupational backgrounds, with the marked exception of the very limited access of Japan's manual workers to business leadership. Our conclusion was that the different rate for each occupation in the three countries could be explained by both the extent of industrial maturity of the country and cultural differences. Our major finding is that Japanese business leaders were recruited more from non-business occupations because Japan was in a less-developed state of industrial maturity. There were also relatively few cases of inheritance in Japanese top executive positions. This practice reflects a certain relation of Japanese culture to achievement.

Are there any changes in origin of the 1970 business leaders in contrast to more recent data from the U.S. and European countries? Direct comparable data are not available. However, social backgrounds of American and European chief executives are known. So we made a separate analysis of the presidents from our entire sample and compared them. It should be noted that the distributions of occupation of father between this president group and all Japanese business leaders in 1970 are different to some degree.

Table 7 provides the comparative proportions of the occupations of fathers of presidents in Japan and Europe. Lower class includes farmers and skilled and unskilled workers. Middle class comprises those whose fathers were salesmen, school teachers, junior civil servants, and office workers. Upper class refers to those whose fathers were business owners, senior executives or professional men. (In the Japanese data 21 percent of small business owners are included in the middle class, since they are mostly small scale and operated mainly by family members or extended family workers.) Almost four-fifths of European chief executives came from the upper class, and only 5 percent of them were from working class families. Even for the middle class chances for chief executive positions are limited. Evidently, social mobility is more closed in Europe than in Japan. Differentiations by social class in Europe are more pronounced than in Japan. Among the European countries the French business environment offers the least opportunity for social mobility.

Table 7. Comparison of the Social Origin of Japanese and European Presidents

	Japan 1970	All Europe 1968	France 1968	U.K. 1968	Germany 1968
Lower class	9%	5%	2%	8%	11%
Middle class	30	16	12	23	16
Upper class	61	79	86	69	73
(Father-son same firm)	(14)	(26)	(34)		
Percent total	100	100	100	100	100
Number total	138	576			

Source: Hall, D. J., Bettignies, H. C. de, and Amado-Fischgrund, G., "The European Business Elite," *European Business*, No. 23, October 1969.

Although we do not have directly comparable statistics for the U.S., R.S. Diamond writes about U.S. chief executives as follows: ". . . the reality is that most chief executives grew up in comfortable middle- and upper-middle-class surroundings. Only 16% are the sons of blue-collar workers or farmers. All the rest got a first hand view of the executive world from fathers with an entrepreneurial frame of mind or who closely served those who did. Forty-five percent of their fathers stood at the very top of the business hierarchy either as founder, chairman of the board, or president of a company, or as a self-employed businessman."[9]

Obviously, inheritance and influential connections are important factors in the recruitment of chief executives even in the U.S. Nonetheless, the U.S. business community is an example of an open society in that a higher percentage of lower class people have access to chief executive positions. Also the leaders of the five hundred biggest U.S. firms indicated that only 5.8 percent succeeded their fathers in the top positions, while in the biggest European firms there are nearly four times as many who took over their father's chair, 26.4 percent, and 34.2 percent in France. Among the Japanese chief executives 8.1 percent said that their fathers were the owners of the same firm and 5.6 percent said that their fathers were executives of the same firm over which they now preside. Thus, 14.1 percent of the Japanese presidents in 1970 assumed their positions through either inheritance or influential connections. From 1960 to 1970 the proportion of father-son in the same firms among the chief executives has declined slightly. The role of inheritance in Japanese presidents at present is not as low as that in the U.S., but it is far less than that in European countries. Furthermore, it should be noted that as far as inheritance across all levels of top executives is concerned, the proportion of inheritance in Japan is as low as in the U.S.

Education of Business Leaders

Let us now examine aspects of formal education of the 1970 Japanese business leaders. Our major findings for the 1960 business leaders were that an overwhelming majority of them received

---

[9]Diamond, Robert S., "A Self-Portrait of the Chief Executives," *Fortune* (May, 1970). It is a survey of chief executives for the five hundred biggest U.S. corporations.

higher education in specialist schools or universities. The business leaders having less education were older and disappearing. The general level of education was even higher than that of the U.S. and the U.K. counterparts. They were trained in a few selected institutions and tend to constitute a homogeneous elite group in terms of educational background.

What are the findings in 1970? Table 8 compares the educational level of the Japanese business leaders in 1960 and 1970 and the general population. It should be noted that the Japanese business leaders studied here received their education about thirty to forty years ago, in which period chances for higher education were few for sons of the lower classes.

Table 8.   Level of Education: 1960 and 1970 Business Leaders and Japanese Total Population

Highest Level of Education	Japanese Total Population of Adult Males*		1960 Business Leaders	1970 Business Leaders
	1960	1970		
Primary school graduate or less	64%	55%	3%	5%
Middle school graduate	27	31	6	
Specialist school graduate	4	4	23	20
University graduate	5	10	66	75
Graduate school	—	—	2	0
Percent Total	100	100	100	100
Number Total	28.5 million	34.1 million	985	1076

*Sources: Bureau of Statistics, Office of the Prime Minister, *1960 and 1970 Population Census of Japan*, 1962 and 1972.

The trend in education for business leaders indicates that top executive positions are increasingly associated with higher education. In 1960 68 percent graduated from universities; in 1970 the figure was 75 percent. Nine percent in 1960 and only 5 percent in 1970 went no further than middle school. Graduates of specialist schools have declined. Since very few go to graduate school the top level of Japan's business world becomes a more homogeneous group in terms of educational attainment. It becomes more and more clear that higher education and success in a business career are closely associated in Japanese society. This relationship is more pronounced in 1970 than in 1960.

In chapter 4 of this book we have indicated that graduates of certain elite universities played a dominant role in the recruiting of business leaders in 1960. We will examine the specialist schools or universities attended and the kind of education received for Japanese business leaders in 1970. Table 9 presents the schools attended. The graduates of Tokyo University alone account for about one-third (36 percent in 1960 and 32 percent in 1970) of recent business leaders.

Another imperial university, Kyoto, provided 11 percent in 1960 and 12 percent in 1970. The proportion shared by these two and the other imperial universities (Kyushu, Osaka and Tōhoku) accounts for over half (53 percent in 1960 and 51 percent in 1970) of Japanese business leaders. Hitotsubashi University and Keiō Uni-

Table 9. Distribution of Specialist School and University Attended by Business Leaders of 1960 and 1970

	1960 Business Leaders	1970 Business Leaders
Tokyo University	36%	32%
Kyoto University	11	12
Hitotsubashi University	10	5
Keiō University	7	6
Kobe University	6	2
Waseda University	5	4
Kyushu University	3	3
Tokyo Institute of Technology	2	2
Osaka University	2	2
Tōhoku University	1	2
Others	17	30
Percent total	100%	100%
Number total	902	1026

versity were the other major recruiting sources of Japanese business leaders. But their proportion has been declining. Other colleges and universities include private and municipal universities and commercial and engineering specialist schools throughout Japan. They recruited 17 percent of the total in 1960 and 30 percent in 1970. These groups have increased most.

It appears that the tendency to recruit business leaders from prestigious universities declined from 1960 to 1970. Especially, Hitotsubashi and Kobe, former commercial colleges, have been losing their positions. These decreases are covered by many specialist schools located throughout Japan. All of these became universities as the result of the educational reform after the Second World War. Major universities still supply the largest majority of business executives, though there is a recent tendency that executive positions are opening for graduates of minor universities that were former specialist schools.

From these data on the relationships between educational institutions and the business community, it is evident that Japanese universities have continued to supply the elite who direct business corporations. It is safe to assume that the rapid growth of the Japanese economy is largely due to the efficient functioning of these executives drawn from the selected universities.

Recent studies on higher education and business recruitment in Japan have explored the relationship between the two. They indicated that "the hierarchical distinctions that grew up among the universities and specialist schools had immediate consequences for career chance."[10] It is a well-known fact that many leading companies take their executive level entrants only from a particular school or schools. The channels of recruitment from university to corporation are well documented in a recent publication.[11] It is indicated that the education and career success of Japanese business leaders bear traits of particularistic orientations.[12]

Furthermore, it should be noted that educational background is

[10]Passin, Herbert, *Society and Education in Japan* (New York: Teachers College, Columbia University, 1965), p. 123.

[11]Azumi,Koya, *Higher Education and Business Recruitment in Japan* (New York: Teachers College, Columbia University, 1969), pp. 50–96.

[12]Smelser, Neil J., and Lipset, Seymour Martin (ed.), *Social Structure and Mobility in Economic Development* (Chicago: Aldine Publishing Company, 1966), p. 32.

so important that influential connections or inheritance do not automatically guarantee either employment or the attainment of executive position in large scale business firms. So the ascriptive status of a man as determined by the occupation of his father has relative importance in determining how much formal education he can get, but higher formal education, especially a diploma from selected universities, is the most important passport to a successful business career. It is clear that success in education provides the basis for a business career. Thus, the same principle has been operating in screening talented men. There has been no change in institutional relationships between the university and the business community over the last decade.

Regarding the relative importance of social class for selecting present business leaders in Japan, we should note that the rareness of opportunity for sons of the lower class is not itself an exclusion by virtue of their class; rather it is due to their lack of the family environment that is so important in determining and stimulating educational achievement.

A university hierarchy has been institutionalized in Japanese society, and graduates of the selected universities are regarded as the ones possessing superior intelligence. It is a common notion in Japan that education should be regarded as the measure of a man's worth. Once a man has been accepted by a prestigious university and holds a diploma, his university achievement changes into an ascribed status for his subsequent career. This is true of every industrial society, but this tendency is strongly emphasized in Japan and in certain other societies. Let us examine these patterns in a comparative way.

International Comparison of the Education of the Business Elite

To direct a large corporation is an increasingly complex task and requires men of great ability. In every industrial country university training has gained in importance for a business career. Let us evaluate the pattern of education among Japanese business leaders in comparison to those of the U.S. and Europe. Table 10 shows the proportion of university graduates among chief executives in the largest corporations in Japan, the U.S. and Europe. Although each country has a different educational system, the general pattern that each country has established between the university and the business community can be clearly seen.

Table 10.   University Attendance by Chief Executives: Japan, United States and European Countries

Education	Japan 1970	U.S. 1970	France 1968	U.K. 1968	Germany 1968
Did not attend university	11%	6%	11%	60%	22%
Attended university	89	94	89	40	78
	100	100	100	100	100

Sources: The U.S. data are from Diamond, *op. cit.*, European data are from Hall, D. J., Bettignies, H. C. de and Amado-Fischgrund, G., "The European Business Elite," *European Business*, No. 23 (October 1969); Japanese data are separate statistics for presidents from our research. Japanese figures include the graduates of specialist schools.

The U.S. chief executives have by far the most education. Ninety-four percent have attended university and 80 percent have at least a bachelor's degree. Forty-four percent received a master's degree and 3 percent hold a doctorate. Of course, the size and complexity of U.S. corporations are two of the reasons that they require college graduates as their chief executives. Furthermore, as a recent writer on U.S. chief executives indicated, "the Thirties and Forties clearly marked the beginning of an era in which young Americans were college-educated on a scale unparalleled anywhere in the world."[13] One-third majored in business administration, 40 percent majored in science and engineering, and 35 percent specialized in law, social sciences and humanities, as shown in table 11.

The French chief executive has received more university education than his European colleagues. Also over half of them (59 percent) studied science and engineering subjects at the École Poly-

---

[13]Diamond, *op. cit.*, p. 181.

technique. This indicates that the French business community places great importance on university education, especially in science and engineering. The writers about the European business elite noted, "the selection procedure for these schools is remarkably tough, and that children from lower class backgrounds stand very little chance of enjoying the educational opportunities that can help them pass through the successive screening procedures."[14]

In Britain there have been relatively few top men with higher formal education. It has been the practice for industry to give more importance to job training than to university training, as we indicated earlier (chapter 4).

Table 11. Field of Study of Chief Executives: Japan, United States and European Countries

	Japan 1970	U.S. 1970	France 1968	U.K. 1968	Germany 1968
Science or engineering	23%	53%	59%	43%	54%
Business or economics	44	32	34	47	29
Law, government or social sciences	24	9	7	10	17
Other	9	6	—	—	—
	100	100	100	100	100

Sources: The same as table 7.

Over three-quarters of German chief executives are university graduates, and more than one-half of these have a doctorate. The bigger the company the more likely is the German chief executive to be a Ph.D.[15]

Some significant patterns in the role of higher education for Japanese business and industry stand out in comparison to the others. Japanese business leaders received university education, but few of them have further graduate and professional training. They limit their education to the bachelor's degree. The proportion with graduate training is very low both in 1960 and 1970. Profes-

---

[14]Hall et al., *op. cit*, p. 53.
[15]*Ibid.*, p. 54.

sional training plays less of a role in Japan. This is quite different from the important role of higher education in the U.S., where 44 percent have a master's degree or higher, and Germany, where more than one-half of the present chief executives hold a doctorate. In Japan professional training itself is not important for a business career, but the general talents of the university graduate are more important. Their professional and executive talents have been developed mainly within the industry and especially within the corporation where they are employed. The development of Japanese executives is the outcome of management training on the basis of university training at bachelor's level.

As in France, Japanese business leaders are educated in certain elite universities. Executive positions in Japanese society have been largely dominated by the graduates of the elite universities. Relationships between one's social class and one's educational achievement in Japan resemble the patterns found in France. Educational achievement largely determines a man's subsequent business career in the two countries. However, the French business community gave more emphasis to science and engineering for business leadership; Japanese industry tends to select its executives from the field of economics (44 percent), law and government (24 percent) and to a lesser degree from engineering and science (23 percent). The proportion of men who studied engineering and science is the lowest in Japan.

Career Pattern

In examining the present age of the Japanese business leaders, we have already noted they are older than their colleagues in Western countries. We found that they are less influenced by inheritance. Let us review the career patterns of Japanese business leaders in comparison to their Western counterparts.

The average age of the Japanese chief executives is 62 years and they entered the business world 40 years ago, around 1930. Forty-four percent of them entered their present firm before 1945. The rest of them joined the present firm after the Second World War.

It is not correct that every top executive stays with the same firm throughout his career. Actually, the great majority have changed their employment. However, the reasons may be largely due to the drastic reorganization following the war and subsequent policies of the occupation forces.

The career patterns of chief executives are statistically summarized in table 12. Japanese presidents are now 62 years old. The average age at which they entered their present company was 35. It took 19 years to attain the chief executive position. Their average age when they reach the position of president is 54 years. They have been in the chief executive position for 8 years. However, it should be noted that while about one-half of the presidents assumed their present position within 5 years and around age 60, a minority stay on as president for a very long time because they have founded the company,or because they have inherited it, or because they have demonstrated their unusual ability in directing it. The chief executives who are appointed on the basis of a bureaucratic career usually work some years longer in the company and attain the chief executive position some years later. He remains in the chief executive position for about 8 years and serves another 4 years or more as the chairman of the board of directors of his company. This pattern is typically found in the largest and established firms.

The second column of table 12 shows statistical figures for European chief executives as a whole. Although there are significant differences between countries, the average chief executive is about 57 years old, joined his present company at around 39, and usually reached the top 8 years later. They stay in the chief executive position longer. It seems that the presidents of U.S. companies have spent more time with their present firms, which they joined at around 32, and trained for much longer before they became president. European companies on the other hand tend to hire more senior managers who have already had a good deal of professional experience and to promote them to the top job in less time.

We had a common notion that American chief executives are more mobile than European executives and that the former are appointed to the top position at a younger age. However, this is not true, but the U.S. chief executives on the average enter the present firm earlier. They take eighteen years to reach the top

Table 12.   Present Age, Age at Appointment and Years in Chief Executive Position: Japan, Europe and United States

	Japan 1970	Europe 1968	U.S. 1966
Present Age	62 years old	57 years old	55 years old
Age entered present company	35	39	32
Age upon reaching position of president	54	47	50
Year required to become president	19 years	8 years	18 years
Years as president	8	10	5
Years in present company	27	16	23

Sources: Hall, D. J., Bettignies, H. C. de and Amado-Fischgrund, G., "The European Business Elite," *European Business*, No. 23, October 1969, p. 48.

within the company. Unlike European presidents, the U.S. presidents will retire earlier or leave for another top job. Therefore, the U.S. presidents are more mobile than the European presidents only in terms of shorter time in the chief executive position and an earlier age leaving the top position.

In comparison with these groups, the career pattern of Japanese presidents is striking. They represent the oldest group. They are with the company the longest and are appointed to the top position the latest. If we take into account that their next expected position is chairman of the board of the directors, the career pattern of Japanese chief executives is characterized by non-mobility. They have the least experience in professional and management training outside their firm or industry. Even though we do not have direct data on the interfirm mobility of 1970 business leaders to compare with that of 1960, it is safe to assume that they consist of the men chiefly selected on the basis of merit within their own firm, as we found in the case of 1960 Japanese business leaders.

Birthplace

In examining the birthplace, region and size of community for the 1960 Japanese business leaders, we concluded that their geographical background closely paralleled that of industrial development; the more industrialization, the more business leaders. During the last ten-year period, substantial industrialization has taken place, and geographical distribution of the Japanese population has shifted to industrial centers. However, the change in geographical distribution of the Japanese population in the beginning of this century was slow as shown in the third and the fourth columns of tables 13 and 14.

Let us examine the regional background of the 1970 Japanese

Table 13. Distribution of 1960 and 1970 Business Leaders by Region of Birth and Population by Region of Residence in 1903 and 1910

Region	1960 Business Leaders Region of Birth	1970 Business Leaders Region of Birth	Japanese Population by Region*	
			1903	1910
Kanto	24%	28%	18%	19%
Kinki	23	23	16	16
Chūbu	18	17	21	21
Kyushu	13	9	15	15
Chūgoku	11	11	11	10
Shikoku	5	4	6	6
Tōhoku	4	4	11	10
Hokkaido	2	2	2	3
Others**	0	2	0	0
Total percent	100	100	100	100
Total number	977	1080	48,543	50,713
			(thousand)	(thousand)

*The figures for Japanese population by region are drawn from Bureau of Statistics, Imperial Cabinet, *Japan Imperial Statistical Yearbook*, No. 25, 1906, pp. 36–7 for 1903 and No. 33, 1914, pp. 42–6 for 1910. Others come from areas outside Japan's four islands, most of them former colonies.

Table 14. Distribution of 1960 and 1970 Business Leaders
by Size of Place of Birth

Size of Community	1960 Business Leaders	1970 Business Leaders	Total Population 1903*	Total Population 1910
Village	30%	15%	72%	69%
Town	27	30	14	15
Small or medium city	19	19	6	6
Five large cities	12	15	4	6
Tokyo	12	19	4	4
Other	0	2	0	0
Total percent	100	100	100	100
Total number	977	1065	48,543 (thousand)	50,713 (thousand)

*Sources are shown in Table 10.

business leaders in contrast to changes in the total population during the period they were born. During the period from 1903 to
1910, the population increased by 1.5 million. This increase took
place in the Kanto, or Tokyo, region, the most industrialized sector, and Hokkaido, then the least-developed area. From 1960 to
1970 the proportion of business leaders from the Kanto region
gained the most, and Kyushu lost the most. The rest of the regions
remained at about the same proportion. It should be noted that
the "others" category includes areas outside the four islands of
Japan, most of them Japan's former colonies. They are a sizable
number in 1970 and zero in 1960.

Next, we will review rural versus urban contributions to business leadership in 1970. Again we find a relatively small population shift in the beginning of this century. There are no drastic
changes of population in the various sizes of community, and there
is only a gradual movement from village to small town and large
city. However, men from villages drastically declined in number
from 30 percent in 1960 to 15 percent in 1970, while all the other
groups increased chances of business leadership. The fact that
villagers could not take advantage of industrialization seems due

to the fact that villagers of this time failed to attend the new higher educational institutions. More than two-thirds of the population were still in villages throughout Japan, but villagers were alienated from industrial leadership to a far larger degree in 1970 than in 1960.

Compared to the contribution of village communities in Japan, that of small town communities is different. The latter are over-represented in leadership positions twice relative to the total population. Moreover, there is a definite trend in 1970 that the larger the city, the more leadership positions. Evidently, sources of Japanese business leaders are away from rural villages to urban and industrial centers, while the largest population still remained in village communities.

Summary and Perspectives

The study of the social backgrounds of the Japanese business leaders in 1960 and 1970 suggests the following perspectives on their future recruitment.

As societies become more industrialized, the amount of elite mobility also increases.[16] Japan's industrialization in particular has been accompanied by a great increase of demand for elite in recent periods. If we compare the 1970 Japanese business leaders to those of 1960, our important finding is the emergence of a certain closing tendency in elite recruitment. Sons of laborers and lower white collar workers are substantially less represented in 1970 than in 1960. Landlords and farmers, who were the single largest source of business leaders in 1960, have been decreasing in proportion. Sons of owners of large business firms have also decreased. The main recruitment sources of business leaders have shifted to sons of executives of large business firms, government officials and professions, all upper white collar groups.

These trends, in general, reflect that administrators or managers, rather than owners, have been gaining as the large recruit-

---

[16]Marsh, Robert M., *Comparative Sociology* (New York: Harcourt, Brace & World, Inc., 1967), pp. 174–8.

ment source for business leaders. It is also clear that in 1970 Japanese business leaders are for the most part recruited from urban industrialized occupations, rather than rural or traditional occupations as in the case of 1960 business leaders. Thus, the 1970 Japanese business leadership positions are more open to the urban upper white collar class, but they are less open to the remaining social groups. In general, a certain exclusiveness in recruitment of the business leaders in 1970 is evident. Current data indicate that the present business elite are recruited from the business class or urban upper white collar class, excluding laborers and lower white collar groups. In comparison to the U.S., the lower-strata Japanese population is under a definite disadvantage for opportunities of movement to elite positions.

Regarding the role of education in the career of Japanese business leaders in 1970, their recruitment pattern operates basically on a merit and achievement principle. Competitive examinations in schooling and competitive careers in the business organization are key features of the system. Candidates for business leadership must hold a diploma from certain selected universities. Thereafter, they have to follow a long competitive career step by step. It is evident that there is a similar principle operating to screen talent in both universities and business organizations. Although now there are some signs that cooperation is lacking between the university and the business community, academic study in economics, law and engineering provides basic training for business careers. Actual business training belongs to the enterprise where the graduate is employed. In this respect there seems a certain particularistic tendency to limit business executives largely to the managerial personnel who devote their whole career to the company. There is no sign of substantial change in these recruitment and training patterns. In the future, Japanese business firms will increase in size. Bureaucratic management will develop further. It is quite probable that the present leading universities will continue to supply most of the candidates for top business positions.

What factors will operate in the recruitment of Japanese business leaders in the future? So far we have described the supply side of the question. However, we have to recognize the significance of the demand side of the question. As we know, direct influence of family social status, especially inheritance of leadership positions, is less and formal education is more important in recruitment of leaders in Japan. There is a reason for this. In order to attain industrialization, Japan had to adopt Western science and technology. The men who studied modern science and technology in universities were more qualified for this task. It is clear that the need for managerial talent has been stronger than traditional social forces. Also rapid industrialization itself provides the condition for larger demand of executive talent and results in greater social mobility.

In the future, as Japanese enterprises continue to grow and to become complex they must appoint more talented men to their directing positions. Individual enterprises are aware that they have to select the best talent ahead of their competitors. Otherwise they will lose their competitive position. Furthermore, in the 1970s Japanese businesses will become involved in international competition. In order to adapt to these changes, Japanese management must nominate successors not only by seniority, past merit and loyalty but also by actual performance. The executive recruitment system from universities and bureaucratic career in business organizations is well established and also functional in producing executive decisions. It is my opinion that Japanese business recruitment will continue the present pattern and adapt to new environmental requirements in a gradual way.

Appendix II

RESEARCH METHODS FOR PART I

Data concerning the 1960 Japanese business leaders were gathered principally by means of a questionnaire that was formulated on the basis of a pilot study conducted in 1959, on the social backgrounds of Japanese political and intellectual leaders as well as business leaders.[1] The total number of subjects selected for the pilot study was rather small (695 men), and responses were received from only 57 percent. Despite the small size of this sample, the experience gained from the research assured us that questionnaires could be used profitably to obtain data on the social background and careers of business leaders. We were also able to determine that responses to questions were generally accurate. Furthermore, this earlier research provided a basis for selection of the sample used in the present study.

For the present study, we selected leaders in various types of important businesses and industries who occupied positions as chairman of the board of directors, president, vice president, and senior managing director. Firms chosen are the largest in Japan, defined in terms of capitalization. A revised form of the questionnaire employed in the pilot study was sent to these business leaders, of whom 985 or 64.6 percent gave usable responses.

Selection of the Subjects

Our basic criterion of selection was that the men must represent

---

[1]Details of the research methods and the scope of the sample are stated in Abegglen, James C. and Mannari, Hiroshi, "Leaders of Modern Japan," *Economic Development and Cultural Change*, IX:1, Part II (Oct. 1960), pp. 100–34.

the business elite and thus provide an accurate sample of the top level business positions in Japanese business and industry in 1960. In studies of American business leaders conducted by F. W. Taussig and C. S. Joslyn in 1928 and W. Lloyd Warner and James C. Abegglen in 1952, the authors reasoned as follows: Wherever possible, the executives in the leading companies in each industry should be included rather than those having positions in minor companies. This is important because the men in the leading companies are undoubtedly capable executives and are more likely to be in a position to furnish information that will be of value than are men who occupy positions in minor companies, where they are often placed as subordinates by the leaders who really control the company and its activities.[2]

We have accepted these premises as appropriate for the study of Japanese business leaders, although our pilot sample included executives of a few small industrial organizations that we thought exerted strong influence on other sectors of the commercial world.

Among several criteria that might be used in determining which are the largest firms, we chose capitalization, because other criteria such as total assets, number of employees, or gross sales are not consistent measures of size throughout the various types of business and industrial firms. Initially we tried to select 400 companies that are commonly regarded in Japan as large business firms. Finally we decided to select only companies with capitalization exceeding one billion yen (approximately $2,780,000 in 1960). The total number of such firms was 396.[3]

We then recorded names of the incumbent chairman, president, vice president, and the two most highly placed or senior managing

[2]Taussig and Joslyn, *op. cit.*, p. 6 and Warner and Abegglen, *op. cit.*, p. 230.
[3]A survey of corporations provides a measure of the activities of the biggest firms in Japan. In April 1960 (several months later than our sampling period) there were 497,206 corporate enterprises in Japan, of which only 415 companies or 0.09 percent of the total had capital exceeding one billion yen. These 415 companies represent over half (57 percent) of the total capitalization of corporate enterprises. Total assets of these firms represented 42 percent of the total; their operation revenues for the 1960–61 term, 27 percent; operation profits and losses for the term, 41 percent; net profits and losses for the term, 43 percent; and number of employees, 16 percent. The foregoing data are drawn from *Hōjin Kigyō Tōkei Nempō* for April 1960–March 1961 (Annual Report of Corporate Enterprises Survey) (Ministry of Finance, Japanese Government, 1961).

directors *(senmu torishimariyaku* and *jōmu torishimariyaku)* of each of these firms. Senior managing directors we have selected stand immediately below the position of president of the firm. As giant firms have developed in Japan, management has become institutionalized, a development often compared to the growth of a bureaucracy, and important positions of this kind have emerged.

The selection procedure thus defined did not resolve all problems. Our sample should include representatives of all types of business and industry. In order to meet this requirement in their American study, Warner and Abegglen[4] selected a representative sample in relation to gross national income of the United States. This procedure was initially followed by us and then rejected after examining the proportions of the whole represented by the different types of business and industry and comparing by type of business the proportions with the relative contribution, by type of industry, to the national income. Considerable disparity was evident, and our selection of numbers of business leaders by type of business or industry was made to accord as nearly as possible with the proportions of capitalization represented by the industries in 1959. (See table 1).

The largest firms in Japan are not equally distributed in accordance with the contribution to national income of the various types of business. In comparison with the share of national income that they provide, the largest firms are especially overrepresented in manufacturing and finance and extremely underrepresented in trade and services. Japan's business and industry tend toward a few giant firms in manufacturing and finance and a great many very small firms in trading and services. If we had selected approximately 19 percent of our sample from trade and 19 percent from service industries, to accord with the contribution to national income of trade and service, we would have reached into small firms and presented a distorted picture.

It must be noted that the 396 companies selected include the seven largest mutual life insurance companies and the nine largest newspaper companies. These were chosen not on the basis of capitalization, but on the basis of their business activities. Mutual

---

[4]Warner and Abegglen, pp. 229–36.

Table 1. Ratio of Sample by Type of Business or Industry and its Contribution to National Income (1959)

Type of Business	Percentage of National Income in 1959 Fiscal Year	Percentage of Firms Capitalized at More Than 1 Billion Yen	Percentage of Original Sample in 1960 Business Leaders
Mining	2.2%	3.2%	3.2%
Construction	6.6	3.1	5.3
Manufacturing	32.4	54.8	52.4
Finance	9.0	14.1	14.1
Transportation, communication, public utility	12.3	13.4	13.6
Trade	18.6	4.4	5.4
Services	18.9	7.0	6.0
Total percent	100.0	100.0	100.0
Total number	8,374 billion	396	1,525

Source: Keizai Kikakuchō, *Kokumin Shotoku Hakusho*, 1959 (The White Paper on National Income) (Tokyo: Ministry of Finance, Printing Bureau, 1961), p. 31.

life insurance companies are not capitalized, yet they perform extremely important functions in the Japanese financial world and are giant firms. The seven companies in question were the largest insurance firms in Japan in both assets and amounts of contracts at the end of 1959.[5] These firms are included in "Finance" in our classification. Newspaper companies do not make their capitalization publicly known. Of the nine largest, six publish newspapers with national circulation and the remaining three publish papers with broad regional circulation. All of these newspaper companies also own radio or television broadcasting subsidiaries with capitalization exceeding one billion yen. These firms are included in "Service" in our classification.

By following the procedure outlined above, we felt that the two most important criteria of selection had been met. The men studied are executives and are with the largest firms in Japan. They

[5]Okazaki, Yutaka, *Seimei·Hoken* (Life Insurance) (Tokyo: Yūhikaku, 1960), pp. 157–73.

also constitute a fairly representative cross section by type of business or industry, with the exceptions we have noted. Our final sample of 396 firms represented a total of 1,525 executives: 106 chairmen, 368 presidents, 224 vice presidents, 355 *senmu torishimariyaku* and 472 *jōmu torishimariyaku*. Men holding the positions of *jōmu torishimariyaku* in the firms concerned far outnumber men in higher positions. In order to avoid distortion of our results by overrepresentation of men in these positions, only one-third of the total number of 1,362 *jōmu torishimariyaku* were included and these were randomly selected.

In selecting companies with capitalization exceeding one billion yen, we used *Kaisha Nenkan, 1960* (Yearbook of Companies, 1960) (Tokyo: Nihon Keizai Shimbun Sha, 1959). This yearbook also includes listings of executive personnel of companies. We listed the positions in the appropriate companies in accordance with our definition and then identified the name of the man occupying the position. During the sampling period there were changes in the capitalization and executive personnel of various firms. We learned of these changes through announcements in the *Nihon Keizai Shimbun*, a major economic and financial journal, and adjusted our sample accordingly. Reference was also made to *Kaisha Yōran, 1960* (Yearbook of Companies, 1960) (Tokyo: Daiyamondo Sha, 1959) to check the accuracy of the *Kaisha Nenkan, 1960*.

The 1960 Questionnaire: Questionnaire Items and Coding

The questionnaire used in the present study is two pages long and contains sixteen questions. The sample appended has been translated into English. Before being mailed each questionnaire was assigned a code number identifiable only by the researchers that indicated for each respondent: the position he held in his company, the type of business or industry, and the size of his firm's capitalization.

The purpose of most of the questions seems self-evident or may easily be inferred from a brief examination of the titles of the chapters of this study. It is useful, however, to make a few comments regarding certain questions and our handling of responses.

Responses to item 2, which requests name of place of birth, were classified as village, town, or city on the basis of the size of the community, as determined by examination of census reports, at the time the respondents were born. Answers to item 7, year of founding of respondent's firm, were often complex, due to histories of the merging and separation of firms, and we were sometimes forced to make arbitrary judgments.

Responses to items 9 and 10, which were designed to collect information on movement from one industry to another and from one firm to another, were not always answered or were not fully answered. When information was not given by the respondents or seemed doubtful for any reason, the researchers drew the desired data from *Jinji Kōshin Roku* (Tokyo: Jinji Kōshin Sho, 1958), which is similar to *Who's Who* and contains detailed biographical information on all of our respondents.

Items 11 and 12, on birth order and adoption, are especially significant in Japan in relation to traditional customs of inheritance.

In classifying occupations of parents, grandparents, and other relatives of our respondents (item 13) we adopted the following policies: (1) our occupational categories should show hierarchical order; e.g., whether tenant-farmer or landlord, owner of small, medium, or large business concern, and, when employment was in private business or public office, whether clerical or managerial; (2) the categories should be comparable to those used in the national census report and comparable with those of similar studies of other countries.

Judgment as to whether business firms (of parents and other relatives) were small, medium, or large was left to our respondents, since no means of gaining truly accurate information on this subject was available. Information given by respondents on the type of business or industry of forebears was, however, surprisingly detailed, and we feel that with the aid of this information, we were able to classify the occupations and sizes of firms fairly accurately. It should be noted that many respondents listed two or more occupations for their fathers, e.g., landlord owning a retail store or mill, and business owner holding a political position. In these cases we chose one as a principal occupation and the others as subsidiaries.

For forebears in civil and military service, we asked respondents to state the last and highest title and the branch of service, and we classified the occupations in accordance with the information given. Specific information was requested on professions, i.e., whether professor, doctor, lawyer, priest, artist, or other.

Item 15 refers to the social status of families of leaders in late feudal times. Specifically, we asked whether the leaders' families were formerly nobles, samurai, or commoners, following the feudal class definitions. We had initially doubted that this question would be answered. However, nearly all persons returning the questionnaire (957 of 985) did answer this question.

Item 16 asks for a statement of religious affiliation. In preparing the questionnaire, it was felt that this question, as well as item 15, might be resented by the respondents. However, only 18 of the 985 respondents failed to answer this question.

Since the responses to the questions on religion do not allow us to present a precise account of the religious affiliations of the 1960 business leaders, we have not included an analysis of these data in the next. Instead we shall simply summarize the responses as follows: Buddhism 84.7 percent; Christianity 5.8 percent; Shintoism 5.3 percent; other 0.2 percent; and no religion 4.0 percent. Census data on the religious affiliations of the total Japanese population in 1960 do not provide information suitable for comparison owing principally to the extensive overlap of Shinto and Buddhist religious affiliation. The national population in 1960 was 93 million, but figures on religious affiliation report 134 million because of multiple affiliation.[6] Regarding religious affiliation, we may note that Buddhism and Christianity are overrepresented.

On the second page of the questionnaire, a blank space was provided for comments on the questionnaire or further remarks concerning the career of the respondent. Some respondents provided additional information helpful in coding responses.

Some remarks are necessary concerning our procedures in measuring the growth of industries and of firms. The expansion of the industries and of the firms with which the business leaders are

---

[6] *JSY*, 1961, pp. 482–3.

associated are discussed in chapter 5. We assumed that differences in the rates of growth of industry and of expansion of individual firms would have an important bearing on the question of occupational mobility. We examined the rate of growth in mining and manufacturing only, because no index showing activity in tertiary industry over the past few decades is available. Within these limits, the expansion of the Japanese economy by different sectors of industry was examined for the period 1935 to 1958 (latest figures available at the time of selection of the sample). An established index of production for mining and manufacturing[7] was used for measuring the rate of growth. The period 1935 to 1958 covers in large part the time span of the business careers of our respondents. It should also be noted that 1935 and 1958 are both years of national prosperity, marked by no special event such as war. An index of production in each industry from 1935 to 1958 provides a measure of the overall rate of increase in production during the period, which is more than two-fold (2.38 times). Increases in each type of industry in 1958 over 1935 are shown below (1935 = 100).

We classified industries that increased more than 4 times as

Table 2. Rate of Growth between 1935 and 1958 by Type of Industry

Type of Industry	Rate of Growth in 1958 over 1935
Electrical machinery	1,270%
Shipbuilding	1,232
Petroleum and petroleum products	544
Machinery, excluding electrical, shipbuilding, and automobiles	451
Paper and pulp	361
General chemical products	319
Iron and steel	240
Rubber	224
Ceramics	205
Foodstuffs	158
Mining	142
Textiles, excluding synthetic	104
All mining and manufacturing	238

[7]Data are derived from *JSY*, 1959, pp. 202–3.

"rapidly expanding"; those that increased 2 to 3 times as "moderately expanding," and those with lower rates of growth as "slowly expanding." Although there are no data of the desired kind on industries that arose or became important after 1935, a recent report[8] indicates that some exceptional expansions have taken place in the synthetic resin, synthetic fiber, and automobile industries. Their rates of expansion from 1951 to 1958 are 25 times, 15 times, and 13 times, respectively. These three industries are therefore included among the rapidly expanding industries in our study. Among respondents in mining and manufacturing industries, 33.2 percent are coded as rapidly expanding, 42.1 percent as moderately expanding, and 24.7 percent as slowly expanding.

The expansion of firms in mining and manufacturing represented by our sample is measured by increases in capitalization from 1950 to 1959. Drastic reorganization of industrial enterprises took place during and after the Second World War. In addition, the great inflation of the early postwar period made it impractical for us to attempt to study company expansion farther back than 1950. Firms represented by this study that increased in capital more than 30 times from 1950 to 1959 were classified as "rapidly growing," firms with increases from 8 to 29 as "moderately expanding," and those with lower rates of increase as "slowly expanding."[9] Among our respondents in mining and manufacturing, 21.3 percent are in the first category, 51.0 percent in the second, and 27.7 percent in the third.

The Questionnaire Returns and Their Accuracy

The questionnaire, together with an explanatory letter signed by the researchers and a supporting letter from the secretary of the Japanese Federation of Employers' Associations (see English translations appended), were sent to a total of 1,525 businessmen, of whom 1,008 responded. Among these, twenty-three were incomplete or otherwise inadequate and were not used in our tables.

---

[8]Research Department of the Ministry of Trade and Industry, *Nihon no Sangyō no Genjō, 1959* (Present Status of Japan's Industry) (Tokyo: 1959), p. 110.
[9]Data on capitalization were drawn from *Kaisha Nenkan 1960*.

The total number of usable responses was 985, or 64.6 percent of the total mailing. The returns were categorized by type of business from information previously obtained on each respondent in the original selection of the sample. Returned questionnaires were examined only by the present authors.

A random sample was later selected from among men who did not return completed questionnaires. Contact was made with these men by letter or telephone in an attempt to determine why they had not responded.

The return of usable responses of nearly 65 percent is high in comparison with the responses in the American studies by Taussig and Joslyn in 1928 and Warner and Abegglen in 1952, which were 57 percent and 48 percent, respectively. The rate of response is substantially higher than that of most mailings of questionnaires. Interest in the subject on the part of Japanese businessmen themselves helped to account for the results. The high rate of response is also no doubt due in large part to the supporting letter from the secretary of the Japan Federation of Employers' Associations. Furthermore, on the advice of the secretary, the researchers enclosed in the questionnaire a brief summary of the findings of their pilot study to inform the subjects as to how their responses would be used. By these devices we gained a higher rate of response than in the pilot study.

The reader might well ask whether the responses to the questionnaire accurately reflect the backgrounds and careers of the 1960 business leaders. This question implies two points of doubt. First, are the men who returned the questionnaire representative of our original sample (of 1,525 men) or are there systematic differences in careers or backgrounds between the men who returned the questionnaire and the men who did not? Second, did the respondents give truthful information on their backgrounds? Several types of evidence were obtained to answer these questions.

In answer to our first question, it is possible to compare the completed questionnaires with the original mailing on several items: type of business, size of business, and positions in business of the respondents. The coded information we had inserted on each questionnaire before mailing allowed us to check these matters for accuracy of responses. As we have already noted, we found the responses highly congruent on these points with data obtained from other sources.

Table 3 compares the type of industry or business of the entire mailing with that of men who returned the questionnaire. As may be noted, the men who returned the questionnaire closely resemble the original mailing in proportions in the various types of business. Some differences may be noted, however. A proportionately greater number of returns came from men in textiles, mining, and machinery. Returns from men in trade and food industries are proportionately lower, and from men in service industries, the lowest of all. A test of differences between mailing and returns by the type of business indicates no statistical significance at the 5 percent level of Chi-square test. On the whole, it appears that the returns reflect fairly accurately the distribution by sector of business of the original mailing.

A comparison of the returns with the total mailing from the standpoint of comparative size of businesses also shows generally high correlation. Men in the largest enterprises (capitalization exceeding twenty billion yen) responded to the questionnaire somewhat less frequently than men associated with firms of medium and small size, but the differences are not statistically significant.

A comparison of returns and the original mailing with respect to business positions shows some difference in the proportions holding the position of chief executive. The 985 usable responses show a proportionate increase in presidents and a decrease in chairmen. The proportions of vice presidents and senior managing directors are essentially the same. Finally, the returns and mailings were compared from the standpoint of geographical location of the respondents. No significant differences were found.

We found, in short, only minor differences between our original sample and the respondents, and on the basis of the points discussed in the foregoing paragraphs, we think it justifiable to regard our final sample of 985 returns as a representative sample.

Some idea of the accuracy of the information given by responses was gained through the procedures we used when no responses were received. Those who did not respond to the original questionnaire were sent a second one, and the responses to this second mailing (297) were examined to see if the men concerned

Table 3. Distribution of Total Mailing and of Returns by Type of Business for 1960 Business Leaders

Type of Business	Number		Percentage		Percentage of return to mailing
	Mailing	Return	Mailing	Return	
Mining	49	34	3.22	3.45	69.38
Construction	81	49	5.31	4.97	60.49
Iron, steel, metal	96	61	6.30	6.19	63.54
Machinery	239	163	15.68	16.66	68.20
Chemicals	191	116	12.54	11.88	60.73
Textile, pulp, rubber	180	130	11.81	13.10	72.22
Food	92	53	6.04	4.97	57.60
Trade	82	47	5.38	5.07	57.31
Finance, insurance	215	145	14.10	14.72	67.44
Transportation, communication	160	104	10.50	10.56	65.00
Power, gas	49	32	3.15	3.25	63.30
Service	91	51	5.97	5.18	56.04
Total	1,525	985	100.00	100.00	64.59

differed in systematic or patterned ways from those who responded to the first mailing. Then, a random sampling of the men who did not reply to either the first or second mailing was contacted by telephone and other means, and completed questionnaires were received from them. This sample not only provided a check on the reliability of the responses we had received earlier, but also disclosed the reasons why some men had failed to answer our previous requests.

For this purpose we chose at random from among the 625 men who failed to respond to our first and second mailings 57 men (9 percent) and sent each of them a third questionnaire with a letter explaining its purpose. Fifteen responses were received. Fourteen additional questionnaires were completed by the researchers from published biographical sources, which included most of the desired information, including occupations of fathers. Contact was made with the 28 remaining men by telephone either directly or indirectly. We telephoned the subject himself whenever possible, and when this seemed impossible, we talked with his wife or his secretary. Twenty-one subjects gave their questionnaire answers over the phone. Some expressed suspicion about the purpose of the questionnaire, but most stated that they had been too busy to comply with our request. Altogether 50 questionnaires were thus completed, of which 36 contained data supplied by the subjects, their wives, or their secretaries.

It was not possible to get completed questionnaires on seven subjects. One subject specifically refused to answer, saying, "The questionnaire is not relevant to my business." The wife of one subject stated, "I need to have permission from my husband to answer your request." Through family members or secretaries, we learned that two men had died, one had recently changed from one firm to another, and one man was abroad. We were able to make no direct or indirect contact whatever with one man. These experiences suggest that almost all of our subjects were willing to cooperate even though they failed to respond to our earlier requests.

Now we turn to the question of the use of our random sample in checking the reliability of responses to the first and second mailings. The three sets of responses (first mailing, second mailing, and the random sample that resulted in fifty completed questionnaires) were checked against each other for consistency. The following variables were selected: age of respondent, educational level of respondent, place of birth, occupation of the respondent's

Table 4. Comparison of Returns from First Mailing, Second Mailing and Random Sample, by Occupation of Father of 1960 Business Leaders

Occupation of Father	First Mailing No.	%	Second Mailing No.	%	Random Sample No.	%	Total No.	%
Laborer	7	1.11	6	2.02	0	0.00	13	1.33
White collar worker	54	8.61	29	9.76	4	8.00	87	8.93
Executive or owner of business	286	45.62	123	41.41	19	38.00	428	43.94
Government official	73	11.64	32	10.78	7	14.00	112	11.50
Professional	54	8.61	34	11.45	6	12.00	94	9.65
Farmer	148	23.61	71	23.90	14	28.00	233	23.93
Other	5	0.80	2	0.68	0	0.00	7	0.72
Total	627	100.00	297	100.00	50	100.00	974	100.00

father, and social status in feudal times of respondent's family. Table 4 shows this comparison by occupation of father. Chi-square comparison shows no significant differences between the men who returned the mailed questionnaires and those who did not. Comparison of the other variables yielded the same results; no significant differences were found in any of the items. On the basis of the results of this comparison and of the other crosschecks discussed earlier, it seems reasonable to think that the information supplied by respondents is generally reliable.

Leaders of Modern Japanese Business Questionnaire
1. Age _____ years (by Western count)
2. Birthplace (Name of village, town, or city)
   _____ Prefecture _____ City or _____ Ward, town,
   district or village
3. Present permanent address
   _____ Metropolis, _____ City or _____ Ward, town,
   province or district or village
   prefecture
4. Highest education (Please fill in or check (X) the appropriate space
   a. _____ None _____ Primary school _____ Higher primary
   graduate school graduate
   _____ Middle school _____ Higher school or
   graduate specialist school graduate
   _____ University _____ Graduate _____ Doctorate
   graduate school (specify degree)
   b. (If more than higher school or specialist school graduate) field of specialization _____
   c. (If more than higher school or specialist school graduate) Name of school _____, and place _____
5. Number of trips abroad _____, length of stays ____, main places visited _____, main purpose of trips _____
6. Highest education of father _____
7. Year of founding of your company _____
8. Year of entering your present firm _____
   Year of attaining your present position _____
9. Your original field of work: manufacturing _____,

engineering _____, research _____, sales _____,
finance_____,personnel_____, other (specify)_____

10. If you have spent more than two years in a position before entering your present company, please note below:

	Period of time	*Type of work*	*Position*
a. From	_____ to _____	, _____	, _____
b. From	_____ to _____	, _____	, _____

11. Your birth order: oldest son _____, or other than oldest son _____

12. Are you an adopted son _____, or other than oldest son _____ ?

13. Please note the specific principal occupation of the following persons:

Type of Occupation	Your father (or foster father)	Your wife's father	Your father's father	Your mother's father	(If adopted) your natural father
*Unskilled or skilled laborer					
Farmer: tenant or small owner					
Farmer: landlord					
Clerk or shopkeeper					
Owner, small business					
Owner, medium or large business (type of business)					
Manager, medium or large business (type of business)					
Clerk or employee in public office					
Public official (What was the last position?)					

** Profession

Other (please specify)

---

*Unskilled and skilled laborer includes common laborers, miners, motormen, factory workers, carpenters and the like.
**In the case of professions, please note specifically whether professor, doctor, lawyer, priest, artist, or other.

14. Is your occupation the same as _____ or different from _____ your father's (or foster father's)?
    Is your present company the same as _____ or different from _____ your father's (or foster father's)?
    Did you have relatives who were in the company _____ or not _____ before you entered the company?
    (If so, what was their relation to you and rank in the company? _____.)
15. Was your family formerly nobility _____, samurai _____, or commoner _____?
16. Is your religion Shinto _____, Buddhism _____, Christianity _____, other _____, or none _____?
    If you have comments about this study or concerning your career, please note them below.

February 15, 1960

Dear Sir:

The topmost leaders of the industrial spheres of each country exert a great influence on the economy and society of their countries. Factual studies are being carried out in the Western countries regarding these leadership groups. Last year we conducted a survey on the social backgrounds of contemporary Japanese leadership groups in political and intellectual circles as well as the business world. This year we are confining our research subjects to the topmost business leaders of present-day Japan and attempting to answer such questions as the following: What kinds of men are the executives in the largest business firms? What is their training and background? How did they reach their present positions? Comparison of our results with the results of various similar studies of foreign countries should illuminate special features of our society.

This survey is purely academic in nature. A select group of subjects has been chosen as a sample after careful investigation. Because the items in the enclosed questionnaire cover personal data, they will be kept strictly confidential by the researchers. The answer to the questions can generally be made by check mark or a simple entry on the form. Although we appreciate the many demands on your time, we request your reply and ask that you forward the completed questionnaire to us.

In case you wish to make comments about this study or supply additional facts concerning your career, we would appreciate your noting them on the reverse side of the questionnaire. Thank you for your attention. Your cooperation will be deeply appreciated.

> Sincerely,
> Assistant Professor of Sociology
> Kwansei Gakuin University
> Mannari Hiroshi
>
> Manager, International Standard
>   Electric Corporation
> Research Associate, Massachusetts Institute of Technology
> James C. Abegglen, Ph. D.

> Japan Federation of Employers' Associations
> 2, 1 Marunouchi, Chiyoda-ku, Tokyo
> February 15, 1960

Dear Sir:

Re: Request for Cooperation in a Study of Industrial Leaders

We call to your attention a very interesting undertaking, an academic study of the highest level of leadership in the economic spheres of modern Japan, the characteristics and trends of modern society in our country, and a comparison with research results already obtained in various other countries. The study will be conducted by Mr. James C. Abegglen, manager, International Standard Electric Corporation, and research associate, Massachusetts Institute of Technology, and Mr. Mannari Hiroshi, assistant professor of sociology, Kwansei Gakuin University, with the assistance of Dr. Kurauchi Kazuta, professor, Osaka University, and president of the Japan Sociological Society, and Dr. Hori Tsuneo, president of Kwansei Gakuin University, with the support of the Asia Foundation.

Last year the principal researchers made a successful pilot survey on the social background of industrial and political as well as intellectual leaders. On the basis of this survey they wish to conduct a more extensive study of business leaders. We believe that the study is worthwhile.

The items of the enclosed questionnaire deal rather briefly with one's birth, job history and the like. Although we appreciate how busy you are, we request your understanding of the purposes of this research, and, on behalf of the researchers and myself, I most earnestly request your cooperation.

                Hayakawa Masaru

                Secretary

                Japan Federation of Employers' Associations

Appendix III

RESEARCH METHODS FOR PART II

Definition of Sample

In order to study continuities and changes of origin of elites over the periods of 1880, 1920 and 1960, we faced difficulties in finding exact criteria for defining who was to be studied.* We adopted the following general definition first; the term *elite* or *leader* refers to persons who hold top positions in business, political organizations, and intellectual communities, whose positions are acknowledged to be powerful and prestigious and who are publicly recognized as leaders. We decided to identify positions or statuses in important hierarchies or organizations. Therefore, without specific reference to the individuals who might be occupying the positions, and without considering fame, reputation, or other indications, we must establish our listing of the positions to be studied at each period of time and ensure that these positions are comparable.

The first question then is: how do we determine the top ranks of Japanese society at three time points? It was decided that about 400 positions would be included in the study sample in each period, and that these would be drawn approximately as follows:

---

*It should be noted that we have conducted our research after the two similar projects had been undertaken. We are grateful to Professor Everett E. Hagen, who made available to us his research data on 175 Japanese business leaders from around 1850 to around 1900. Professor R. P. Dore generously let us check our collected data against his data. His sample includes 2,300 males born before 1890 who died after 1880 and achieved sufficient eminence to be included in the biological dictionary *Nihon Dai Jinmei Jiten* (Tokyo: Heibonsha, 1958). Their research data were especially helpful in defining our research sample and collecting data, although we felt these two studies also have some weakness in defining who is to be studied. Their results have been reported in the following works: Hagen, Everett E., *On The Theory of Social Change*, (Howewood, Illinois: The Dorsey Press, Inc., 1962), pp. 349–52; R. P. Dore, "Mobility, Equality and Individuation in Modern Japan," in R. P. Dore (ed.), *Aspects of Social Change in Modern Japan* (Princeton; Princeton University Press, 1967).

100 from the several categories of political leadership; 100 from the group described as intellectual leaders: and 200 from the business community. These quite arbitrary totals were decided on since the figures would be sufficient to allow for such broad statistical manipulation as might be necessary in drawing comparisons between and within the several groups. It should be noted that in effect the sample has been selected backward over time, beginning with those positions judged to be the most important in 1960 and then for the 1920 and 1880 periods.

Sampling of 1960 Elite

In a pilot study* on Japan's elite, we defined our sample in political, intellectual, and business sectors in Japanese society. It was further decided that political leaders would here be defined as including cabinet members, leaders in the Diet, officials of the political parties, and senior members of the civil service. No empirical basis for weighting the sample with one or another of these groups presented itself, and a simple equal division among them was seen as desirable. On further consideration a fifth category was added to the political leader group: trade union leaders. The inclusion of this group of leaders in the political category might be debated, but the trade union movement in Japan is indeed considerably political, and the close connection between the trade unions and the minority Socialist Party made inclusion of this group of leaders useful as a counterbalance to the bias toward conservative leaders that selection on the basis of cabinet and Diet status would cause.

The term "intellectual leaders" is not entirely felicitous, but no better term could be found. In Japan the role and status of the members of the university community, and the influence and authority of the artist, critic, and journalist, are such as clearly to provide social leadership. While hardly homogeneous in major activities, these made up a group distinguishable from the political and business groups. Arbitrarily it was determined that the intellectual leader group as defined for this study would include professional

*The details of sampling and data collection are stated in Abegglen, James C. and Mannari, Hiroshi, "Leaders of Modern Japan: Social Origins and Mobility," *Economic Development and Cultural Change*, Vol. IX, No. 1, Part II, October, 1960.

men–doctors, lawyers, priests, and the like–the leaders of the academic community, leading journalists, critics, and authors, and finally leaders in the entertainment fields–actors, musicians, and artists.

Of the three categories of leadership established for this sample, the business community causes least difficulty in definition and selection. The number to be included in this group was made larger than the others, primarily because of interest in undertaking comparisons with results obtained in research in other countries. Since the total was to be rather small, however, it was decided to include in the sample only the men holding the topmost positions in the largest business organizations. In addition, the influence of business associations in Japan suggested the need to include senior officers of certain leading business associations as well.

With this broad definition of the sample desired for the survey, the invaluable assistance of two groups of authorities was obtained in the task of specifying the men to be studied. The Research Department of Mainichi Shimbun Sha, a major newspaper publishing firm, undertook the tedious work of naming the positions and men that, in the judgment of the staff of the department, are the foremost leaders of the political and intellectual communities in present-day Japan.

Since we planned to collect data by mailing questionnaires, we had expected about one-half or two-thirds of returns out of total mailing. In order to collect 100 responses each from political and intellectual leaders, we had to have a total of 300 to 400 individuals. The Mainichi experts in fact selected for the study a total of 335 persons, 171 in the political sphere and 164 in the intellectual community. It was the judgment of the members of the Research Department that these 335 were the leaders of Japan in 1959 in these two areas, and that there was a marked division, or falling-off, below this number of persons. While the department members could agree that the 335 men named were indeed leaders, when additional names were proposed such agreement was lacking. Therefore, the authors were advised that the 335 men listed would be an adequate and thorough sample of the topmost stratum of political and intellectual leaders. The department's judgment was accepted, and the mailing list then included 335 men from these two areas.

The Research Department of the Diamond Publishing Company, one of Japan's leading publishers of business books, journals and directories, undertook to select the business leader sample. Here again a similar result occurred: after the selection of some 350 names, it was stated that these formed one stratum, after which a great many more names would need to be included since general agreement would be lacking as to whether a given man was or was not a leader. In the case of the selection of businessmen, the list provided by the Diamond Publishing Company was later reviewed by the secretary of the Japan Federation of Employers' Associations. With the addition of about 10 names to the listing, the federation's staff agreed that the list did indeed represent Japan's top level contemporary business leadership.

The final mailing list then included 360 businessmen, 171 political leaders, and 164 persons in scholarly, professional, artistic, or journalistic pursuits. After sending questionnaires to these 695 men, we received 412 responses: 212 from business leaders, 100 from political leaders, and 100 from intellectual leaders. The details of administration of questionnaires, representativeness of these responses, and accuracy of answers tested are stated elsewhere. These responses provide us the data for Japan's elite in 1960, as shown in table 1, Sample of Japan's Leaders: 1880s, 1920 and 1960.

Sampling of 1920 Elite

We had a listing of around 400 positions that we believed to be the 400 top men of Japan in 1950–60. Now, regarding the Taishō elite, a listing should be prepared to provide a 1 to 1 equivalence. In other words, a civil service position for 1959–60 should have a 1920 equivalent beside it. Then it would be necessary to find out who filled that position in 1920, and finally to obtain the necessary background data for that man. Some of the positions for 1920 may not be identical with 1959–60, but should be as nearly equivalent as possible.

*Abegglen and Mannari, *op. cit.*, pp. 130–34. It should be noted that in addition to the total responses in the pilot research, we have received more answers through remailing.

Table 1. Sample of Japan's Leaders: 1880s, 1920, 1960

	1880s	1920	1960
Total Sample	384	400	412
Political Leaders			
Cabinet members	10	10	10
Diet leaders	16	16	16
Party leaders	18	18	18
Higher civil servants	40	38	38
Labor leaders	—	18	18
Total	84	100	100
Intellectual Leaders			
Professional	22	22	22
Religious	(10)	(10)	(10)
Law	(5)	(5)	(5)
M.D., etc.	(7)	(7)	(7)
Scholars and professors	41	41	41
Journalists and writers	20	20	20
Artists	17	17	17
Total	100	100	100
Business Leaders			
Mining	10	8	8
Construction	4	4	4
Steel, metal, etc.	4	12	12
Machinery	11	34	36
Chemicals (includes cement, pharmaceuticals, ceramics, glass, etc.)	20	26	28
Textile, etc.	33	24	25
Food	18	12	13
Trading	29	10	11
Finance and insurance	40	34	36
Public utilities	22	26	27
Other services	9	10	12
Total	200	200	212

We found that in some cases, after the man occupying the equivalent 1920 position had been identified, it was not possible to obtain the needed biographical data. Thus, we attempted, in drawing up the list of equivalent positions for 1920, to also list alternatives. For example, since we had ten cabinet members in the 1959–60 sample, any ten of the twelve cabinet ministers of 1920 might be considered equivalent. We used in our sample only ten, depending on which men it was possible to get background data about. Then, our first task was to draw up a master list of positions. After the positions were identified, the men's names were listed. After sampling policy was decided, the actual political and intellectual leaders were identified by Professor Sadahira Motoshiro of Kwansei Gakuin University through his specialized knowledge of modern political and cultural history in Japan. His listing for political and intellectual leaders was reviewed and concurred in by a staff member of the Research Department of the Mainichi Shimbun, which had selected the 1959–60 sample for political and intellectual elite. The major references for the sampling are the following:

1. *Kokumin Nenkan,* 1920 and 1921 (Kokumin Newspaper Yearbook) (Tokyo: Kokumin Shimbun Sha, 1920 and 1921).
2. *Mainichi Nenkan,* 1920 and 1921 (Mainichi Newspaper Yearbook) (Osaka: Mainichi Shimbun Sha, 1920 and 1921).
3. *Naikaku Shokuin Roku,* 1920 and 1921 (Personnel list of the Japanese Government) (Tokyo: Cabinet Printing Office, Japanese Government, 1920 and 1921).
4. Others: Almanacs of labor, religion, art, journalism, entertainment, etc.

The 1920 sample of business leaders was selected by the author familiar with the sampling of the 1959–60 counterparts. In order to control comparability of the 1920 and 1960 samples, we selected eight positions in mining in 1920 as the same proportion we selected in 1960. Similarly the same proportions in banking and insurance were identified in 1920 parallel to the 1960 sample. In selecting leaders, we examined the capitalization of companies in each sector of business and industry in 1920, using the following references:

1. *Kabushiki Kaisha Nenkan,* 1920 and 1922 (Yearbook of Limited Stock Companies) (Osaka: The Research Department, Nomura Shoten, 1920 and 1922).

2. *Tōyō Keizai Kabushiki Kaisha Nenkan, No. 1* (Tōyō Keizai's Yearbook of Limited Stock Companies) (Tokyo: Tōyō Keizai Shimpō Sha, 1921).
3. *Kokumin Nenkan,* 1920 and 1921 (Kokumin Newspaper Yearbook) (Tokyo: Kokumin Shimbun Sha, 1920 and 1921).
4. *Mainichi Nenkan,* 1920 and 1921 (Mainichi Newspaper Yearbook) (Osaka: Mainichi Shimbun Sha, 1920 and 1921).
5. Meiji Taishō Shi Kankōkai (ed.) *Meiji Taishō Shi:* 15 Vol. (History of the Meiji and Taishō Periods) (Tokyo: Jitsugyō no Sekai Sha, 1929).
6. Sawamoto, Moko, (ed.) *Nihon Sangyō Shi.* 2 Vol. (History of Japanese Industry) (Tokyo: Teikoku Tsūshin Sha, 1928).
7. Kinukawa, Taichi, *Hompō Menshi Bōseki Shi,* 4 Vol. (History of Japan's Cotton Textiles) (Osaka: Nihon Mengyō Club, 1937).

In adapting this method of sampling, we could not always include all the largest firms in the Japanese business world at the time, but we included the largest in each category of industry. Mining and trading were the leading businesses and industries at the time. The capitalization of such companies in our 1920 sample was distinctly larger than that of other types of business. Construction and chemical industries were markedly smaller in capitalization. We selected the same proportion of positions in each category in 1920 as in 1960, in accordance with rank of capitalization. The number of leaders selected and capitalization in various industrial sectors are shown in the following table:

Our method of sampling had two difficulties. First, we did not take into account development of the Japanese economy in the two periods of time. Second, we did not take into account changes of industrial structure in the two different periods.

Sampling of 1880s Elite

The selection of the Meiji elite was more complex. This period was the beginning of Japan's industrialization. The positions of political, intellectual, and business leadership in the 1880s are often unlike those of 1920 and 1960. However, we carried our sampling policy throughout the three points of time with a little operational modification.

One important modification was to extend the sampling period

Table 2. Sample of 1920 Japanese Business Leaders

Type of Business and Industry	Number of Leaders Selected	Capitalization Largest and Smallest
Mining	8	100–10 million yen
Construction	4	3–1
Iron and steel	12	30–2
Machinery	34	50–1.5
Chemical industry	26	22–1.5
Textile	24	50–1.2
Food	12	40–2.5
Trade	10	100–10
Finance	34	100–3
Public utility	26	440–3
Other	10	2.5–0*
Total	200	

*A few (e.g., chambers of commerce) were not capitalized.

from the one year of 1880 to five or ten years: political and intellectual leaders for 1880–1885; business leaders for 1880–89. By using five or ten, rather than one year for this period, it was possible to obtain enough positions to compare with the later samples.

The selection of political and intellectual leaders was undertaken by Professor Sadahira Motoshiro, who selected their counterparts in the 1920 sample. In selecting political leaders, he tried to identify positions comparable to those in 1920, despite the fact that the political system was fluid in the 1880–85 period. These positions are identified either for 1880 or for 1880–85. There was no organized labor movement in 1880–85, so our sample of Meiji political leaders does not include labor leaders. Thus, the total of political leaders of the Meiji period was 84 instead of 100. The intellectual leaders were selected by Professor Sadahira in the same way.

The references used for selecting Meiji political and intellectual elite are the following:

1. Kanai, Yukiyasu, (ed.), *Meiji Shiryō Ken'yō Shokumu Honinroku* (Appointments of Meiji Senior Administrative Officials) 2 vol. [n.p.] 1903. (Publisher not specified. It is assembled from various sources. This is reproduced and published by Tokyo: Kashiwa

Shobō, 1967). This work includes all appointments of higher civil, military, educational and legislative branches of the Japanese Government from 1868 to 1902.
2. Ōtsuka, Takematsu, (ed.), *Hyakkan Rireki.* 2 vol. (Career of Senior Officials) (Tokyo: Nippon Shiseki Kyōkai, 1927).
3. Miyake, Yujirō, (ed.), *Shin Nihon Shi,* 5 vol. (New History of Japan) (Tokyo: Manchōsha, 1926).
4. Meiji Taishō Shi Kankōkai, (ed), *Meiji Taishō Shi,* 15 vol. (History of the Meiji and Taishō Periods) (Tokyo: Jitsugyō no Sekai Sha, 1929).
5. Department of History, Kyoto University, ed. *Nihon Kindai Shi Jiten* (Handbook of Japan's Modern History) (Tokyo: Tōyō Keizai Shimpō Sha, 1958).

The business leaders of the Meiji period were selected by Dr. Yunoki Manabu, an economic historian at Kwansei Gakuin University. He originally selected 240 business leaders according to our sampling policy. Among the total 40 were alternatives. The extension of the sampling period from 1880–85 to 1880–89 was necessary because we could not identify 200 major business leaders for 1880–85 alone. Since most of the firms did not have capitalization in that period, the selection of firms and leaders could not be based on that or any other single criterion. Instead, Dr. Yunoki selected business leaders in reference to production, selling, or capitalization through examining reliable historical records of each field of business and industry. Again eight positions in mining (comparable to 1920 and 1960) were selected. We could not find comparable numbers of leaders in steel and machinery, because these fields were not yet developed. For the same reason, 50 percent of the Meiji business leaders were drawn from mining and manufacturing and 50 percent from tertiary industry, instead of 60 percent and 40 percent as in the 1920 and 1960 samples.

The major references for the Meiji business sampling were the following:
1. Sawamoto, Moko, (ed.), *Nihon Sangyō Shi* 2 vol. (History of Japanese industry) (Tokyo: Teikoku Tsūshin Sha, 1928).
2. Meiji Taishō Shi Kankōkai, (ed.), *Meiji Taishō Shi,* 15 vol. (History of the Meiji and Taishō Periods) (Tokyo: Jitsugyō no Sekai Sha, 1929).

3. Miyake, Yujirō, (ed.), *Shin Nihon Shi,* 5 vol. (New History of Japan) (Tokyo: Manchōsha, 1926).
4. Kōgyōkai, (ed.), *Nihon Kōgyō Shi,* 13 vol. (History of Japan's Industrial Enterprise) (Tokyo: Kōgyōkai, 1925–28).

The 240 business leaders in 1880–89 whom the researchers judged to have held positions equivalent to those of the 1920 and 1960 samples were further reviewed by Dr. Horie Yasuzō, professor of economic history, Kyoto University. He identified 160 business leaders from our list and added several names to our list. The foregoing sampling methods can be illustrated as follows:

Type of Elite Leader	1960 Position	1920 Equivalent Position	1920 Alternative Equivalent	1880–89 Equivalent Position	1880–89 Alternative Equivalent
Political	Ambassador to the U.S.	Ambassador to the U.S.	Ambassador to the U.K.	Minister to the U.S.	Minister to a major Western country
Intellectual	Artist	Artist	Artist	Artist	Artist
Business	President of Fuji Steel, Ltd.	President, large metal processing company		President, heavy manufacturing company	

This method of sampling posed some problems, but we found this type to be the best procedure for accurate identification of trends over the three periods.

Overlapping Sample of Japan's Elite: 1880, 1920 and 1960

Some problems were posed by the overlapping of two sample groups. Many of the Meiji elite assumed influential positions, either by achievement or on an ascriptive basis, at a young age and stayed in top positions for a prolonged period. We examined the resulting overlapping to see whether it gave any bias to our research results. We had tried to avoid overlapping; however, our sampling policy—to select men in comparable positions in 1880, 1920, and 1960—made some overlapping inevitable.

A total of 29 cases in the Taishō sample appeared also in the Meiji sample, and 11 among the 1960 sample were in the Taishō sample. Most cases of overlapping are in the same elite group, but 7 out of 40 overlapping cases appear in different elite sectors. Among the 1920 business leaders, 15 men had held positions of leadership in 1880–89. Most were the founders of the enterprise and remained in the chief executive position for a long period.

Data Collecting

Data were collected for the 1959–60 sample by mail questionnaire. The administration of research and reliability tests of answered responses are reported elsewhere.* Data for the 1920 sample were collected next, and then data for the 1880 sample, in three steps:

For the primary step for collecting data, we used the following:
1. *Dai-Jimmei Jiten,* 10 vol. (Great Biographical Dictionary) (Tokyo: Heibonsha, 1958).
2. *Jinji Kōshin Roku* (Who's Who) (Tokyo: Jinji Kōshin Sho) (6th ed., 1921, 5th ed., 1918, 2nd. ed. 1908, and lst ed., 1903).

These two sources provided in most cases sufficient data on education, career, and achievement, but they lack details of the family origins that we are most interested in.

As a second step, we used vast numbers of autobiographies and biographies in the biographical sections of Kwansei Gakuin University Library, Kobe University Library, Kyoto University Library, and the library of Mainichi Shimbun Sha. These libraries provided not only individual biographies but cumulative biographies of politicians, scholars, lawyers, physicians, and businessmen. Some of these biographical publications used for collecting data are the following:

Hagihara, Yoshitarō, *Teikoku Hakushi Retsuden* (Biographies of Imperial Doctoral Degree) (Tokyo: Keigyō Sha, 1890).
Haraguchi, Reizei, (ed.), *Kōmei Daigennin Retsuden* (Biographies of Eminent Lawyers) (Tokyo: 1886).
Jitsugyō no Sekai Sha, (ed.), *Zaikai Bukko Ketsubutsuden,* 2 vol. (Biographies of Deceased Eminent Businessmen) (Tokyo: Jitsugyō no Sekai Sha, 1936).

---

*Abeggler, James C. and Mannari, Hiroshi, *op. cit.*, pp. 130–4.

Kiyoura, Tsunemichi, *Jitsugyō 50 Nenshi*, 5 vol. (History of 50 Years of Business) (Tokyo: Jitsugyō Kyōiku Shinkōkai, 1937).

Sugiura, Eiichi, *Chūkyō Zaikaishi* (Business History of Nagoya) (Nagoya: Chūbū Keizai Shimbun Sha, 1956).

Tamura, Eitarō, *Nihon no Sangyō Shidōsha* (Japan's Industrial Leaders) (Tokyo: Kokumin Tosho Kankōkai, 1944).

Tsuboya, Zenshirō, *Jitsugyōka Hyakketsu Den*, 6 vol. (One Hundred Biographies of Businessmen) (Tokyo: Tōkyōdō Shobō, 1892).

Umezawa, Hikotarō, (ed.), *Kindai Meii Issekiwa* (Stories of Modern Eminent Physicians) (Tokyo: Nihon Ijishimpō Sha, 1937).

Yamadera, Seijirō, *Tōkyō Jitsugyōka* (Businessmen in Tokyo) (Tokyo: Gyokushu-kan, 1892).

The Research Department of the Mainichi Newspaper Company greatly aided us by permitting use of its files on eminent figures in all fields. Many questions regarding higher officials and labor leaders in the 1920 period were answered from these files.

As one of the researchers participated in an interdepartmental seminar on modernization at Kyoto University, that biographical collection also became available to us. The seminar members provided us not with only biographical data but also advice for selecting the samples.

The collection of local histories in the Department of Sociology and the central library of Kyoto University provided another source for answering questionnaires as well as checking the accuracy of our collected data. These histories contain biographies of eminent men. For business leaders large numbers of company histories provide biographies of company founders and early chief executives.

Finally, to obtain other data, we wrote to local librarians, local historians, town and village offices, companies, and in a few cases descendants of men in the early samples. (Copies of the questionnaire and our accompanying letter follow.) We introduced our research interest by sending a reprint of the research results of our study of the 1960 elite. Some respondents gave us names of more adequate informants, and we traced them.

Faculty of Sociology
Kwansei Gakuin University
Nishinomiya City

Assistant Professor of Sociology   Research Associate
Kwansei Gakuin University   Massachusetts Institute of
Mannari Hiroshi   Technology
    James C. Abegglen, Ph. D.

May _____ , 1961

Dear Sir:

We have been engaged in a research project on Japan's leaders and investigating social backgrounds of these men. Some of the research findings were reported in a journal of the University of Chicago, and a reprint of the Japanese translation, April issue 1961 of *Americana* is attached. We wish to have you read it. Parallel to this study, we plan to examine the origins and careers of Taisho (1920) and Meiji (1880–89) leaders and analyze the process of elite recruitment in the course of Japan's modernization. We have already filled out our research items by using biographies and *Who's Who*. However, it is difficult to identify detailed information of occupation of father or family feudal status, which is important to our study. Therefore, we are requesting this information from descendants, local offices or libraries, or local historians who are related to the leaders. These leaders are selected on the basis of holding comparable positions in 1960 and 1920, and were identified by scholars specializing in the modern history of Japan. While we appreciate the many demands on your time, we request your reply and ask that you forward the completed questionnaire to us. We plan to publish the findings of this research. If you are interested in reading these, please note this on the questionnaire.

Our questionnaire covers detail, so please feel free to write whatever you know. We will appreciate it very much if you could indicate further informants in case you do not know. With best regards.

Sincerely,

Japan's Elite in 1880s Period Questionnaire

Name _____ (Born _____ Died _____ year) Name of
Position _____

Please check or fill out the underlined space

1. Birthplace
   (Name at time of birth) _____ Kuni _____ Gun _____
      Town or village
   (Name at present) _____ Prefecture _____ City/
      County _____ Town or Village
   (Name of feudal domain in Tokugawa period) _____
2. Occupation or family feudal status of father and paternal grandfather
   a. If his father was a samurai, specify family fief, family rank,
      or official position _____
      If his father was a villager, specify whether country samurai,
      village headman, landlord, trader, manufacturer, or tenant
      farmer _____
      If his father was a townsman, specify type of business, and
      whether wholesale or retail _____
   b. What was the social status of his grandfather? Same as
      father _____ different _____ Specify _____
   c. If he was adopted, specify status of real father _____
3. Education and training of subject
   a. No education _____ had education _____
      unknown _____
   b. If he had education, name of school _____
      teacher _____
   c. Details _____
4. Other questions
   a. Has a biography of him been published? _____ If so,
      specify _____
   b. If the biography is a rare book, indicate library or man who
      has a copy _____
   c. Other information _____
5. Any other informant: name _____ address _____
   If you have comments on the questionnaire or further remarks
   concerning the subject, please note below.

Appendix IV

LISTS OF FAMILY FEUDAL STATUS AND OCCUPATIONAL BACKGROUNDS OF JAPAN'S ELITE GROUPS, 1880–1960

Table 1. Feudal Origin of Meiji Elite

Feudal Status		Specific Position of Father	
Kuge or daimyo	*13*	Imperial family	1
		Minister, councilor, general in imperial court	4
		"*Kuge*" (position not specified)	3
		Monseki (priest)	2
		Daimyo	3
Samurai	*178*		
Upper Class	19	Minister of daimyo	7
		Manager for daimyo	5
		Other senior retainer of daimyo	3
		Vassal of shogun	3
		"Upper samurai" (position not specified)	1
Middle Class	52	District magistrate	8
		Financial and other magistrate	11
		Lieutenant of daimyo	10
		Lesser retainers of daimyo	8
		"Middle class samurai" (position not specified)	15
Professional	47	Physician for daimyo	30
		Confucian scholar	7
		Artist for daimyo	3
		Calligrapher	2
		Japanese classic scholar	2
		Professor of Western studies	1

		Other professions	2
Lower Class	60	Lower class retainer	15
		Subordinate to retainer	6
		Foot soldier	4
		Other lower class samurai	5
		"Lower class samurai" (position not specified)	28
		Other samurai (rank not specified)	2
Farmer	*59*		
Country samurai	12	*Gōshi* (country samurai)	12
Village headman and landlord	36	Village headman	16
		Village headman and trader or manufacturer	3
		Landlord	13
		Landlord and trader or manufacturer	4
Farmer	11	Owner-farmer	6
		Peasant or tenant	5
Townsman	*131*		
Professional	25	Town physician	10
		Artist or entertainer	9
		Priest	5
		Scholar	1
Merchant or businessman	101	*Sake* or *shōyu* maker or dealer	18
		Dealer in rice, sugar, tea or tobacco	11
		Purveyor to shogun and daimyo	10
		Dry goods store owner	10
		Lumber and construction	8
		Textile trader or manufacturer	8
		Druggist	6
		Money exchanger	6
		Steel wholesaler	3
		Manufacturer, machinery or ceramics	3
		Other retailer or wholesaler	18

Other	5	Bantō (clerk)	2
		Religious sculptor	1
		Coal miner	1
		Messenger	1

(Total: 381)
(Unknown: 3)

Table 2. Feudal Origin of 1920 Elite

Feudal Status		Specific Position of Father	
Kuge or daimyo	*8*	Shogun	1
		Daimyo	3
		Monseki (priest)	3
		"Kuge" (position not specified)	1
Samurai	*159*		
Upper class	25	Minister of daimyo	7
		Vassal of shogun	5
		Manager for daimyo	3
		Other senior retainer for daimyo	3
		"Upper samurai" (position not specified)	7
Middle class	21	District magistrate	4
		Financial or other magistrate	4
		Retainer of daimyo	4
		Lieutenant of daimyo	2
		"Middle class samurai" (position not specified)	7
Professional	21	Confucian scholar	7
		Physician	7
		Japanese classic scholar or calligrapher	4
		Artist	3
Lower class	46	Foot soldier	12
		Lower class retainer	7

		Subordinate to retainer	6
		"Lower class samurai"	
		(position not specified)	21
Samurai (rank not specified)	46	Satsuma	5
		Chōshū	4
		Kanazawa	4
		Tosa	3
		Aizu	2
		Saga	2
		Other class	26
Farmer	*99*		
Country samurai	15	*Gōshi* (country samurai)	15
Head villager and landlord	71	Landlord	32
		Village headman and landlord	31
		Landlord and trader or manufacturer	8
Farmer	13	Owner-farmer	5
		Peasant or tenant	8
Townsman	*124*		
Profession	26	Town physician	11
		Arist or entertainer	7
		Scholar or teacher	4
		Priest	4
Merchant	86	Retail store owner	30
		Sake or *shōyu* maker	12
		Dry goods store owner	10
		Wholesaler or broker	10
		Mining or manufacture	10
		Money exchanger	8
		Construction or lumber merchant	6
Artisan, Laborer	12	Carpenter	4
		Factory laborer	4
		Machinist	2
		Miner	2
(Total: 390)			
(Unknown: 10)			

Table 3. Occupation of Father: 1920 Leaders

Occupation of Father		Specific Occupation of Father	
Laborer	1	Silkweaver	1
Farmer	11	Owner-farmer	5
		Tenant or peasant (ownership status not specified)	6
Landlord	71	Landlord	36
		Landlord and village headman	16
		Landlord and trader or manufacturer	10
		Gōshi	9
White Collar Worker	17	House steward	3
		Bantō (clerk in merchant firm)	2
		Clerk in central government office	4
		Clerk in local government office	6
		Teacher	2
Owner, Small Business	52	Retainer	25
		Wholesaler or broker	9
		Mining or manufacturing	9
		Sake or *shōyu* maker	7
		Owner, small business (not specified)	2
Owner or Executive, Large Business	76	Banking and insurance	20
		Trade (foreign or domestic)	15
		Mining, steel, machinery, chemical	12
		Sake and food industry	8
		Transportation or public utility	6
		Textile or paper	3
		Construction	3
		Other service business	8
		Owner, large business (not specified)	1

Government Official	*36*	Senior official (e.g., prime minister, privy councilor)	14
		Ministry of Justice	3
		Ministry of Home Affairs	3
		Ministry of Finance	2
		Imperial court	1
		Military officer: Major	2
		Admiral	1
		Mayor or senior official in local office	10
Profession	*58*	Professor or scholar	17
		Doctor	18
		Religious (Buddhist 4, Shinto 2)	6
		Artist (actor 7, painter, writer, etc.)	13
		Lawyer	4
Samurai	*77*	Upper class	23
		Middle class	15
		Lower class	19
(Total: 399) (Unknown: 1)		Position not specified	20

Table 4. Occupation of Father: 1960 Leaders

Occupation of Father	Number	Specific Occupation of Father	
Laborer	4	Boatman	1
		Blacksmith	1
		Steel worker	1
		Shipyard worker	1
Farmer	35	Tenant farmer or owne farmer (no other known occupation)	33
		Owner farmer and textile mfg.	1
		Farmer and fisherman	1
Landlord	70	Landlord (no other occupation specified)	52

		Landlord and village or town mayor	12
		Landlord and retail store owner	3
		Landlord and factory owner	3
White Collar Worker	38	Clerk in merchant firm	11
		Clerk in central government office	14
		Teacher	9
		Clerk in local office	4
Owner, Small Business	61	Retailer	11
		Sake or *shōyu* maker	10
		Wholesaler or broker	8
		Construction and manufacturing	4
		Other service	8
		Owner, small business (not specified)	20
Owner, Large or Medium Business	62	Steel, machinery, chemical mfg.	13
		Banking and insurance	11
		Transportation and public utility	9
		Trader (foreign or domestic)	8
		Sake and food industry	7
		Textile and paper	5
		Construction	5
		Other service business	3
		Owner, large or medium business (not specified)	1
Manager, Large or Medium Business	32	Banking or insurance	13
		Steel, machinery, chemical	9
		Trading	3
		Food industry	3
		Textile	2
		Other service business	2
Government official	45	Senior official (e.g., councilor, cabinet secretary)	8

		Ministry of Justice	6
		Ministry of Home Affairs	4
		Government engineer	3
		Ministry of Foreign Affairs	3
		Lower house of Diet	2
		Military officer: General	2
		Colonel	4
		Major or senior staff in local office	7
		Principal of primary or high school	3
		Postmaster	2
		Position unknown	1
Profession	54	Doctor	21
		Religious (Shinto 2, Buddhist 4, Christian 2)	9
		Artist (actor, author, painter, etc.)	7
		Lawyer	6
		Professor	6
		Engineer	2
		Other profession	3
Other	5	Samurai	3
		No occupation	2

(Total: 406)
(No Answer: 6)

BIBLIOGRAPHY

Note: Only those published items which have been cited in the text or footnotes of this volume are included in this listing.

Abegglen, James C., *The Japanese Factory* (Glencoe, Illinois: The Free Press, 1958)

Abegglen, James C. and Mannari, Hiroshi, "Leaders of Modern Japan: Social Origins and Mobility," *Economic Development and Cultural Change* (Chicago: University of Chicago), IX:1, Part II (Oct. 1960)

Aonuma, Yoshimatsu, *Nihon no Keieisō* (The Managerial Class in Japan) (Tokyo: Nihon Keizai Shimbun Sha, 1965)

Azumi, Koya, *Higher Education and Business Recruitment in Japan* (New York: Teachers College, Columbia University, 1969)

Bettignies, H. C. de, "Leaders Across the Ocean: Comparing American and European Chief Executives," *European Business*, no. 26, Summer 1970.

Bureau of Statistics, Imperial Cabinet, *Japan Imperial Statistical Yearbook*, No. 7, 1888.

_____ No. 23, 1904.

_____ No. 25, 1906.

_____ No. 33, 1914.

_____ No. 48, 1929.

_____, *Shokugyō, Kokusei Chōsa Hōkoku*, Vol. II (Occupations: 1920 National Census Report, 1929)

_____, *Shokugyō to Sangyō: 1930 Kokusei Chōsa Hōkoku* (Occupation and Industry: Census Report of 1930), 1935.

_____, Office of the Prime Minister, *Japan Statistical Yearbook 1961* (Tokyo: Japan Statistical Association, 1962)

_____, *Japan Statistical Yearbook*, 1970.

_____, *1960 and 1970 Population Census of Japan*, 1962 and 1972.

Clark, Colin, *The Conditions of Economic Progress*, 2nd ed. (London Macmillan, 1951)

Copeman, G. H., *Leaders of British Industry* (London: Gee & Company, 1955)

Dai Bukan (The Great Directory of Samurai), Vol. 10 (Tokyo: Daigō Sha, 1936)

Dai-Jinmei Jiten, 10 vol. (Great Biographical Dictionary) (Tokyo: Heibonsha, 1958)

Department of Japanese History, Kyoto University (ed.), *Kindaishi Jiten* (Handbook of Modern History) (Tokyo: Tōyō Keizai Shimpō Sha, 1958)

Diamond, Robert S., "A Self-Portrait of the Chief Executives," *Fortune* (May 1970)

Dore, R. P., "Mobility, Equality, and Individuation in Modern Japan," in *Aspects of Social Change in Modern Japan*, edited by R. P. Dore (Princeton: Princeton University Press, 1967)

_____, *Education in Tokugawa Japan*, (Berkeley and Los Angeles: University of California Press, 1965)

Erickson, Charlotte, *British Industrialists* (London: Cambridge University Press, 1959)

Foote, Nelson N. and Hatt, Paul K., "Social Mobility and Economic Advancement," *American Economic Review*, Vol. 43 (May 1953)

Fujita, Gorō, *Nihon Kindai Sangyō no Seisei* (The Development of Modern Japanese Industry)(Tokyo: Yūhikaku, 1948)

Fukuchi, Shigetaka, *Shizoku to Samurai Ishiki* (Samurai Consciousness) (Tokyo: Shunjū Sha, 1956)

Furushima, Toshio, *Kisei Jinushi no Seisei to Tenkai* (Development of Parasitical Landowners) (Tokyo: Iwanami Shoten, 1952)

Glass, D. V., *Social Mobility in Britain* (London: Routledge and Kegan Paul, Ltd., 1954)

Gregory, Frances W. and Neu, Irene D., "The American Industrial Elite in the 1870s—Their Social Origins," in *Men in Business*, edited by William Miller (Cambridge, Massachusetts: Harvard University Press, 1952)

Hagen, Everett E., *On the Theory of Social Change* (Homewood, Illinois: The Doresay Press, Inc. 1962)

Hagihara, Yoshitarō, *Teikoku Hakushi Retsuden* (Biographies of Imperial Doctoral Degree) (Tokyo: Keigyō Sha, 1890)

Hall, D. J., Bettignies, H. C. de, and Amado-Fischgrund, G., "The European Business Elite: an Exclusive Survey in Six European Countries." *European Business*, No. 23, October 1969.

Haraguchi, Reizei, (ed.), *Kōmei Daigennin Retsuden* (Biographies of Eminent Lawyers) (Tokyo: 1886)

Hirano, Yoshitarō, *Nihon Shihonshugi Shakai no Kikō* (The Mechanism of Japanese Capitalism) 6th ed. (Tokyo: Iwanami Shoten, 1949)

Hirschmeier, Johannes, *The Origins of Entrepreneurship in Meiji Japan* (Cambridge, Massachusetts: Harvard University Press, 1964)

Hōjin Kigyō Tōkei Nempō (Annual Report of Corporate Enterprises Survey) (Ministry of Finance, Japanese Government, 1961)

Inkeles, Alex and Rossi, Peter H., "National Comparisons of Occupational Prestige," *American Journal of Sociology*, 61 (Jan. 1956)

Ishikawa Ken, *Nihon Shomin Kyōikushi (Educational History of Japanese Commoners)* (Tokyo: Tōkō Shoin, 1934)

———, *Terakoya* (Tokyo: Shibundo, 1960)

———, *Tokugawa Jidai ni okeru Gakkō no Hattatsu* (Development of Schools in the Tokugawa Period) (Tokyo: Iwanami Shoten, 1951)

Jinji Kōshin Roku (Who's Who) (Tokyo: Jinji Kōshin Sho) (20th ed., 1958, 6th ed., 1921, 5th ed., 1918, 2nd ed., 1908, and 1st ed., 1903)

Jitsugyō no Sekai Sha, (ed.), *Zaikai Bukko Ketsubutsuden*, 2 vol. (Biographies of Deceased Eminent Businessmen) (Tokyo: Jitsugyō no Sekai Sha, 1936)

Kabushiki Kaisha Nenkan, 1920 and 1921 (Yearbook of Limited Stock Companies) (Osaka: The Research Department, Nomura Shoten, 1920 and 1921)

Kaisha Nenkan, 1960 (Yearbook of Companies, 1960) (Tokyo: Nihon Keizai Shimbun Sha, 1959)

Kaisha Yōran, 1960 (Yearbook of Companies, 1960) (Tokyo: Daiyamondo Sha, 1959)

Kanai, Yukiyasu, (ed.), *Meiji Shiryō Ken'yō Shokumu Honinroku*, 2 vol. (Appointments of Meiji Senior Administrative Officials), 1903.

Kanno, Watarō, *Nihon Kaisha Kigyō Hassei-shi no Kenkyū* (Study of the Origins of Japanese Company Enterprises) (Tokyo: Iwanami Shoten, 1931)

Keizai Kikakuchō, *Kokumin Shotoku Hakusho,* 1959 (The White Paper on National Income) (Tokyo: Ministry of Finance, Printing Bureau, 1961), p. 31.

Keizai Tōkei Kenkyūsho, (ed.), *Nihon Keizai Tōkei Shū* (Collected Economic Statistics for Japan) (Tokyo: Tōyō Keizai Shimpō Sha, 1960)

Kerr, Clark, Dunlop, John T., Harbison, Frederick, and Myers, Charles, *Industrialism and Industrial Man* (Cambridge, Massachusetts: Harvard University Press, 1960)

Kinukawa, Taichi, *Hompō Menshi Bōseki Shi,* 4 vol. (History of Japan's Cotton Textiles) (Osaka: Nihon Mengyō Club, 1937)

Kiyoura, Tsunemichi, *Jitsugyō 50 Nenshi,* 5 vol. (History of 50 Years of Business) (Tokyo: Jitsugyō Kyōiku Shinkōkai, 1937)

Kodama, Kota, "Bakuhantaisei," *Sekai Daihyakka Jiten* (Encyclopedia of the World), Vol. 23 (Tokyo: Heibonsha, 1958)

Kōgyōkai, (ed.), *Nihon Kōgyō Shi,* 13 vol. (History of Japan's Industrial Enterprise) (Tokyo: Kōgyō Kai, 1925–28)

Kokumin Nenkan, 1920 and 1921 (Kokumin Newspaper Yearbook) (Tokyo: Kokumin Shimbun Sha, 1920 and 1921)

Kubota, Akira, *Higher Civil Servants in Postwar Japan: Their Social Origins, Educational Backgrounds, and Career Patterns* (Princeton: Princeton University Press, 1969)

Lenski, Gerhard E., *Power and Privilege* (New York: McGraw-Hill, 1966)

Lipset, Seymour Martin and Bendix, Reinhard, *Social Mobility in Industrial Society* (Berkeley and Los Angeles: University of California Press, 1959)

Lockwood, William W., *The Economic Development of Japan, Growth and Structural Change, 1868–1938* (Princeton: Princeton University Press, 1954)

Mainichi Nenkan, 1920 and 1921 (Mainichi Newspaper Yearbook) (Osaka: Mainichi Shimbun Sha, 1920 and 1921)

Management Succession (London: The Acton Society Trust, 1956)

Mannari, Hiroshi and Abegglen, James C., "The Japanese Busi-

ness Leaders in 1960 and 1970: Their Social Origins, Education
and Career Patterns," *Social and Cultural Background of Labor-
Management Relations in Asian Countries* (Tokyo: The Japan Institute of Labour, 1972), pp. 43–67.

Marsh, Robert M., *Comparative Sociology* (New York: Harcourt,
Brace & World, Inc., 1967)

Marx, Karl, "A Note on Class," in *Class, Status, and Power,* 2nd
ed., edited by Bendix, Reinhard and Lipset, Seymour Martin,
(New York: The Free Press, 1966)

Matsumoto, Yoshiharu Scott, "Contemporary Japan, the Individual and the Group," *Transactions of the American Philosophical
Society,* New Series Vol. 50, Part I, January 1960.

Meiji Taishō Kokusei Sōran (General Statistics for the Meiji and
Taishō Periods) (Tokyo: Tōyō Keizai Shinpō Sha, 1927)

Meiji Taishō Shi Kankōkai (ed.) *Meiji Taishō Shi:* 15 Vol.
(History of the Meiji and Taishō Periods) (Tokyo: Jitsugyō
no Sekai Sha, 1929)

Meiji-Zenki Zaisei Shiryō Shūsei (Materials on Financial and Economic History in the Early Meiji Period) (Tokyo: Kaizōsha,
1931), XVIII.

Miller, S. M., "Comparative Social Mobility," *Current Sociology,*
IX:1 (1960)

Ministry of Education, *Monbushō Nempō,* 1890–1910 (The Annual
Report of the Ministry of Education, 1890–1910)

Ministry of Education, *Monbushō Nempō* (The Annual Report of
the Ministry of Education, 1924)

Ministry of Education, *Gakusei 80 Nenshi* (Eighty Years' History
of Educational System) (Tokyo: Finance Ministry Printing
Bureau, 1954)

Ministry of Education, *Nihon no Seichō to Kyōiku* (Japan's Growth
and Education) (Tokyo: Teikoku Chihō Gyōsei Gakkai, 1962)

Miyake, Yujirō, (ed.), *Shin Nihon Shi,* 5 vol. (New History of
Japan) (Tokyo: Manchōsha, 1926)

Naikaku Shokuin Roku, 1920 and 1921 (Personnel List of the Japanese Government) (Tokyo: Cabinet Printing Office, Japanese
Government, 1920 and 1921)

Namiki, Masayoshi, "The Farm Population in the National Economy Before and After World War II," *Economic Development and Cultural Change* (Chicago: University of Chicago), IX:1, Part II (Oct. 1960)

Naoi, Atsushi, "Keizai Hatten to Shokugyō Kōzō no Hendō" (Occupational Structure of Japan and Economic Development), *Nihon Rōdō Kyōkai Zasshi*, Vol. 12, No. 12, Dec. 1970.

Newcomer, Mabel, *The Big Business Executive* (New York: Columbia University Press, 1955)

Nihon Shakai Gakkai Chōsa Iinkai, *Nihon Shakai no Kaisōteki Kōzō* (Hierarchical Structure of Japanese Society) (Tokyo: Yūhikaku, 1958)

Nishihira, Shigeki, *Shokugyō no Shakaiteki Hyōka* (Social Evaluation of Occupations) (Tokyo: Tōkeisūri Kenkyūjo, 1965)

Odaka, Kunio (ed.), *Shokugyō to Kaisō* (Occupation and Stratification) (Tokyo: Mainichi Shimbun, 1958)

Ohkawa, Kazushi and Rosovsky, Henry, "The Role of Agriculture in Modern Japanese Economic Development," *Economic Development and Cultural Change* (Chicago: University of Chicago), IX:1, Part II (Oct. 1960)

Okazaki, Yutaka, *Seimei Hoken* (Life Insurance) (Tokyo: Yūhikaku, 1960)

Ōtsuka, Takematsu, (ed.), *Hyakkan Rireki*, 2 vol. (Career of Senior Officials) (Tokyo: Nippon Shiseki Kyōkai, 1927)

Passin, Herbert, *Society and Education in Japan* (New York: Teachers College, Columbia University, 1965)

Research Department of the Ministry of Trade and Industry, *Nihon no Sangyō no Genjō, 1959* (Present Status of Japan's Industry) (Tokyo: 1959)

Rostow, W. W., *The Stages of Economic Growth: A Non-Communist Manifesto* (New York: Cambridge University Press, 1960)

Sansom, G. B., *Japan, A Short Cultural History* (New York: Appleton-Century-Crofts, Inc., 1943)

Sawamoto, Moko (ed.), *Nihon Sangyō Shi*, 2 vol. (History of Japanese Industry) (Tokyo: Teikoku Tsūshin Sha, 1928)

Schumpeter, Joseph A., *Imperialism and Social Class*, tr. by Heintz Norden (New York: Augustus M. Kelley, Inc., 1951)

Sekiyama, Naotarō, *Kinsei Nihon no Jinkō Kōzō* (Structure of

Population in the Modern Period in Japan) (Tokyo: Yoshikawa Kobunkan, 1957)

Smelser, Neil J. and Lipset, Seymour Martin, "Social Structure, Mobility in Economic Development," in *Social Structure and Mobility in Economic Development,* edited by Smelser, Neil J. and Lipset, Seymour Martin (Chicago: Aldine Publishing Company, 1966), pp. 1–50.

Smith, Thomas C., "Landlords' Sons in the Business Elite," *Economic Development and Cultural Change* (Chicago: University of Chicago), IX:1, Part II (Oct. 1960)

———, "Japan's Aristocratic Revolution," *The Yale Review,* Vol. 50, No. 3, (March 1961)

———, "Merit As Ideology in the Tokugawa Period," *Aspects of Social Change in Modern Japan,* edited by Dore, R. P. (Princeton: Princeton University Press, 1967)

Spaulding, Robert M. Jr., *Imperial Japan's Higher Civil Service Examinations* (Princeton: Princeton University Press, 1967)

Sugiura, Eiichi, *Chūkyō Zaikaishi* (Business History of Nagoya) (Nagoya: Chūbū Keizai Shimbun Sha, 1956)

Tamura, Eitarō, *Nihon no Sangyō Shidōsha* (Japan's Industrial Leaders) (Tokyo: Kokumin Tosho Kankōkai, 1944)

Taussig, F. W. and Joslyn, C. S., *American Business Leaders* (New York: MacMillan Co., 1932)

Tōkyō Shi Kazoku Tōkei (Tokyo City Family Statistics) (Tokyo Shiyakusho, 1935)

Tominaga, Ken'ichi, "Occupational Mobility in Japanese Society: Analysis of Labor Market in Japan," *The Journal of Economic Behavior,* II:1 (April 1962)

———, "Shakaiidō no Sūsei Bunseki 1955–1965" (Trend Analysis of Social Mobility, 1955–1965), *Japan Sociological Review,* Vol. 21, No. 1, June 1970, pp. 2–24.

———, "Shakaiidō no Katei Bunseki" (Process Analysis of Social Mobility), in *Kaikyū to Chiikishakai* (Class and Community), edited by Tominaga, Ken'ichi and Kurasawa, Susumu (Tokyo: Chūō Kōronsha, 1971), pp. 133–89.

———, "Studies on Social Stratification and Social Mobility in Japan: 1955–1967," in *The Study of Japan in the Behavioral Sci-*

ences, edited by Norbeck Edward, and Parman, Susan, Rice University Studies, Vol. 56, No. 4, Fall 1970, pp. 130–49.

Tōyō Keizai Kabushiki Kaisha Nenkan, No. 1 (Tōyō Keizai Yearbook of Limited Stock Companies) (Tokyo: Tōyō Keizai Shimpō Sha, 1921)

Tsuboya, Zenshirō, *Jitsugyōka Hyakketsu Den*, 6 vol. (One Hundred Biographies of Businessmen) (Tokyo: Tōkyōdō Shobō, 1892)

Tsuchiya, Takao, *Nihon Shihonshugi no Keieishi-teki Kenkyū* (Study of the Managerial History of Japanese Capitalism) (Tokyo: Misuzu Shoten, 1954)

Umezawa, Hikotarō, (ed.), *Kindai Meii Issekiwa* (Stories of Modern Eminent Physicians) (Tokyo: Nihon Ijishimpō Sha, 1937)

Veblen, Thorstein, *The Theory of the Leisure Class* (New York: The Viking Press, 1931)

Vogel, Ezra F., *Japan's New Middle Class* (Berkeley and Los Angeles: University of California Press, 1963)

Warner, W. Lloyd and Abegglen, James C., *Occupational Mobility in American Business and Industry* (Minneapolis: University of Minnesota Press, 1955)

Weber, Max, *Essays in Sociology* (Translated by Gerth, H. H. and Mills, C. Wright) (London: Routledge & Kegan Paul, Ltd., 1948)

Yamada, Yūzō, *Nihon Kokumin Shotoku Suikei Shiryō* (Descriptive Statistical Data on National Income in Japan), revised ed. (Tokyo: Tōyō Keizai Shimpō Sha, 1957)

Yamadera, Seijirō, *Tōkyō Jitsugyōka* (Businessmen in Tokyo) (Tokyo: Gyokushū-kan, 1892)

Yasuda, Saburō, *Shakaiidō no Kenkyū* (Studies in Social Mobility) (Tokyo: Tokyo Daigaku Shuppan-kai, 1971)

Yoshino, M. Y., *Japan's Managerial System* (Cambridge, Massachusetts, and London, England, The MIT Press, 1968)

INDEX

Abegglen, James C.: 252; studies by, 94, 237–238, 245
ability: role of, in occupational mobility, 82, 127, 202, 229
academic-industrial cooperation: 199
achievement: in executive recruitment, xxi, 18, 35, 173, 235, 263
Acton Society: 197
adoption of heirs: among 1960 business leaders, 109–113; role of, 103, 241; in Tokyo families in 1934, 110, 112
age
—of business leaders: *1880s*, 133; *1920*, 140; *1960*, 16, 33–34, 79, 87–93, 145; *1970*, 208–209
—of intellectual leaders, 1960: 145
—of non-Japanese business leaders: European presidents, 211; United Kingdom, 16; United States, 1952, 16; United States, presidents, 211
—of political leaders, 1960: 145
Alger-style heroes: 147
apprenticeship: and training of leaders, 162–164, 166, 169, 173, 188, 199, 201, 202
Austria: and foreign education of 1920 Japanese intellectual leaders, 174

bakufu: 135–136
Bendix, Reinhard: 17, 54, 84
birth order: in Tokyo families in 1934, 112–113; of 1960 business leaders, 111–112; role of, in inheritance, 241
birthplace
—by region: of 1920 leaders, 140;

of 1960 leaders, 114–117, 231–232; of 1970 leaders, 231–232
—by size of community: of 1880s leaders, 134; of 1920 leaders, 141; of 1960 leaders, 100, 114, 117–121, 145–146; of 1970 leaders, 231–233
bureaucracy: in firm management, xxi, 127; in government, 189
bureaucratic careers: of business leaders, 147, 157, 196, 201
bureaucratic managers: xxi
business elite: definition of, xxi–xxiii. SEE ALSO business leaders
business hierarchy: and occupations of fathers, 93–96
business leaders: definition of, xxi, xxii, 132; of 1970, 205

cabinet members: among political leaders, 132, 255, 259
capitalism: and business leadership, 122
capitalization: of corporate enterprises, 237n, 240; of firms of business leaders, 77–78, 246, 259, 260, 262
career patterns: of Japanese business leaders, xxi, 85–93, 156–158, 195–196; of European presidents, 229–230; of Japanese presidents, 228–230; of United States presidents, 229–230
census data
—Japan: *1872*, 134; *1883*, 10, 13, 15, 37, 144; *1886*, 134; *1903*, 114–119, 121, 231–232; *1910*, 231–232; *1920*, 13–15, 24, 27–28, 56, 147–149, 214; *1930*, 212–215; *1960*, 14–15, 116, 121,

DATE DUE